Against the Market

V

Against the Market

Political Economy, Market Socialism
and the Marxist Critique

DAVID McNALLY

VERSO

London · New York

First Published by Verso 1993
© David McNally 1993
All rights reserved

Verso
UK: 6 Meard Street, London W1V 3HR
USA: 29 West 35th Street, New York, NY 10001–2291

Verso is the imprint of New Left Books

ISBN 0 86091 431 3

ISBN 978-0-86091-606-2

British Library Cataloguing in Publication Data
A catalogue record for this book is available from the British Library

Library of Congress Cataloging-in-Publication Data
A catalogue record for this book is available from the Library of Congress

Set in Monotype Baskerville by Ewan Smith
48 Shacklewell Lane, London E8 2EY
Printed and bound in Great Britain by Biddles Ltd
Guildford and King's Lynn

Contents

Preface   viii

Introduction   1

1   **Origins of Capitalism and the Market**   5

Creating the Market in Labour: from
Feudalism to Capitalism   7
From Petty Production to the Factory System   24
Market Competition and Proletarianization   30
The Working Class and the Industrial Revolution   34

2   **Justice and Markets: the Ambiguous Legacy
of Adam Smith**   43

Virtue and Commerce: against Mandeville   46
Sympathy, Communication and Exchange   50
Dependence, Independence and Wage-Labour   53
Exploitation, Equity and the Market   55
Moral Economy and the Market   58
The Economics and Politics of Social Classes   59

3   **The Malthusian Moment: Political Economy
versus Popular Radicalism**   62

Popular Radicalism and the Poverty Debate   63
Alternatives to Radicalism: 'Humanitarianism' and
the Poverty Debate   71
Against the Right of Subsistence: Malthus's First *Essay
on Population*   75

Poor Laws Under Attack: Later Editions of the *Essay
on Population*   78
The Malthusian Legacy, 1: Anglican Social Thought   91
The Malthusian Legacy, 2: Classical Political Economy   93
The Malthusian Legacy, 3: The Poor Law Debate   97

4 **Exploitation, Inequality and the Market:
   The Making of Popular Political Economy**   104

Popular Political Economy: the Forerunners   106
Owenism and Political Economy   112
Popular Political Economy: Labour, Exchange,
   Money, Co-operation   117
From Theory to Practice: the Labour Exchange
   Experiment   133

5 **'Proudhon Did Enormous Mischief': Marx's
   Critique of the First Market Socialists**   139

Proudhon, Property and Political Economy   139
Marx and Proudhon: from First Encounter to
   Poverty of Philosophy   146
The Poverty of Philosophy: Petty Bourgeois Socialism
   under Attack   150
A Battle Continued: Marx's 'Economy' and the
   Critique of Proudhon   154
Capital: 'The Real Battle Begins'   159

6 **Beyond the Market**   170

Wage-Labour, Accumulation and Market Regulation   175
The Political Economy of the Working Class   184
Five Objections: Individuals, Needs, Abundance, Plan
   and Transition   188
The Question of Calculation   197
Socialized Markets or Market Reformism?   213

Conclusion   218

Notes   225

Index   255

For Adam

Preface

I began work on this book in the summer of 1990, in the aftermath of the democratic uprisings of 1989 in Eastern Europe. At a moment when the permanent victory of the liberal ideology of the market was being triumphantly proclaimed, I set out to interrogate the origins of this ideology as a means of developing its socialist critique. My work was interrupted twice in 1991 by the pressing need for practical involvement in struggles against the tyranny of the market. First, by participation in the movement against the Gulf war, an example of the imperialism built into the world market. And, second, by involvement in a solidarity campaign for two national strikes of public sector workers, the Canadian Union of Postal Workers and the Public Service Alliance of Canada. Completion of this book may have been delayed by participation in these struggles, but the vitality and solidarity of anti-war activists and rank-and-file workers striking against market-imposed austerity reaffirmed my belief in the struggle for a socialist society beyond the market. I hope this study may make a small contribution to that cause.

Colin Barker, Chris Harman, Ellen Meiksins Wood and Neal Wood all read a draft version of this book. I am grateful for their many comments and criticisms. Robin Blackburn and I carried on a spirited correspondence over the arguments I develop in chapter 6. While we have agreed to disagree on many matters, I would like to think that our polemic strengthened my final product. Joanne Boucher was a constant source of encouragement while she undertook some important writing of her own. I hope I can do as well by her. During the period in which I was working on this book, my son Adam accompanied me on demonstrations and picket lines whose significance he is beginning to understand. I dedicate this work to him.

Introduction

We live in a period of glorification of the market. The crisis of much of the socialist Left, brought on by the collapse of Stalinism, has resulted in a spate of articles and books proclaiming the end of socialism and Marxism, indeed, the end of history itself. Many on the Left, for too long insufficiently critical of the Stalinist regimes, too much inclined to depict them as some kind of socialist or 'post-capitalist' societies, have collapsed to varying degrees in the face of this ideological assault. They have emerged as 'born-again' adherents of the market. The great defect of socialism, they maintain, has been its hostility to the market, its tendency to counterpose central planning to market allocation of goods and services. Therein they find the germ of Stalinist totalitarianism; labour camps, police repression, the denial of elementary civil and democratic rights – all these and more are said to have derived from a messianic commitment to planning over markets. If socialism is to lay claim to any future, they argue, it will only be a socialism which whole-heartedly embraces the market.[1]

At times this embrace of the market verges on a complete capitulation to the most extreme market fetishists, Ludwig von Mises and Friedrich von Hayek, and their diatribes against economic planning. According to Mises and Hayek, rational economic decision-making is impossible without private ownership of the means of production and the establishment of monetary prices for commodities in fully competitive markets. Socialism thus represents for them a system of economic chaos; in such a society 'it would be impossible to speak of rational production any more'.[2]

This right-wing critique looms large in recent discussions of the economics of socialism. Robin Blackburn, in an attempt at a sweeping evaluation of socialism in the aftermath of the anti-Stalinist revolutions in Eastern Europe, makes the Mises–Hayek assault on planning a central part – one might argue *the* central part – of his account of the crisis of modern socialism. Impressed by 'the acuteness of the theoretical critique developed by Mises and Hayek', Blackburn suggests that socialists have yet to construct an adequate reply. In so doing, he echoes the sentiment of Geoff Hodgson, who judges that Hayek offered a 'brilliant critique' of centralized planning, and of Alec Nove, who commends the suggestion that a future socialist commonwealth might erect a statue to Mises, as one of the few who grasped the real difficulties of economic planning.[3]

Yet these authors do not appear to grasp the scale of the concession they are making to the anti-socialist argument. Wlodzimierz Brus and Kazimierz Laski, however, do seem to recognize what is at stake. Their recent book, *From Marx to the Market*, suggests that the 'half-way house' of market socialism 'is still exposed to criticism from the extreme liberal position' represented by Mises and Hayek. 'If marketization is the right direction of change', they argue, 'it must be pursued consistently' – which means accepting not just markets for consumer goods, but capital markets, unemployment and economic crises. And this, they acknowledge, involves openly disavowing both Marxism and any project of socialist transformation of society. If the market is the solution, they write, then 'not only the original Marxist promise has to be cast aside as anachronistic, but also the very concept of transition from capitalism to socialism'.[4]

This formulation has the merit of highlighting the real terms of the debate. For what is at stake is not an argument over different mechanisms of socialist economy, but, rather, the survival of socialism itself as an alternative to capitalism. For the logic of the modern cult of the market is a thoroughly anti-socialist one. If the market is the solution, then, as Brus and Laski note, socialism and Marxism are finished. The choice before us, therefore, is *socialism or the market*. This is not to suggest that markets can be eliminated overnight. On the contrary, markets would have to play some role for a considerable period of time in the transition to socialism. It is to insist, however, that this transition involves a struggle *against* the market; that socialist economy rests on principles antithetical to those of the market.

This book thus takes issue with the 'turn to the market' which dominates much of modern socialist thought. While written from a standpoint that is uncompromisingly hostile to the idea that Stalinism ever represented some form of socialism, it is equally uncompromising in its criticism of market socialism.[5] Indeed, it is my view that there is an interesting symmetry in the shift of many on the Left from an adherence to the state as the agency of socialist construction to an embrace of the market. While market socialism is often presented as an alternative to statism, to the domination of civil society by the state, in fact both 'statist socialism' and 'market socialism' assume that society cannot function except through alienated institutions and mechanisms which evade popular control. Both perspectives dismiss Marx's view that a 'free association of the producers' represents a viable alternative to social and economic regulation by either the state or the market.

A central premiss of this study is that Marx's socialism was simultaneously anti-statist and anti-market. It could not be otherwise for a revolutionary who theorized socialism as the self-emancipation of the working class and a transition to a society of freedom. In what follows, I attempt to sketch out one side of Marx's position: his critique of commodities, money and the market. I endeavour to show that Marx systematically engaged with, and rejected, the idea that the market could serve as a central mechanism of socialist economy, and that this rejection was underpinned by a serious and profound argument about the nature of commodities, money and the market – an argument of which modern-day adherents of market socialism show little understanding.

In order to make sense of Marx's critique, I attempt, first, to trace the rise of a capitalist market system in Britain; second, to explore the way in which that system was theorized by classical political economists from Adam Smith to David Ricardo; and, third, to outline the development of a working-class critique of that political economy which naturalized capitalist exploitation of labour. In so doing, I endeavour to show that the first popular critics of political economy accepted key aspects of the ideology of the market – in particular the idea that production for exchange by isolated producers is the natural foundation of all economy. As a result, these critics held that exploitation was not inherent in the market system; that it resulted, rather, from a distortion of the true principles of market exchange. This was the Achilles' heel of popular political economy: its failure to emancipate itself from market ideology, which was expressed in its frequent attempts to utilize the more humane market economics of Adam Smith against anti-working class economists like Malthus.

It is the burden of my argument that popular political economy could not develop a coherent critique of capitalist exploitation without a break from market ideology, and the form it took in Smith's work. For this reason, I complete this study with an examination of Marx's theory of the commodity and money, and his critique of those socialist writers who remained wedded to the market. The latter were, I argue, the first market socialists. And Marx's critique of them anticipates all the flaws one finds in the writings of those who today attempt to combine socialism and the market.

With the focus on the initial movement of socialist thought from Smith to Marx, I set out to show in chapter 1 that the key to capitalism *is the market in human labour-power*. In chapters 2 and 3, I describe how ideological justification of the full consequences of the labour market, a task carried through by Thomas Robert Malthus, required a jettisoning by political economists of the moral presuppositions of Adam Smith's economics. I then show in chapter 4 how the first popular critics of political economy attempted to employ Smith's theory of fair and equitable commodity exchange in free markets as the basis of their criticism. Only then do I turn, in chapter 5, to Marx and his powerful critique of those socialist theorists who hoped to construct a socialism via the market, who sought to eliminate exploitation while retaining commodities, prices and money. Finally, chapter 6 uses Marx's critique to confront modern market socialists.

Central to this study, therefore, is the claim that an important debate over 'market socialism' began in the 1820s, a debate that was central to Marx's critique of political economy. In an important sense, then, this book represents an attempt to recover that debate, and its historical and theoretical context, as a contribution to the modern controversy over the economics of socialism. For that reason, it also represents a challenge to participants in the modern debate: a challenge to clarify essential terms, to come to grips with the way in which Marx theorized 'the commodity' and 'money', to take a stand for or against Marx's position that is in the first instance informed by this earlier debate. Finally, I attempt to show that, if socialism means the emancipation of labour, then at the heart of its project must be the liberation of human life activity from the dictates and the 'laws' of the impersonal market. In a fundamental sense, then, this journey through history and political economy is about the very meaning of socialism.

1

Origins of Capitalism
and the Market

There is a great evasion at the heart of market socialism: the question of the market in human labour-power. This evasion is all the more remarkable in that nothing more distinguished Marx's critique of classical political economy than his attempt to theorize the commodification of labour-power as the secret to the workings of capitalism. Yet market socialists generally have argued as if the issues at stake involved merely technical questions of economic distribution. In so doing, they have engaged in a process of fetishization, of depicting relations between human beings and the labour they perform as consisting simply of material relations between things.

The ultra-liberals by whom many market socialists appear mesmerized are 'fetish-worshippers' in the extreme. Mises's work *Human Action: A Treatise on Economics* is a classic case in point. There we are told that 'labor is a scarce factor of production. As such it is bought and sold on the market.' And that 'man deals with other people's labor in the same way that he deals with all scarce material factors of production'.[1] In the Mises–Hayek world-view this is all to the good; indeed, the capacity of the market to treat labour as a scarce material factor of production is what makes economic rationality possible. It is a sign of the enormity of the intellectual retreat represented by market socialism that most of its proponents have tacitly accepted the ultra-liberal equation of the market with rationality. To be consistent, of course, they should then argue that the creation of the market in human labour-power constituted a decisive step towards a more rational form of society. They hesitate in the face of such an admission, however, sensing perhaps that it would mean the abandonment of any serious argument for socialism.

Yet here the market-worshippers have consistency on their side, albeit the consistency of crude apologists for capitalism. Take the case of Mises. Having extolled the virtues of the labour market, his exultant raptures know no bounds. Capitalism and the industrial revolution were unmitigated blessings. The first factories 'emptied the poor houses, the workhouses and the prisons. They converted starving beggars into self-supporting breadwinners.' And these glorious developments were no accidental by-product of industrial capitalism. After all, 'the very principle of capitalist entrepreneurship is to provide for the common man'; indeed, 'cheap things for the many, was the objective of the factory system'.[2]

Most market socialists will pull up short in the face of such bald-faced apologetics. They will claim to oppose the inequalities of unbridled market competition, to be appalled by the horrors of the early factory system. They will insist that they wish merely to alert socialists to the 'acutness' of the critique of economic planning advanced by Mises and Hayek, a critique we allegedly ignore to our own peril. While dismissing the prescriptions advanced by the ultra-liberals, they might contend that they wish to engage their critique in order to overcome the dogmas and the blindspots which have brought socialism to its present crisis.

Yet such protestations feign too much innocence. For the very core of the Mises–Hayek critique of capitalism is the equation of economic rationality with market competition. And it is not accidental that the predominant trend in market socialist thought is to accept competition, money and market prices as essential to any 'feasible socialism'. For at the heart of market socialism is the fetishized view of money, commodities, prices and markets which achieves its most vulgar form in the tradition of Mises and Hayek. Moreover, as I demonstrate below, that tradition has a history, rooted in Malthus's vulgarization of Smithian economics, and in the way Malthus's position was used to attack the working class during the era of popular radicalism and the industrial revolution (1790–1848).

But before turning to these debates in political economy, I set out in the remainder of this chapter to reconstruct their prehistory in the era of emergent English capitalism. By exploring some of the crucial historical moments in the development of fully capitalist market relations, I attempt to highlight four things.

First, following Marx's hints in this direction, I argue that the separation of labourers from their means of production is the key to the rise of capitalism. Second, I show that this separation was no gradual, harmonious process, but that it involved force and suffering. Third, I outline how the emerging working class fought bitterly to prevent its complete subjugation to the laws of the market. Finally, I discuss the way in which classical political economy was enlisted – and reconstructed – as an ideological weapon in the battle to subject workers to the brutal discipline of the capitalist market. Having set out this background, I then proceed in subsequent chapters to examine the confrontation between bourgeois and working-class political economy, a confrontation that culminated in Marx's critique of the capitalist market system.

Creating the Market in Labour: from Feudalism to Capitalism

In Marx's account of capitalism the essential nature of the system is defined by a unique relationship of production – that between 'owners of money, means of production, means of subsistence' on the one hand, and 'on the other hand, free workers, the sellers of their own labour-power, and therefore the sellers of labour'. The 'confrontation of, and contact between' these two different classes of commodity owners – owners of means of production and 'owners' of labour power – establishes the capital/wage-labour relationship: 'with the polarization of the commodity market into these two classes, the fundamental conditions of capitalist production are present'.[3]

This definition of the essential social relation which constitutes capitalism is not meant to serve as an adequate historical account of the rise of capitalism. Such an account would have to bring together a number of interconnected phenomena: the crisis of European feudalism; the attempt to 'externalize' that crisis through war and foreign expansion; the internal efforts at resolving this crisis through intensified exploitation of the peasantry, the drawing of bourgeois wealth into the economic circuits of the state, attempts to tax noble wealth; and so on. For this reason, war, civil war, revolution, colonialism, the slave trade would all figure in any comprehensive account. But for these phenomena to lead towards a transition to capitalism, they had to result, in one way or another, in the expropriation of the peasantry and the creation of a class of 'free workers' who lack 'any means of production of their own'. Central to the genesis of capitalism, therefore, are those historical processes which bring about the separation of a large and growing proportion of the labouring population from means of production which could provide them with an adequate subsistence. It follows that the emergence of a *labour market* is central to the rise of capitalism. And, emerging

out of an overwhelmingly agricultural society, the origins of the
capitalist labour market must be sought in 'the expropriation of the
agricultural producer, of the peasant, from the soil'.[4]

It is clear that capitalist social relations did develop directly out
of the decline of English feudalism. From the late fourteenth century
onward, the traditional manorial economy and peasant village
community were slowly but decisively replaced by an increasingly
stratified rural society based around large farms, rich tenant farmers
and a growing agrarian proletariat. Over the same period, the less
traditional open communities, found often in woodland and pastoral
areas, experienced a substantial growth of rural industries. To be
sure, this emerging system of agrarian capitalism was not pure-bred.
It developed through a complex process of reaction against, and
adaptation to, the traditions of manorial and peasant economy. But
however much these traditional relations restrained the drive towards
rural capitalism, they could not halt it. Between 1400 and 1640 rural
England was irreversibly transformed. A society based on peasant
labour for large landlords, or upon largely self-sufficient peasant
farming and domestic industry, was replaced by a society where
agricultural production was carried on increasingly by wealthy
capitalist tenant farmers who hired propertyless or almost propertyless
labourers, and where traditional domestic production of manufactures began to give way to embryonic forms of capitalist organization.

This transformation of English rural society went through a
number of crucial phases. The most important of these are the great
feudal crisis of the fourteenth century; the 'golden age' of peasant
prosperity during the economic recovery of the fifteenth century;
the activation of the land market, the expansion of the landed class,
and the drive towards commercial agriculture and enclosure associated with the religious Reformation and the massive sale of Church
lands which began in 1536; the landlord offensive of 1590–1640, which
saw a doubling of rents as a result of consolidation, enclosure and
a squeeze on the small tenants; and the widespread expansion of
petty commodity production.[5]

With the resolution of the Civil War and the stabilization of its
achievements in 1688–9, the stage was set for the great consolidation
of agrarian capitalism and the emergence of industrial capitalism
which characterized the eighteenth century. All of these processes
contributed to an irreversible transformation of the peasantry, as
from the ranks of this class there emerged both embryonic capitalists
and semi-proletarians. This increasing social differentiation of the

peasantry, which spelled its end as a distinct class, is a key measure of the capitalist transformation of the English economy. The economic and social processes at work were piecemeal and uneven; nevertheless their cumulative effects were dramatic and irreversible. Whereas the typical medieval peasant had held between 8 and 30 acres of land, during the period 1450–1550, 'peasant' estates of 150–200 acres became more and more common. Some peasant holding were substantially larger. Indeed, yeoman estates in grazing areas might stretch to 500–600 acres.[6]

Table 1.1 Number of Landless Peasants in England and Wales 1086–1640

Date	Population (millions)	% of peasants not tied to a manor	Number of landless peasants
1086	1.1	6	66,000
1279	3.3	10	330,000
1381	2.1	2	42,000
1540–67	2.8–3.0	11–12	308,000–360,000
1600–10	3.75	35	1,312,500
1620–40	4.5–5.5	40	1,800,000–2,200,000

Source: Lachmann, *From Manor to Market: Structural Change in England, 1536–1640* (Madison: University of Wisconsin Press, 1987), p. 129.

Meanwhile, the poorest peasants were being reduced to the status of cottagers with only a few acres of land. And once the social differentiation of the peasant community had proceeded, its poorest members were especially vulnerable. Previously, the commonality of peasant circumstances had cemented a solidarity within the village community which was crucial to resisting assaults by lords. In the changed circumstances of the sixteenth century, however, the richest peasants often stood to gain from lordly attacks on poor peasants and on traditional communal practices. Yeoman farmers were themselves expropriators of the village poor; moreover, they were often the ones best situated to expand their holdings if lords evicted poor cottagers or enclosed and divided common lands. When they moved to evict, consolidate and enclose, lords now often encountered a divided peasant community incapable of concerted action in defence of custom and tradition.

The differentiation of the peasantry thus often rebounded to the benefit of a vigorous landlord who 'could carry these tendencies to their logical conclusion and become himself the final accumulator of all holdings.[7] This was especially true during the sixteenth century, when economic conditions favoured a conversion of arable land to pasture, especially for sheep farming. Throughout this period, then, the traditional peasant community was undermined as layers of better-off peasants became wealthy yeoman farmers, some entering the ranks of the gentry, while others were pauperized and proletarianized – and on a massive scale. One calculation of the number of landless peasants in England and Wales shows a dramatic escalation concentrated in the hundred years from 1540 to 1640 (Table 1.1), thus reinforcing the view that by the sixteenth century the English peasant community consisted of 'a chain stretching from a mere cottager up to a petty capitalist'.[8]

The impulse towards capitalist farming did not emanate only from the peasant village community. The growth of trade and industry created new capitalist fortunes, expanded markets for agricultural products and generated a flow of bourgeois investments in land. Equally important were the social and economic effects of the Reformation and the sale of Church properties which brought about one quarter of all English lands on to the market. As a result of this new fluidity of the land market, whole new gentry strata were created, as wealthy yeomen and urban bourgeois purchased or leased new holdings. Alongside these developments went the use by lords of their newly acquired land to create large enclosed farms for rental to wealthy tenants. The sale of Church lands thus accelerated the social differentiation of the peasantry, the trend towards enclosure and consolidation, and the increasing presence of large capital farms.

That there were tendencies towards the creation of large farms and the employment of wage-labour throughout the sixteenth and seventeenth centuries is hardly a point of dispute among historians.[9] The crucial area of debate concerns the social basis of these changes. Whereas mainstream historiography has treated the trend towards larger farms as an essentially technical development based on the advantages of 'economies of scale', socialist historians have seen this tendency as one aspect of a complex process of transformation in the class relations of English agrarian production.[10]

Concentration of land, enclosure and social differentiation were well advanced long before the parliamentary enclosures of the period 1760–1830, as landlords sought to create farms in the 200–300 acre range (and larger in pastoral areas), which could be leased to wealthy tenants. These prosperous tenants were able to pay larger rents on the basis of the higher productivity of improved, market-oriented farming sustained by capital investment on the land. But the creation of large farms was not an automatic process; it required getting rid of small occupiers. Consolidation of scattered strips of land and enclosure of open fields contributed to precisely that, hitting hardest at the small tenant with 10–30 acres.[11] Thus a central consequence of the creation of large farms was a shift in the distribution of English lands from peasant to aristocratic hands. By the end of the seventeenth century, English landlords controlled as much as 70–75 per cent of cultivable land, thus leaving owner-occupiers with some 25–30 per cent. The contrast with France is marked. There, peasants held 45–50 per cent of cultivable land, often in the form of scattered open fields.[12] This sharp discrepancy between patterns of agrarian landownership in England and France was well established by the second half of the eighteenth century – *prior* to the great wave of parliamentary enclosure. And these trends were to continue, especially under the impact of the parliamentary enclosure movement. Their cumulative effect was massive. Indeed, one historian has estimated that the period 1690–1873 saw small peasant owners lose between 3 and 4 million acres of land.[13]

Much ink has been spilled over whether there was a dramatic decline in the number of small tenants during this period. This, however, is not the crucial issue. Whether small tenants held on to tiny tracts of land is of much less importance than the radical alteration of their social existence as loss of land, open fields and common rights made their land holdings a less and less viable means to economic self-sufficiency. Those poor tenants who stayed on the land, clinging to small plots and cottages were no longer 'tenants' in the meaningful sense of the word. Increasingly, they were semi-proletarianized rural labourers, whose families combined farming and wage-labour in order to make ends meet.

Such shifts in the social distribution of land were part of an agrarian social revolution. It was not simply the techniques of agricultural production which were revolutionized; more important, the social relations of agricultural production were radically transformed. Indeed this revolution in social relations was crucial to the systematic extension of the technical revolution in agriculture. New techniques of crop rotation, drainage or marling, for example, were only viable on large, enclosed 'capital farms', where wealthy tenants could dispose of about £500 of working capital, make substantial investments and benefit from the enclosures and improvements carried out by the owners of the land.[14] Both rents and profits rose on improved commodity-producing farms. Indeed, it has been suggested that enclosure led to a doubling of rents, thus justifying what were often quite substantial investment costs associated with this means of improvement. Not surprisingly, the decisive century of 1690–1790 – in which 'agrarian capitalism came fully into its inheritance' – saw a general doubling of rents.[15]

Since the early 1950s, orthodox liberal historiography has maintained that, rather than being the great loss for the poor depicted by populist and socialist historians, enclosure actually contributed to major improvements in the conditions of the bulk of the rural population. Instead of dispossessing small tenants and depopulating villages, enclosure is said to have stimulated demand for agricultural labour, the effects of which can be measured in population increases in enclosed villages.[16] This line of argument was seen as reinforcing the earlier view of Clapham, according to whom growth of an agrarian proletariat in the period 1688–1832 was slow and relatively insignificant. Modern liberal historiography has thus sought to portray the emergence of agrarian capitalism, and the associated phenomena of consolidation and enclosure, as gradual, peaceful processes, which were beneficial to all major groups in English society.[17] These arguments deserve critical examination in any discussion of enclosure.

Enclosure involved 'the emancipation from the rules of communal cultivation of part or all of the lands used for purposes of tillage or pasture'.[18] It thus represented a social transformation of the organization of agricultural production involving the destruction of communal practices. This is why the 'spatial rearrangement' involved when peasants traded and reorganized small plots should not be included in the term. And for this reason it is to the enclosure wave of the Tudor period that we look for the origins of the social revolution which reshaped English farming.

A wave of enclosure swept parts of England during the second half of the fifteenth century. By 1500 almost half the country was enclosed, with the remainder consisting of open fields. After the 1520s, the rate of enclosure slowed, only to pick up again in the seventeenth century.[19] Tudor enclosures were concentrated in the Midlands, and often involved massive dislocation and depopulation as a result of the shift from arable farming to sheep and cattle grazing. Indeed, as much as 80 per cent of all enclosure during the period 1485–1607 took place in the Midlands, resulting in perhaps 20 per cent of the land in that region being enclosed.[20]

Contrary to interpretations that emphasize parliamentary enclosure after 1760, it is now clear that the greatest wave took place during the seventeenth century and the first half of the eighteenth. Nearly 30 per cent of England was enclosed in the years between 1600 and 1760. Indeed, on the eve of the parliamentary enclosure movement, England was already 75 per cent enclosed.[21] This is not to minimize the great burst of activity between 1760 and 1830 in which some 6 million acres of land were enclosed by Act of Parliament; it is to insist, however, that the resort to Parliament characterized only the last phase in a centuries-long process when enclosure by other means had run its course.

Parliamentary enclosure has rightly been described as a 'massive violence exercised by the upper classes against the lower'.[22] It was a concentrated use of state power to expropriate land and dispossess small producers; and it was a crucial phase in the capitalist transformation of English society. But those historians, including some early socialist writers, who laid almost exclusive emphasis on parliamentary enclosure often underestimated the degree to which it was merely the violent completion of a process which had started two centuries earlier. The latter was Marx's view. 'The prelude to the revolution that laid the foundation of the capitalist mode of production', he wrote, 'was played out in the last third of the fifteenth century and the first few decades of the sixteenth. A mass of "free" and unattached proletarians was hurled onto the labour-market by the dissolution of the bands of feudal retainers.' And as crucial moments in this continuing process, Marx identified 'the spoilation of the Church's property, the fraudulent alienation of the state domains, the theft of the common lands, the usurpation of feudal and clan property and its transformation into modern private property'. Parliamentary enclosure was thus for Marx one of many acts of 'ruthless terrorism' by the ruling class which 'conquered the field for capitalist agriculture, incorporated the soil into capital, and created for the urban industries the necessary supply of free and rightless proletarians'.[23]

The Marxist case should not rest, therefore, on the impact of parliamentary enclosure alone. Nevertheless, even in this area three fatal flaws can be identified in the liberal account. The first concerns the effect of parliamentary enclosure on the labour market. One important recent study has shown that, during the main period of parliamentary enclosure, population rose in both enclosed and unenclosed villages, and that the rate of growth was no faster in the former. Enclosure cannot therefore be said to have had a uniquely stimulative effect on population growth. The same study also demonstrates that there was a 'positive association' between enclosure and migration out of villages. Finally, a definite correlation has been established between the extent of enclosure and reliance on poor rates.[24] The heart of the modern liberal account has thus been refuted; indeed, the older socialist picture now seems remarkably accurate – parliamentary enclosure resulted in outmigration and a higher level of pauperization.

The second flaw in the liberal position centres on the claim that there was no dramatic trend towards the elimination of small farmers during the period of parliamentary enclosure. Mingay has written, for example, that 'modern understanding of the slow pace of the "agricultural revolution" and of the effects of parliamentary enclosures does not, in general, support the old view that a major decline of small farmers occurred between 1760 and 1830'.[25] Once again, the focus should not be placed exclusively on enclosure by Act of Parliament. After all, Mingay recognizes that the number of smallholders did decline significantly during the hundred years prior to the great wave of parliamentary encosures (1650–1750).[26] Thus, debate merely over the effects of parliamentary enclosure unnecessarily restricts the frame of reference. Yet, Mingay's treatment of even this last phase of enclosure tends to substitute static, numerical considerations for a full social analysis by minimizing the qualitative changes which parliamenatry enclosure wrought on the small tenant. This can be seen by scrutinizing the way in which the orthodox liberal account uses the notion of the 'small farmer' during this period.

As Mingay has noted in another context,

> the very small farmers – occupiers of perhaps 25 acres and less – could hardly survive without some additional form of income; the land itself, unless used for specialized production or amply supplemented by common, would hardly yield sufficient to pay the rent and keep the family.[27]

He goes on to point out that only in rare circumstances could such small occupiers engage in specialized farming for the market. Yet the other means of support – farming 'amply supplemented by common' – is precisely that which was being destroyed by parliamentary enclosure, to the tune of six million acres via enclosure Act (about one-quarter of the cultivated area of England) and another 8 million acres by 'agreement'.[28] The impact of enclosure on small tenants, whose lands were inadequate to procure subsistence, can only have been dramatic, forcing them into growing reliance on wage-labour – as proponents of enclosure said it should.

Before turning to look at that impact, let us further pursue the situation of the small tenant. For, while it is true that many clung to the land, it is also true that the rural poor came to hold ever smaller tracts. J.R. Wordie has documented this trend on the Levenson-Gower estates during the period 1714–1832. He shows that over these years the number of farms in the 20–200 acre range fell sharply. At the same time, the acreage of large farms grew. Most important, the great majority of those holding 20 acres or less had fewer than 5 acres; indeed, a majority held less than a single acre. Yet, according to the analysis put forth by Mingay, these were all 'small farmers'. In reality, the majority were proletarians who held on to small plots as a supplement to their wages. Behind the alleged 'survival of the small farmer', one thus discovers the growing proletarianization of the rural poor.[29]

This brings us to the third flaw in the liberal account: its systematic underestimation of the size of the agrarian proletariat. By insisting that every owner of land be treated as a non-labourer – indeed, as an 'entrepreneur' – liberal economic historians have obscured the marked growth of a rural proletariat during the rise of agrarian capitalism. This can best be seen in the way Clapham continually underestimated the size of the agrarian proletariat in both 1688 and 1831, an underestimation which has entered into the modern liberal orthodoxy.[30] Clapham took as his starting point Gregory King's figures on the social structure of England in 1688. He then lumped freeholders of the 'better sort' together with 'lesser' freeholders and tenant farmers to construct an 'entrepreneur class'. Then, on the basis of estimates of the number of rural labourers, he concluded that the ratio of wage-labourers to employers of labour ('entrepreneurs') in rural England was 1.74:1.

It is not difficult to detect a central error in this argument. Once we realize that most 'lesser freehold' families would not have employed any wage-labourers, and that a large proportion of the members of many of these families would have been engaged in wage-labour themselves, it is clear that the actual ratio would be much higher. If we simply eliminate the families of 'lesser freeholders' from the equation, we then get a ratio for rural labourers per rural employer of about 3:1, rather than Clapham's 1.74:1. In reality, the actual ratio would almost certainly have been higher, given that many 'lesser freeholder' families would have had a member or members engaged in wage labour on the land or in local industry.

We get a similar result with the figures Clapham derived for the early nineteenth century based on the census of 1831. According to the census, there were some 686,000 'labouring families' in agriculture. In addition, there were 144,600 'entrepreneur families' employing labour, and 130,500 'entrepreneur families' employing no labour. According to Clapham, this gives us a ratio of agrarian capitalists to agrarian proletarians of 2.5:1. But eliminate the 130,500 'entrepreneur families' employing no labour from the equation – since these should hardly qualify as agrarian capitalists – and we get a ratio of 4.7:1, nearly twice Clapham's ratio.[31]

King's figures, properly scrutinized, thus indicate that the degree of proletarianization in English agriculture was *much* higher than the orthodox liberal account suggests, about twice as high at both points in time. Indeed, the degree of proletarianization was already greater by 1688 than what Clapham claimed for Britain 150 years later. Moreover, the actual ratio would almost certainly have been higher, given that a growing proportion of small occupiers would have been entering the labour market over this period. Finally, use of such aggregate figures tends to ignore the growing preponderance of large farms as employers of labour. Using sample figures from the 1851 Census, for example, John Saville has shown that farms which employed ten labourers or more accounted for 42.3 per cent of all employment of rural wage-labour.[32]

Table 1.2 Proportion of English Peasants Employed as Wage-labourers, 1096–1688

Date	% of peasants employed as wage labourers
1086	6
1279	10
1381	2
1540–59	11
1550–67	12
1600–10	35
1620–40	40
1688	56

Source: Lachmann, *From Manor to Market*, p. 17.

Despite the efforts of liberal historians to minimize the pace and the extent of the social revolution in the English countryside, it is clear that a fundamental transformation was at work. 'The domestic economy of the whole village was radically altered', wrote Hoskins about the Midlands peasant.[33] And at the heart of that radical alteration was the transformation of the more or less self-sufficient peasant into a wage-labourer, the dimensions of which are indicated in Table 1.2.[34]

These figures are consistent with numerous studies which suggest that labourers made up between one quarter and one third of the population of Tudor and early Stuart England, and constituted about one half the population by the time of the Civil War.[35]

The emergence of an agrarian proletariat was crucial to the creation of large capitalist farms and developing rural industries. This was so for two reasons. First, small tenants had to be dispossessed of land in order to bring about consolidation of large farms. Second, these dispossessed producers were then subjected to the pressure to accept wage-labour on large farms and/or in local industries as one means of procuring an adequate subsistence. Contrary to much modern historiography, it was here that parliamentary enclosure was often decisive, as contemporaries were generally aware. To be sure, proletarianization was not the creature of enclosure. Indeed, the transformation of rural poor into wage-labourers proceeded even in regions largely unaffected by parliamentary enclosure, as a result of heavier exactions by lords, peasant indebtedness and the increased pressure of specialization for the market. In this sense, the enclosures of 1760–1830, which concentrated on common lands, were simply 'a special case of a general situation: the growing inability of tiny marginal cultivators to hold out in a system of industrialised manufactures and capitalist agriculture'.[36] But this 'special case' was often an inextricable part of the general process; and frequently it sealed the fate of the small tenants or cottagers by making them irreversibly reliant on wage-labour for their subsistence.

Many rural wage-labourers in Tudor and Stuart England continued to maintain a garden or small farm and exercise common rights. In many villages, a clear majority of the working population combined farming with wage-labour; a large proportion of the rural poor had more than one industrial by-employment. Joan Thirsk has estimated, for example, that as many as one half of all small farmers in seventeenth-century England engaged in one or more industrial employment.[37] Probably one quarter of the farming population of England spent some of their working hours in the woollen industries during this period.

And it was not just the rural poor who combined wage-labour with farming. This was characteristic also of relatively skilled labourers, such as carpenters, masons, coopers, wheelwrights and ploughwrights.[38] What we are dealing with throughout this period, then, is a sort of semi-proletariat, a group that lacked enough land to maintain economic self-sufficiency, but that could at the same time use its own production (either for consumption or for the market) as a substantial supplement to wages. As Marx put it, the agricultural proletariat of this time was composed on the one hand of peasants, and on the other hand, of 'an independent, special class of wage-labourer'. The latter, however,

> were also in practice peasants, farming independently for themselves ... Moreover, like the other peasants, they enjoyed the right to exploit the common land, which gave pasture to their cattle, and furnished them with timber, fire-wood, turf, etc.[39]

So long as the degree of capitalist development was such that agrarian and rural industrial employers did not need a substantially larger class of full-time wage-labourers, this arrangement was satisfactory for economic purposes. But as agrarian and industrial capitalism developed in the eighteenth century, the elements of economic self-sufficiency which wage-labourers retained became a hindrance, pulling them periodically out of the labour market and providing them with elements of both material and psychological independence. Thus, as the economic demand for a growing full-time proletariat increased, so did the pressure to expropriate completely the land or access to land of the semi-proletariat.[40] This is what made the battle over common lands so important, as these generally constituted the most important insurance against outright proletarianization and the poverty that came with it.

It should come as no surprise that the standard of living was generally much higher in those areas where labourers managed to combine industrial work with farming; in regions where agriculture was separated from rural industries, on the other hand, labourers were usually poor. Moreover, it is clear that 'important though the labourer's individual smallholding was, the vital factor in his fortunes was his rights of common.'[41] Access to commons meant that labourers could graze animals, gather wood, stones and gravel, dig coal, hunt and fish. These rights often made the difference between subsistence and abject poverty. Arthur Young estimated, for example, that the value of a cow in terms of milk and butter equalled the wages of a fully employed labourer.[42] Yet cows usually could not be kept once grazing rights on the commons were lost. For this reason one historian accurately notes that 'the labourer's rights of common formed part of a carefully integrated economy, whose balance could rarely be altered without serious consequences for the commoners themselves'. Moreover, 'poor though they seem, those rights alone added a few simple graces to an otherwise bare existence, and bred in the labourer a sense of hope and independence'.[43] It was precisely these elements of material and spiritual independence that many of the most outspoken advocates of enclosure sought to destroy.

Eighteenth-century proponents of enclosure were remarkably forthright in this respect. Common rights and access to common lands, they argued, allowed a degree of social and economic independence, and thereby produced a lazy, dissolute mass of rural poor who eschewed honest labour and church attendance, and whose idleness resulted in drunkenness, riotous behaviour and moral laxity. Denying such people common lands and common rights would force them to conform to the harsh discipline imposed by the market in labour. 'The use of common lands by labourers operates upon the mind as a sort of independence', wrote Mr Bishton in the *Report on Shropshire*, prepared for the Board of Agriculture in 1794. Enclosure of the commons would put an end to this state of mind. Once deprived of commons, he argued, 'the labourers will work every day in the year, their children will be put out to labour early' and 'that subordination of the lower ranks which in the present times is so much wanted, would be thereby considerably secured'.[44]

The argument for enclosure as a means to destroying 'independence' was echoed throughout the next half-century. As the Poor Law Commissioners of 1834 stated in their *Report*, 'we can do little or nothing to prevent pauperism; the farmers will have it: they prefer that the labourers should be slaves; they object to their having gardens, saying, "The more they work for themselves, the less they work for us."'[45] Similar statements were made to the 1844 Select Committee on Enclosures. 'They will *not* seek for labour until they are compelled to do it', a witness from Newbury in Berkshire told the Committee. Describing one parish, he claimed that only as a result of a recent enclosure did the poor now constitute 'a respectable class looking up to the wealthier classes for labour'. Indeed, 'respectability' was defined regularly in terms of objective dependence on one's betters. Another witness told the Committee:

I think there is no comparison whatever between the *moral state* of persons who gain their livelihood by day-labour and those who occupy a cottage and garden, and perhaps a small encroachment in the neighbourhood of a common, and who live as cottiers, not as labourers.[46]

The moral inferiority of the former was linked invariably to the slower pace of independent farming and the alternative to wage-labour this provided. 'In sauntering after his cattle', wrote one agriculturalist, 'he acquires a habit of indolence. Quarter, half and occasionally whole days are imperceptibly lost. Day labour becomes disgusting; the aversion increases by indulgence; and at length the sale of a half-fed calf, or hog, furnishes the means of adding intemperance to idleness.'[47] Advocates of enclosure thus made much more than a narrowly economic case for enclosure of the commons; their argument was fully social, emphasizing that elimination of the means to economic independence was essential to creating a disciplined labour force. The campaign for enclosure of common lands was presented as a great moral crusade designed to eliminate idleness, intemperance and riotous behaviour, and to render the poor sober and respectable.

Indeed, by the time of the 1834 Poor Law Commission, the discourse of 'independence' had been radically redefined. Now that the bulk of enclosure had taken place, it was poor relief that represented the labourer's main buffer from the market. Rather than attacking the 'independence' made possible by rights to common, the *Poor Law Report* attacked 'dependence' on poor relief, and advocated a new form of 'independence' – utter reliance of the labourer upon the wages he or she could procure through the market.[48]

Liberal historians have often recognized that the emergence of a modern working class is vital to capitalist development. 'A malleable and trained workforce was central to an industrializing country', one has written.[49] But they have shown little inclination to investigate the actual processes of proletarianization. Contemporaries were not so reluctant. Advocates of enclosure, as we have seen, regularly stressed that a disciplined class of wage-labourers could not be created without enclosure of common lands. As one put it, enclosure was necessary in order to break through 'acquired habits of idleness and dissipation and a dislike to honest labour'.[50] Thus, while far from singularly responsible for reducing the poor to dependence upon wage-labour, enclosure can reasonably be said to have 'hurried the process whereby rural labour became wage dependent'.[51]

By eliminating their most important source of self-provisioning, enclosure removed a crucial buffer between the labourers and the labour market. And there can be no doubt that this contributed to the impoverishment of many. By the late eighteenth century, between one quarter and one half of village populations relied upon poor relief. It is especially significant that we find a strong correlation between the extent of enclosure and per capita poor relief.[52] As Chambers and Mingay put it in a remarkably frank comment on the contemporary debate over rural poverty: 'whatever the merits of the controversy, both sides recognized that poverty was increasing in the countryside. Even the protagonists of enclosure were obliged to admit this unpalatable fact.'[53]

Here, then, we encounter an important insight into the liberal concept of economic rationality. What is 'rational' is not what provides the greatest degree of comfort and security to the labourers – as we have seen, access to commons greatly augmented both. 'Rational' was that which enabled the employer to minimize costs through a steady supply of labourers desperate for wage-work. Yet, 'cost-minimization', as the economics textbooks call it, involved efforts to subject workers more thoroughly to the market, and this as a rule impoverished a good many of them. For this reason, marketization and proletarianization had to be presented as parts of a great moral crusade which would subject labourers to a 'rational' order, which they instinctively resisted.

In terms of agrarian social history, enclosure was at the heart of the process of proletarianization. But alongside enclosure went two other processes which centrally contributed to throwing labourers on the mercy of the labour market: the decline of 'service' and of various allowances and perquisites which provided a supplement to the labourers' wage; and the growing attack on the traditional poor law.

Service in husbandry remains one of the least studied phenomena in English agrarian history. Yet it is hard to underestimate its significance. Between 1574 and 1821 about 60 per cent of youths between 15 and 24 were servants. Almost one half of all farm households hired servants. Moreover, servants constituted between one third and one half of the hired labour force in English agriculture during this period.[54] Service in husbandry was traditionally an annual affair. Servants were hired for a year, lived in their masters' homes, and were paid largely in the form of room and board. For the servant, one year's residence in a parish was the legal basis for a 'settlement' and a claim for support under the poor law in the event of economic distress. For farmers, service provided a guaranteed labour force at an established cost, and was thus an insurance against labour shortage or rising costs for day labourers.[55]

The extinction of farm service was concentrated during the fifty years from 1780 to 1830. A number of phenomena were at work here. The growth of large farms specializing in one or a handful of agricultural products meant that demand for labour was more sporadic; hiring of servants on an annual contract made less and less economic sense, especially in a period of labour surplus.[56] Similarly, during a phase of rising food prices, farmers preferred to pay wages than to have to absorb subsistence costs for servants. In addition, parishes which were confronted with rising poor rates, as a result of relative overpopulation, wished to avoid further increases in rates by reducing or eliminating annual service contracts which gave their holders legal settlement.

This does not mean, however, that annual service was simply replaced by day labour. On the contrary, there was a tendency for the terms of service to become shorter; indeed, some farmers offered 51-week contracts in order to avoid parish settlements. Contracts were often substantially shorter. In practice, weekly contracts tended to become daily since farmers paid nothing for days when labour could not be performed. The decline of service thus took the form, not of an overnight elimination, but of a process in which service shaded 'imperceptibly into forms of weekly or day labour'.[57]

By 1830 farm service was a thing of the past in the south of England. Alongside its decline went the demise of payments in kind, a long-standing set of practices according to which labourers received a share of farm produce in the form of milk or grain; were allowed to graze livestock; received clothing or gloves; or could acquire a rent-free cottage and land.[58] For the farm servant, the decline of payments in kind, like the decline of service, 'reduced him, except at harvest when every hand was needed, to nothing but a precarious cash-wage, which might or might not cover his modest subsistence costs'.[59] Moreover, as we have already indicated, the decline of service was linked to attacks on the old poor law since annual service was often the means by which young people in early modern England established a legal parish settlement.

The Elizabethan Poor Law, based on laws from 1597 and 1601, was in reality a patchwork of local arrangements by which the village poor were to be subsidized by their parish in times of distress. There was enormous variation in the forms of support provided, given the lack of central administration which characterized a system controlled by local gentry. According to the Act of Settlement (1662), however, the poor were the responsibility of their official parish of settlement. For the large farmer, the poor law system had important advantages: first, it guaranteed a local supply of labour by tying the poor to a specific locale; second, the whole of the property-owning population paid poor rates, effectively subsidizing the labour costs of the largest employers of farm labour.[60] As well as a buttress against hunger and social strife, then, the poor law was an effective method of subsidizing wages and guaranteeing a workforce to capitalist farmers.

In *The Wealth of Nations*, Adam Smith railed against the restrictions on personal mobility created by the Act of Settlement. 'There is scarce a poor man in England of forty years of age', he argued, 'who has not in some part of his life felt himself most cruelly oppressed by this ill-contrived law of settlements.'[61] But, whatever truth there was to this, the poor themselves saw much else in the system of parish relief. For, restrictive though it may have been, the poor law was also a 'right' for the poor – a guarantee of subsistence. And an important guarantee it was. Estimates suggest that in the late eighteenth and early-nineteenth centuries between one quarter and one half of village populations depended on parish relief. It has been further suggested that in 1830 the average English farm labourer relied on poor relief for at least 15 per cent of his income, and in some regions the percentage would have been much higher. From the 1790s, expenditure on relief rose steadily, more than doubling to 4.2 million pounds in the ten years up to 1803, surpassing five million pounds in 1815, and soaring to nearly eight million pounds by 1818.[62] Moreover, much more than unemployment relief and pensions had been included in traditional relief practices. Keith Snell notes that

> Besides unemployment relief and pensions, parish payments were made for shoes, pattens or boots, clothes of all sorts, furniture (especially bedding), rents, fuel (coals), childbed linen and other lying-in expenses (such as payments to the midwife), flour, meat, marriage costs, burial shrouds, laying-out expenses, gravedigging and other burial costs, pensions and cleaning costs for elderly paupers, payments to neighbours for nursing, smallpox inoculation, or even spectacles.[63]

Thus, however disquieting the restraints imposed by the laws of settlement, the poor had a vested interest in their maintenance. Indeed, certificates acknowledging legal settlement were treated as a form of property, and were passed from father to son. The 'moral economy' of the poor included, then, a sense of various rights to subsistence comprising common rights, the notion of a just price for grain and bread, and the right of settlement and a claim on the parish.[64]

From the 1780s onwards, the traditional poor law came under the same sort of attack as had common lands. Increasing numbers of writers denounced parish relief as yet another method by which the poor were relieved of the necessity of honest labour and by which wage rates were artificially elevated, since no poor person would be expected to work for less than they could draw from the parish. A series of writers – Thomas Alcock, Joseph Townsend, Arthur Young, Edmund Burke, Thomas Robert Malthus – launched sustained attacks on these customary rights in the name of markets, morals and political economy. The ensuing debate constitutes one of the main themes of the present study. Before turning to that debate over property and political economy, however, we must complete our survey of the rise of capitalism and the formation of the working class.

From Petty Production to the Factory System

Thus far our discussion has focused on social transformations in agricultural production. Yet the processes I have described were closely connected with changes affecting manufacturing, for industrial development during the rise of capitalism was intimately associated with changes on the land. Agrarian historians have come to identify two main kinds of rural community in early modern England. The first is the traditional open-field arable community tightly organized round the church and manor house. The second is the more enclosed community found in the grazing and woodland areas, communities which tended to be much less subject to gentry control.[65] The latter areas, especially those with substantial common lands, experienced significant population growth throughout the Tudor and Stuart period, as the landless poor moved in search of industrial work and land on which to erect a cottage and keep a garden and a few animals. It was in such regions – characterized by a dense population, smallholdings, access to commons, and a pastoral agriculture which demanded little hired labour – that rural industries grew.

Since pastoral agriculture did not generate a large demand for hired labour, many of the semi-proletarianized poor resorted to industrial by-employments: spinning, weaving, nailing, etc. The majority of these small producers, while not hired wage-labourers, were nevertheless subordinated to larger master-manufacturers and/ or merchants who provided access to markets and materials. Only those who successfully accumulated and moved into marketing themselves were in a position to escape this subordination to larger capitalists. Often, retention of a small farm, and the extra revenues and/or food production it provided, made such a transition possible.

Rural England in the early modern period thus exhibited two main patterns of economic development: one based on large-scale arable farming; the other involving regions which combined pastoral agriculture with growing rural industries. The result was 'the division of the country into cereal surplus areas and areas of pastoralism with rural domestic industry'.[66] It is for this reason that historians speak of 'two Englands' in 1600: one characterized by open field arable husbandry organized around the traditional village community; the other developing in pasture woodland areas where a growing population subsisted on tiny holdings and provided a ready labour force for cloth-making, mining, metal-working and scores of other domestic industries.[67] Yet, the phrase 'two Englands' is too sharp, implying differentiation, but not symbiosis. It is important to recognize that this division exemplified the kind of regional and sectoral specialization characteristic of an economy being reshaped by the market forces of emergent capitalism.

As one historian has noted, 'England's trade – in wool, leather, grain, hops, minerals – grew directly out of her land and farms'.[68] For this reason, it is an error to see industrial development in the Tudor and Stuart period as something divorced from agriculture. Moreover, it is crucial to recognize that rural society still provided the most important market for manufactures. While tens of thousands of lords and wealthy merchants consumed a range of luxury goods, the mass market was generated by the demand from agricultural households for a small number of essential commodities: nails and knives; small tools and implements; fittings for houses and farm buildings; wooden or earthenware cooking and eating vessels; footware and textiles. Most manufacturing in early modern England involved production of commodities such as these, although a number of areas specialized in exports. Not only did the mass market for manufactures originate in agricultural households; into the eighteenth century, domestic manufacture by farming households

continued to make up the principal form of industrial production.
And much of this industrial output originated in apparently 'agricultural' communities. So widespread was industrial work in such
communities that about half of those who farmed the land in early
modern England appear also to have engaged in at least one form
of industrial work. It is in these communities of 'peasant-workers'
or 'farmer-craftsmen' that we discover some of the major roots of
'industry before the industrial revolution'.[69]

The Sheffield region was famous for its metalworking. With a
parish population of roughly 5,000 in the 1670s, the area had 600
smithies. The majority of metal craftsmen lived in rural or semi-
rural communities, had only one or two domestic hearths and
continued to combine agricultural pursuits with industrial production. The same basic pattern can be detected in cloth production
in north-east Lancashire. Here the 'farmer-craftsman' dominated
the scene, alternating pastoral farming with seasonal clothmaking.
This system of domestic production by small clothiers who also
engaged in agriculture characterized much of industrial Lancashire
and Yorkshire.[70] So interrelated were agriculture and industry that
historians of the Huddersfield woollen industry have used the term
'yeoman-clothier' to characterize the dominant figure in the industry
during the period 1500–1700. Herbert Heaton in fact found that the
word 'yeoman' was often a synonym for 'clothier' in Yorkshire
throughout this same period. Similarly, J.W. Gough has shown
that labourers who devoted most of their productive energies to
mining also described themselves as husbandmen or yeomen.[71]

Industrial growth in the early capitalist period did not proceed
by way of the separation of agriculture and industry and the rise
of the factory. For a quite important period, industrial production
was dominated by a domestic system inextricably connected with
agriculture. Thus, a study of the personal estates of seventy-nine
building craftsmen in Lincolnshire – carpenters, masons and
thatchers – found that over 50 per cent of them had agricultural
possessions.[72] It is for this reason that early industrialization did not
immediately translate into urbanization; on the contrary, it most
often involved the growth of rural industries. This is readily apparent
in the case of the industrial Midlands of the early modern period
which comprised

> a countryside in course of becoming industrialized; more and more a
> strung-out web of iron-working villages, market-towns next door to
> collieries, heaths and wastes gradually and very slowly being covered

by the cottages of nailers and other persons carrying on industrial occupations in rural surroundings.[73]

Yet from these early shoots, an economy based on urban industrial production would blossom. Like yeoman farming, petty manufacturing would experience the impact of primitive accumulation and give birth to more fully capitalist forms of production.[74]

While there is no exact point of transition between petty commodity production and capitalist production which can be marked with precision, the essential features of this process can be clearly delineated. In essence, they involve the metamorphosis of peasant craftsmen or yeoman manufacturers into merchants and employers, who subordinate the labour of a growing number of small producers, and who market their own output (and that of others). These processes can be illustrated in the cases of some of the industries we have already discussed.

In the Sheffield metalworking industry it is clear that 'the new industrial leaders of the second half of the eighteenth century emerged from a peasant-craftsman background'.[75] The leading ironmasters, the Walkers, Booths, Doncasters, Marshes, Shores, Broadbents and Roebucks, all came from small nail-making and cutler families and went on to become founders of the region's main ironworks. The influence of these rising families of small producers extended beyond single industries and regions. It was Dr John Roebuck who sponsored the young James Watt and established the famous Carron Ironworks in Scotland. Moreover, these manufacturers often had an impact which extended from industry to transportation, marketing and banking. 'It was men such as these who were instrumental in getting the Don Navigation Act passed, in establishing the first banks in Sheffield, and in opening up new avenues of trade. They played a fundamental part in launching the Industrial Revolution in the Sheffield region.'[76] One observes a similar pattern in the metalworking industries of the Midlands. Families such as the Turtons, Lowes, Simcoxes and Jessons rose to prominence on the basis of the nail industry of West Bromwich. By the end of the eighteenth century, iron forges and furnaces, rod mills and blade mills were to found 'along every suitable piece of the Tame and its tributaries'. These metalworking families too came from the ranks of yeoman producers.[77] The same picture emerges in the Huddersfield woollen industry where a whole layer of new gentry families rose from the ranks of the yeomanry during the sixteenth century.[78]

Like wool, the cotton industry was organized along quite different lines from one region to the next. The West Riding of Yorkshire tended to be dominated by small independent producers; much of Lancashire experienced 'putting-out' by large merchants. Yet in both cases, many substantial capitalists emerged from small manufacturing backgrounds. The West Riding woollen industry provides one of the clearest examples of this phenomenon. It is estimated that there were 4,000–5,000 clothiers in the region in 1765. The bulk of these were small producers employing little labour from outside the home. As early as the 1740s and 1750s, however, a number of the larger clothiers in the Halifax area were bypassing the merchants of Leeds and breaking into both local and export markets on their own.[79]

In the West Riding it was manufacturers, not merchants, who built most woollen mills. Indeed, of the mills built in Leeds and Huddersfield before 1835, only one in six were financed and operated by individuals of mercantile origin.[80] The same phenomenon has been observed in the case of the textile mills in the Calder Valley below Dewesbury. John Goodchild has shown that, of those scribbling and fulling mills established between 1780 and 1800 whose origins can be established, nine were developed by clothiers, six by merchants and another two by joint-stock companies. Equally important, one of the region's largest and most innovative mills was initiated by Benjamin Hallas, a master clothier who came from a long line of handloom weavers.[81]

To focus on the development of small producers into merchants and large employers – what Marx called the 'really revolutionary way' towards capitalism – is not to deny that in many areas industrial capitalism emerged out of merchant-controlled putting-out systems.[82] It is to insist, however, that we closely inspect these systems; for often they reveal yet another form in which small producers developed into merchants and employers. Indeed, the great weakness of recent theories of 'proto-industrialization' as applied to England is their tendency to assume that a linear path of development accounts for industrialization, one in which urban merchant capital stimulated by expanding foreign markets seizes control of peasant production, erects putting-out systems and proletarianizes the peasant producers.[83] Yet any serious examination of the relationship of merchants to English industry is forced to conclude that many 'merchants' had developed in precisely the way described by Marx, as small producers who undertook direct marketing of their product (and that of others), and employed putting-out and factory labour.[84] The Huddersfield woollen industry provides a case in point:

Neither was the demarcation between clothier and merchant as rigid as is sometimes thought ... A few of the more substantial clothiers did, in fact, dress their pieces, and probably those of their neighbours, and were merchants in all but name.[85]

The research of S.D. Chapman on the Midlands' textile industry illustrates the same pattern. Chapman demonstrates that many Midlands hosiers 'climbed from the ranks of frame operatives to the position of merchants', kept their own workshops, owned 50 to 100 frames, and used 100 to 150 more, thus providing employment for about 800 domestic workers.[86]

Understanding the way in which mercantile and industrial capital frequently combined in the same hands in early modern England requires us to redraw our picture of the putting-out system. Too often commentators have forgotten that master-manufacturers regularly combined direct employment of wage-labour with putting out. Indeed, even early factory masters often continued putting-out operations. Moreover, many of the 'merchants' who engaged in large-scale putting-out had come from the ranks of the small masters.[87] This is not to deny that some with exclusively mercantile interests moved into putting-out or went on to build mills. It is to insist, however, that many large capitalists did not develop in this way, and that many 'merchants' had actually climbed from the ranks of the small manufacturers and continued to combine industrial and mercantile activities.[88]

Moreover, contrary to many misconceptions, the putting-out system did not close off the path by which small producers developed into full-fledged capitalists in their own right. Even the Lancashire cotton industry, largely organized by 'merchants' who put out materials for work by domestic labourers, provided avenues for the 'revolutionary' path to industrial capitalism. Indeed, in its early stages, putting-out in Lancashire involved not so much the distribution by merchants of materials to individual spinners and weavers as the provision of cotton to small country employers who 'put out' these materials to the direct producers. These country manufacturers 'formed an intermediate class of middlemen-manufacturers, employing the spinners and fustian weavers of their districts, and standing on a footing of some independence in relation to the Manchester linen draper'. Country manufacturers were often well positioned to establish their own connections with London merchants, to move into local wool dealing and finishing processes, and to accumulate capital on a significant scale. Wadsworth and Mann point out that 'although most of the weavers and spinners were employees under one form or another of the putting-out system, the system was not a closed one ... It was a short step from weaver to putter-out, and from putting-out agent to manufacturer.'[89]

To be sure, for every small producer who made the transition to merchant and industrial capitalist, dozens of others failed. Yet this was merely another way in which social differentiation took place within the ranks of small producers and created both indigenous capitalists and proletarians. And this phenomenon of class differentiation among petty commodity producers is a central moment in the total process of primitive accumulation of capital. François Crouzet depicts this aspect of capitalist industrialization with great clarity:

> there were many individuals whose main occupation was actually in industry, but who were also small, part-time farmers, with, as borderline cases, those who had just enough land to maintain one horse and/or cow.

> A selection process took place among these people in the late eighteenth and early nineteenth centuries. Many had to retreat, became cottagers doing handloom weaving and were eventually absorbed into the proletariat. But there was also a superior class of artisans-cum-farmers, who had greater resources and, probably, more ability and more luck than others. They, or their sons, succeeded in becoming putters-out, then merchant-manufacturers, and eventually they established a factory.[90]

Market Competition and Proletarianization

Alongside outright expropriation of the bulk of the peasantry, then, the disintegration of feudalism unleashed new forces of petty commodity production as some small producers, emancipated from feudal exactions, increasingly produced for the market. In the context of a growing labour market, competition favoured those producers who could accumulate sufficiently to employ more and more wage-labourers. It was these capitalist producers, tending to concentrate production at one site, who were able to lower average costs of production (through economies of scale and successful exploitation of labour) and thereby force smaller producers into decreasingly viable strategies of 'self-exploitation' in their desperate efforts to produce according to average costs of production. But the long-run trend was for these smaller producers to be bankrupted and driven into the ranks of the proletariat. Thus, just as class differentiation took place within the ranks of the peasantry, so it did among petty producers in manufactures. It is this phenomenon Marx had in mind when he claimed that capitalism develops on the 'tomb' of petty production, and when he described the dissolution of 'private property based on the labour of its owner' as a central aspect of primitive capitalist accumulation.[91]

Marx's point here is particularly relevant to any full understanding of the capitalist market. The key to that market, as we have seen, is the commodification of labour-power. The necessity for the majority to enter the labour market in order to procure their means of subsistence radically transforms the whole of economic life. It means that all inputs and outputs of a production process will tend to be 'marketized' and 'monetized'. Generalized commodity production is thus possible only if labour-power exists as a commodity on a large scale. For this reason Marx writes that 'this one historical pre-condition comprises a world's history'.[92]

Moreover, in the context of a far-reaching labour market, petty commodity production will tend to be transformed into fully capitalist production through processes of market competition. Indeed, competition will generate a growing labour market as numbers of small producers are regularly bankrupted and proletarianized. It follows that, just as proletarianization is the key to creating a fully capitalist market, so that market, once created, will continually reproduce proletarianization – and on a growing scale. Moreover, market competition in such a context means constant pressures to raise levels of labour exploitation as a condition for the survival and reproduction of the producing unit. Proletarianization and intensified exploitation are thus inherent in all market processes where labour-power exists as a commodity on a significant scale.

One can readily see these tendencies at work in the early history of industrial capitalism in Britain as battles for survival among manufacturers intensified pressures on employers to drive down real wages or boost levels of labour productivity (and exploitation) through industrial and technological reorganization. These tendencies achieved their classic form in the automated factory, where living labour is subjected to a discipline embodied in the objective structure and rhythm of machinery. But the growth of the automated factory in sectors like cotton and iron did not automatically give rise to machine production elsewhere.

As Marx pointed out, an industrial revolution in one sphere often intensifies pre-factory forms of production in other sectors, while also creating entirely new forms of sweated labour. Nevertheless, the development of the automated factory means that machine production 'now plays the determining role everywhere'. It does so either by drawing domestic industry into its orbit – as 'an external department of the factory, the manufacturing workshop, or the warehouse' – or by forcing capitals in other spheres to engage in ever more 'shameless' forms of exploitation in order to maintain a competitive footing. The result is that, while manufacture, handicrafts and domestic work continue to exist, they are 'totally changed and disorganized under the influence of large scale industry' and reproduce and overdo 'all the horrors of the factory system'. Thus, while the industrial revolution does follow a basic pattern determined by the appropriateness of the automatic factory to capitalist exploitation, this revolution 'is accomplished through a variegated medley of transitional forms' – a medley in which handicrafts, manufacture, and domestic production continue, albeit in ways largely determined by the dynamics of mechanized production.[93]

What was common to the working class of this period, then, was not the experience of factory labour, which was confined to a minority throughout most of the nineteenth century, but the experience of intensified exploitation. Whether they worked on the land, in the factory or workshop, or in the home as output labour, workers were subjected to more intense forms of labour (often under more direct and systematic control from the supervisor, master or employer). The rise of more fully capitalist relations of production increased pressures towards specialization and division of labour. This involved significant changes as well in the role of the family and women's labour.

The evidence suggests that prior to 1760 labourers' families had a more flexible and equal division of labour than that which developed during the era of the industrial revolution. Access to commons, the viability of much independent commodity production within the household and freedom from substantial reliance on wage-labour created some space for a more diversified family economy, embracing men, women and children. To be sure, this domestic economy was often harsh and oppressive; but it also provided both men and women opportunities for a degree of independence which later contracted. And in the case of women, the increasing shift of production away from the household contributed to a more rigid division of labour between the sexes. One observes this trend most clearly in the case of industries in which domestic organization gave way to centralized workshops and factories. In the words of Ivy Pinchbeck,

Women's work was most varied where the influence of capital in the trade was negligible, as among the small Yorkshire clothiers. When every process from the fleece to the woven piece of cloth was undertaken in the home, the women of the family commonly assisted in all the operations. Big capitalistic production, on the other hand, meant a division of labour in which women were relegated to certain occupations, the number of which tended to be reduced as capitalistic organization developed.[94]

Men often resisted these developments as much as women. They complained of losing the assistance of their wives and children, and objected to the notion that increased wages were adequate compensation for the loss of a previous way of life.[95] Yet the trend was largely irreversible. As household and site of production were increasingly separated, the economic independence of women, especially women with children, declined. Child-rearing and upkeep of a household were more and more detached from production for the market; as a result, working-class mothers played a decreasing role in commodity production.[96] Part and parcel of these developments was a sharp reduction in the range of jobs done by women. As Pinchbeck showed, well into the eighteenth century women were apprenticed to an enormous number of trades – from goldsmiths, stone-masons, engravers and furniture makers to clothiers, weavers, doctors and dentists. Yet in the nineteenth century a dramatic contraction took place in the trades open to women. The separation of agriculture and industry, the rise of the large workshop and factory, and the tendency towards increasing specialization all conspired to reduce the range of economic options for women: factory work was available in a few trades and domestic service grew; but more and more women with children found themselves on the margins of the market economy.[97]

These changes were part of a radical transformation in the substance and rhythm of everday life. And at the heart of this transformation was the destruction of those elements of independence which had protected workers and their families from utter subjection to the market. Despite specific differences in their experiences, workers shared a common sense of loss of control and intensification of labour. During the years 1780–1832, as E.P. Thompson notes, the English working class felt a series of grievances arising from

> changes in the character of capitalist exploitation: the rise of a master-class without traditional authority or obligations: the growing distance between master and man: the transparency of the exploitation at the source of their new wealth and power: the loss of status and above all

of independence for the worker, his reduction to total dependence on the master's instruments of production: the partiality of the law: the disruption of the traditional family economy: the discipline, hours and conditions of work: loss of leisure and amenities: the reduction of the man to the status of an 'instrument'.[98]

It was in these ways that the whole working class experienced the industrial revolution. However much their work situations varied, all workers felt the impact of the new dynamics introduced by the rise of the factory during a period of sharpening capitalist competition. These new dynamics involved a radical recasting of relations between capital and labour, and produced the great social struggles in which the workers began to define themselves as a class.

The Working Class and the Industrial Revolution

Harold Perkin has written that 'a regular, disciplined, reliable labour force was – and is – the most hazardous requirement of an industrial revolution'.[99] Hazardous it was, because workers resisted the manifold processes by which they were made entirely reliant on the vagaries of the market in labour and subjected to the pressures (both direct and indirect) of mechanization. The battle to create a disciplined proletariat was fought as a campaign against anything that provided labourers with an element of independence from the labour market. We have examined perhaps the most important of these conflicts in the previous chapter – the enclosure debate which played a central role in the creation of a large and growing proletariat, and which was often conducted in terms of an attack on the 'independence' of labourers with a cottage or access to common lands. According to the developing precepts of political economy, the propertylessness of the majority was the indispensable prerequisite to the advance of civilization – which, ironically, was defined in terms of the displacement of common ownership by private ownership of productive resources.[100]

The debate over enclosure was not the only arena in which the argument over labour, property and political economy was conducted. There were many other interrelated issues around which this battle raged between 1780 and 1834. Five of these particularly deserve comment in the context of this study: (1) perquisites and embezzlement; (2) apprenticeship; (3) labour discipline; (4) property, crime and punishment; (5) poor law policy. Each one of these debates focused on the need to render the working class utterly reliant on wage-labour. I intend here to deal with the first four of these issues, leaving a discussion of poor law policy for a later chapter.

Perquisites and Embezzlement

The idea that labour should be paid exclusively in terms of a money wage was foreign to the experience of many workers in the eighteenth and early nineteenth centuries. By-products of the production process were commonly considered the rightful property of the labourers. To take just two examples, it was customary for weavers to take 'thrums' – the weft ends left on the loom after the removal of finished cloth – and for shipwrights to appropriate 'chips' – waste scraps of wood which could be used or sold as firewood – as a supplement to the money wage. These perquisites were widely considered to belong to the labourers as a form of 'property' established and sanctioned by long-standing custom.[101]

In the environment of intensified labour and heightened capitalist competition which emerged in the second half of the eighteenth century, many of these perquisites were redefined in law as forms of 'theft', as embezzlement of property which rightfully belonged to the employer. Associations for the prosecution of embezzlement were formed by masters, modelled perhaps on those created by rural gentry for the enforcement of game laws and prosecution of poachers. These associations employed inspectors to search workers' homes for 'stolen' materials and provided funds for prosecutions. By 1777 the penalty for embezzlement had increased to three months in a house of correction, up from fourteen days in 1749.[102]

The attack on perquisites was not simply an attempt to minimize costs, although it was that in part; it was also an attempt to impose a stricter labour discipline by establishing both the right of the employer to full ownership of all the products of the labour-process, and the complete reliance of employees on their money wage. In large measure, the issue at hand was the imposition of 'the money-form as the exclusive basis of the material relation' between capital and labour.[103] The same issue was central to the dispute over apprenticeship.

The Apprenticeship Debate

The Statute of Artificers and Apprentices of 1563 required that any practitioner of a wide variety of crafts had first to serve a seven-year apprenticeship under a master craftsman. In return for honouring their obligations under the Act, apprentices were often boarded in the home of their master or mistress, and, as with service in husbandry, the latter were commonly expected to provide food, clothes and tools, and to pay entry fines or company dues at the end of the seven-year term. Rather than an arrangement determined by a free labour market, apprenticeship entailed a regulated, customary relationship in which the money-wage played an often secondary role.[104] In practice, however, the Act had never been enforced systematically, and as the eighteenth century progressed it was consistently violated and modified. Thus, the mean length of apprenticeships declined from six and a half years in the 1750s to four years by 1795. During the 1820s and 1830s, apprentices completed their apprenticeships at about seventeen years of age, as opposed to nearly twenty years of age before 1780. Moreover, the increase in apprenticeships that were illegal, and in those that were terminated by decision of the masters, or by apprentices running away suggests a steady deterioration in the conditions of this relationship.[105]

The dilution of apprenticeships elicited a twofold response: a decline in the real wages of artisans and a concerted attempt by the latter to enforce and to strengthen the stipulations of the Act of 1563.[106] Not surprisingly, the employers' campaign against apprenticeship was conducted in terms of the language of political economy and *laissez-faire*; apprenticeship laws were denounced as violations of natural liberty and free trade. During the debate of 1810–11 on the petitions of cotton weavers, for example, Parliament had pronounced that the weavers' proposals to enforce apprenticeship infringed 'on personal liberty in that most essential point, the free exercise of Industry, of Skill, and of Talent'.[107] Similarly, the artisans' campaign of 1812–14 to strengthen the apprenticeship laws was met with the argument that all such legislation should be repealed, since this would force workers to become more industrious. As one such proponent put it,

> Repeal that statute, and all combinations will cease; wages will rise or fall in proportion to the real demand for labour, and mechanics and manufacturers will be induced, by the competition incident to the freedom of employment, to work with much more care and industry.[108]

The artisan campaign to strengthen apprenticeship was a vast and well-organized movement involving a petition bearing 32,000 signatures sent to the House of Commons in April 1813, followed by another with more than 60,000 names.[109] Central to the campaign was an argument which defined labour as a form of property which should be subject to protection in law. The public appeal issued as a result of the artisan meeting held at the Freemasons' Tavern on 14 January, 1814 spelled this out clearly:

> The apprenticed artisans have, collectively and individually, an unquestionable right to expect the most extended protection from the Legislature, in the quiet and exclusive use and enjoyment of their several and respective arts and trades, which the law has already conferred upon them *as a property*, as much as it has secured the property of the stockholder in the public funds; and it is clearly unjust to take away the whole of the ancient property and rights of any one class of the community, unless, at the same time, the rights and property of the whole commonwealth should be dissolved, and parcelled out anew for the public good.[110]

By rejecting the artisans' arguments, and by repealing the apprenticeship clauses of the Statute of Apprentices in July 1814, Parliament announced that it would not recognize the accumulated knowledge and skills acquired by apprenticeship as a form of 'property' eligible for legal protection. We shall return below to the debate over property and political economy which found expression in the conflict over apprenticeship. What needs to be emphasized for the moment is that, whether we accept that the repeal of the apprenticeship clauses represented the removal of 'the last major legislative limitation on the labour market', it clearly did reflect 'the need of capitalist employers for a mobile labour force whose supply and price would be determined by the 'natural' laws of a free labour market'.[111] Moreover, this victory for the capitalist labour market was to be reaffirmed with the defeat in July 1835 of Fielden's Bill to fix wages in the handloom weaving trades, a defeat that was re-enacted several times between 1837 and 1840.[112]

Constructing Labour Discipline

The virtue of Perkin's statement, quoted at the beginning of this section, is that it indicates the immense difficulties associated with the construction of a disciplined industrial proletariat. This is especially clear in the case of factory labour. Workers generally resisted employment in factories, associating them with coercion, punishment and loss of independence. The design of factories along the lines of houses of correction did much to encourage this association. For this reason, early factories often used indentured labour, usually that of children. Even here, enormous difficulties were encountered. Figures for one mill indicate that fully one third of apprentices died, absconded or had to be sent back to parents and overseers between 1786 and 1805.[113]

In addition to the problem of attracting employees, the early factory masters also encountered that of inculcating habits of punctuality, regularity, and industry. The pre-industrial workforce followed a unique rhythm of work and leisure. The practice of 'St. Monday' (taking Monday as a holiday from work) was widespread, as was the taking of numerous feastdays throughout the year. By no means should the domestic system be glorified; nevertheless, 'however intermittent and sweated its labour, it did allow a man a degree of personal liberty to indulge himself, a command over his time, which he was not to enjoy again'. It was the element of 'command over his time' which the early factory masters sought especially to eliminate. 'Time was the new idol – together with care, regularity and obedience.'[114] Central to the creation of labour discipline, therefore, was a new experience of time which was materially embodied in bells, clocks, clocking in, fines for lateness and absenteeism, and so on. It should go without saying that the battle to impose factory discipline was a battle over the very culture of life, labour and leisure.[115]

This battle was often depicted by the practitioners and ideologists of early industrial capitalism as a great moral crusade for social improvement. Thus, Josiah Wedgwood maintained that he sought 'to make *Artists* ... [of] ... mere *men*', and to 'make such *machines* of the *men* as cannot err'. Difficult though this operation might be, Wedgwood conceived it in heroic terms: 'It is *hard*, but then it is *glorious* to conquer so great an Empire with raw, undisciplin'd recruits.'[116] In addition to the bell and the clock, Wedgwood introduced a sweeping set of work rules. Nevertheless, the success of the factory masters at inculcating industrial discipline, while real, should not be exaggerated. Wedgwood, for example, completely failed to control the potters' attendance of fairs and wakes. When a riot broke out at his pottery at Etruria in 1783, he called for military repression; the end result was the arrest and conviction of two men, one of whom was hanged.

It was generally coercion such as this, not incentive, which instilled the new labour discipline. Pollard sums up the balance of the experience when he writes that the modern industrial proletariat was introduced to its role not so much by attraction or monetary reward, but by compulsion, force and fear. It was not allowed to grow as in a sunny garden; it was forged over a fire by the powerful blows of a hammer ... The typical framework is that of dominance and fear, fear of hunger, of eviction, of prison for those who disobey the new industrial rules.[117]

This is confirmed by the questionnaires returned to the Factory Commissioners in 1833, which showed that of 614 incidents of the use of discipline to enforce obedience among factory children, 575 of these were coercive – ranging from corporal punishment to dismissal – whereas a mere 34 cases showed attempts at positive inducement to obedience.[118]

Often, mechanization was the only way to break working-class resistance by establishing a rhythm of production materially embodied in the machine rather than in the skills of the labourers. As Sadler's parliamentary committee reported in 1831–2, in a statement which reinforces Marx's view that 'machinery ultimately forced the worker to accept the discipline of the factory'.[119] But especially during the early transition to industrial capitalism, the use of state power was never far from sight, and was called in whenever the employer could not sustain discipline on his own. And use of state power involved more than periodic use of troops; it also involved whole new arrangements governing crime and punishment.

Property, Crime and Punishment

The emergence of new definitions of property and crime has received increased attention in recent years. The Black Act 1723, for example, criminalized a range of activities which had long been considered legitimate exercises of customary right: appropriating timber, underwood, hedges and fruit from trees; taking fish from ponds; damaging woodlands and orchards; and so on.[120] Similarly, the laws on embezzlement described above represented an assertion of newly defined rights of property against communal and customary rights. Not only did the law increasingly punish transgressions of capitalist property rights, it also sought to punish those who tried to elude the discipline of the employer and the labour market. The Vagrancy Act 1744, for instance, endowed magistrates with the power to whip or imprison beggars, peddlars, gamblers, strolling actors, gypsies, and 'all those who refused to work for the usual and common wages', and it bestowed on them the right to imprison 'all persons wand'ring abroad and lodging in alehouses, barns and houses or in the open air, not giving a good account of themselves'. The emphasis on disciplined adherence to wage-labour was often made explicit. Blackstone explained that one of the reasons for criminalizing the taking of rabbits was to inhibit 'low and indigent persons' from pursuing the hunt rather than 'their proper employments and callings'.[121] In a variety of ways, then, eighteenth-century law was recast in order more effectively to subjugate workers to the discipline of the labour market: by punishing 'vagrancy' (avoidance of wage-labour), and by eliminating alternatives to waged work – hunting, fishing, wood gathering, the taking of thrums and chips.

This extension of the rights of property, the assault on supplementary forms of income, the decline of real wages in numerous industries and the more powerful assertion of capitalist authority combined to produce an escalation in the crime rate. Moreover, as transportation declined as a form of punishment (largely because of the war with America), the prison population soared. John Howard, philanthropist and prison reformer, estimated that the number of imprisoned had increased 73 per cent between 1776 and 1786. Accompanying this was the increasing severity of punishment: the number of persons executed in London between 1783 and 1787 was 82 per cent higher than it had been in the previous five-year period. This trend was exacerbated by the trade depression and mass unemployment, which followed the end of the Napoleonic Wars, resulting in a sharp rise in the number of people committed to trial, a trend that continued into the 1840s.[122] Not only did the law create a whole new set of 'crimes' against the rights of property; the era of the industrial revolution also saw a radically new conception of the nature of punishment, a conception that was embodied in the order of the penitentiary.

Understood in ideological terms, the development of the penitentiary was an expression of the liberal English materialism which contributed to the construction of bourgeois society. Central to this doctrine was the notion that human beings could be remade, by a combination of coercion, education and changed circumstances, to create a disciplined and industrious labour force. In the first instance this required, as we have seen, eliminating those conditions which sustained the material and spiritual independence of the labourers – be they common rights, perquisities, or apprenticeship laws. At the level of the factory, it involved moulding people to the exigencies of industrial production, as expressed in Wedgwood's conviction that he would 'make such *machines* of the *men* as cannot err'. In terms of legal punishment, it involved a growing commitment to the idea that means would have to be found to discipline the mind as well as the body by forcing the prisoner to internalize the new moral code, to accept his guilt as an idler, thief, vagrant or rebel.

Arguments proliferated to the effect that prisons should combine 'correction of the mind' with correction of the body; that conscience must be relied on to 'hold a man fast when all other obligations break'; and that this would be achieved by means of a system of correction based on 'softening the mind in order to aid its amendment'.[123] Central to these views was the notion that solitary confinement was the most effective way to break down the psychological resistance of offenders, to soften their minds and transform their consciences. Perhaps the clearest formulation of the view that penitentiaries could remake prisoners was to be found in Bentham's famous arguments on behalf of his Panopticon, where he described penal correction as 'a species of manufacture' which employed 'its particular capital', i.e. the material form of the penitentiary with its proposed system of cells, supervision, labour and punishment.[124]

The new ideologists of the penitentiary thus advocated a mode of discipline designed to *reform* and *correct* offenders, not merely to inflict punishment on them. By the 1820s, however, these arguments were modified by others, which called for a concerted effort to worsen the conditions of prisoners. As in the campaign against the old poor law, proponents of an attack on prisoners' conditions claimed that the latter lived better than many British labourers. As a result, diets were reduced, floggings were increased and unproductive labour on the treadmill was introduced. At the same time, a series of Acts passed between 1823 and 1831 increased the powers of magistrates, provided for the building of new prisons and created a new police force in an effort to broaden the material means for enforcing the growing rights of property.[125]

The creation of the 'free' labour market was thus the result of decades of coercive measures, embodied in a regime of law and punishment, designed to destroy communal property rights and establish the unfettered sway of capitalist private property. Moreover, as we have seen, the creation of a fully marketized economy was essential to the construction of those property relations. For the labour market presupposed the *destruction* of communal property and reproduced the dispossession of the labourers. Rather than the natural outgrowth of economic life, the 'free market' was the product of class policy and class power. It was this reality that Karl Polanyi had in mind when he coined his memorable phrase: '*laissez-faire* was planned'.[126] And theorists of the developing working class knew it. As a result, at the same time as workers resisted their increasing subjugation to the labour market, working-class writers sought to launch a theoretical assault on the principles which underpinned the planned creation of the 'free' market in labour. Inevitably, this required a theoretical confrontation with political economy.

2

Justice and Markets: The Ambiguous Legacy of Adam Smith

> Did Dr. A Smith ever contemplate such a state of things? it is in vain to read his book to find a remedy for a complaint which he could not conceive existed, viz. 100,000 weavers doing the work of 150,000 when there was no demand (as 'tis said) and that for half meat, and the rest paid by Poor Rates.[1]

So testified Thomas Ainsworth, a ruined man, about the depression in the British cotton trade which followed the Napoleonic wars. What is most important in Ainsworth's statement, at least for our purposes, is his reference to Adam Smith, which identifies an important problem. For central to Smith's theory of growth in the *Wealth of Nations* was the notion that capital accumulation inevitably involved an increase in employment and wages. Yet the experience of the British economy in the half-century after the publication of the *Wealth of Nations* in 1776 seemed directly to controvert Smith's analysis. Instead of increased prosperity and security for 'the sober and industrious poor', as Smith called them, commercial society appeared to offer greater misery and poverty. The result was that Smithian political economy underwent a marked bifurcation: on the one hand, defenders of the status quo stripped Smith's economic theory of its commitment to rising employment and wages (and hence of its ethical dimension) in order to justify the ill fortunes of labourers as necessary and inevitable; on the other hand, critics of emerging industrial capitalism used Smith's theories of growth and distribution in order to indict poverty and the factory system. As a result, by the 1820s, 'Smithian' apologists for industrial capitalism confronted 'Smithian socialists' in a vigorous, and often venomous, debate over political economy.[2]

The term 'Smithian socialists' immediately invites surprise. Wasn't it Smith, after all, who constructed an idealized image of bourgeois society which became a cornerstone of ideological defences of capitalism? Certainly this is the dominant view. Yet working-class radicals did not see things that way. While they directed substantial energies into a campaign against political economy, their targets were usually Malthus and his Ricardian adherents. And they often used Smith's work as a weapon in their campaign against these political economists. That Smith's name was invoked by dogmatic defenders of the capitalist market is of no little historical import. But the Smithian legacy was a contested one. Understanding why this was so, and how an apologetic bourgeois version of Smith came to prevail, is crucial to grasping the evolution of political economy and socialism during this period.

But the question of the Smithian legacy is of more than historical interest, particularly because modern ideologists of the market continue to claim Smith as a prophet of ultra-liberalism. Friedrich von Hayek, for example, is moved to assert that 'the foundation of modern civilization was first understood by Adam Smith'.[3] And the foundation of modern civilization that Smith apparently first grasped is the 'spontaneous order' of the competitive market. According to Hayek, human civilization involves a long struggle against 'primitive instincts' such as solidarity, benevolence and the impulse to put the needs of the community first. These instincts underpin socialism and all theories of social justice. Yet the greatness of modern society consists in the substitution of 'artificial rules' which free the individual from the primitive constraints imposed by communal impulses and enable unfettered competition to establish a 'spontaneous order' conducive to liberty and prosperity.[4]

Hayek claims Smith's famous discussion of the division of labour in Book One of the *Wealth of Nations* as the germ of the modern theory of market society.[5] Yet there is something disingenuous about Hayek's attempt to enlist Smith as a warrior against those inherited instincts which lead to the valuing of benevolence. For the best scholarship on Smith has demonstrated that at the heart of his thought was a considered attempt 'to reconcile the old ethics and the new economics'.[6] Rather than reject all previous ethics, Smith sought to work some of their central elements into a moral and jurisprudential theory which could outline a means of sustaining justice and benevolence within a commercial society. This inevitably produced an enormous tension in his thought as he struggled to weave morality and the market into a new theoretical synthesis.

Ludwig von Mises, Hayek's teacher and predecessor, at least

acknowledged the ambiguous legacy of Smith in this regard, noting in *Theory and History* that the author of the *Wealth of Nations* 'could not free himself from the standards and terminology of traditional ethics that condemned as vicious man's desire to improve his own material conditions'.[7] In an effort to appropriate the Smithian legacy to his own ends, Hayek prefers to ignore these aspects of Smith's thought, to smooth out its tensions and flatten it into a homily for the market. Subtly, however, he has come to put greater emphasis on Smith's adversary, Bernard Mandeville, as the first prophet of the cult of the market. But in depicting the author of the *Wealth of Nations* as a Mandevillean, Hayek is engaged in nothing less than a wholesale vulgarization of Smith's thought.

Given the obvious nature of this vulgarization, it is ironic that much recent scholarship has presented a 'new' image of Smith which looks remarkably like a much older picture. A long-standing line of interpretation depicted the author of the *Wealth of Nations* as 'an unconscious mercenary in the service of a rising capitalist class in Europe' and as 'the prophet of the commercial society of modern capitalism'.[8] Recent interpretations have arrived at a more theoretically subtle and informed image of Smith by setting the *Wealth of Nations* alongside its author's first work, *The Theory of the Moral Sentiments* (1759), and students' notes of his *Lectures on Jurisprudence* from his tenure at Glasgow University. The author of the *Wealth of Nations* thus emerges as a much more sophisticated and profound theorist than earlier images had suggested. Notwithstanding these modifications, the final image offered in the new interpretation is remarkably similar to the traditional one. In one of the most influential volumes in this area, we are informed, for example, that Smith was engaged in a 'defence of modernity' and that 'Smith's argument remains the core of modern capitalism's defence of itself'.[9]

The new interpretation situates Smith in a long line of jurisprudential theorizing which, rejecting classical civic humanist concerns for a virtuous society of publicly spirited citizens, gave priority to the rights of individuals to pursue their economic well-being free from traditional moral and social restraints.[10] In this view, Smith's theory adopts the individualistic co-ordinates of economic 'rights' and 'liberties' as an alternative to those of the virtuous republic; its coherence thus derives from a preoccupation with those political conditions which protect the rights of individuals to free exercise of their labour and their property. In place of the conflict between virtue and corruption, Smith's argument is said to have substituted that between personal liberty and public restraint. The result is a sharp depiction of Smith as a defender of capitalism and a theorist of 'possessive individualism'. It follows from this view that classical economists such as Ricardo and Mill were correct to see themselves as the heirs of Smith; and that early socialist writers had no right to lay claim to the author of the *Wealth of Nations*.[11]

The jurisprudential interpretation has generated some important insights into the overlapping and interlocking lines of argument that run through the *Wealth of Nations*. But, by constructing its argument in so thoroughly one-sided a fashion, it fundamentally distorts our image of Smith. In a manner similar to Hayek, albeit with much greater theoretical sophistication, it has treated the *Wealth of Nations* as if all that really matters are the early chapters of Book One on the division of labour and exchange, and Book Five on the tasks of the legislator in a system of economic liberty. Ironically, as one commentator notes, 'the *economic* analysis of the *Wealth of Nations*' has had 'a shadowy existence' in recent debates over Smith.[12] Equally significant, the connection between Smith's moral philosophy and his theory of economic exchange has been obscured.

It is the object of this chapter to outline the very real tensions that run through Smith's thought, tensions that derived from his ingenious but untenable effort to reconcile 'the old ethics with the new economics'. I endeavour to show that Smith's 'economics' presuppose his moral theory and its jurisprudential component, and that the transformation of his thought into an apologetic bourgeois ideology required a systematic vulgarization, a process in which Malthus played a central role. Finally, I argue in subsequent chapters that Smith's 'solution' could not survive the changed circumstances of the transition to industrial capitalism. The disintegration of his system was therefore inevitable. Equally inevitable were the efforts of both apologists for and critics of early industrial capitalism to base their arguments on that work which held sway over the entire field of political economy – the *Wealth of Nations*.

Virtue and Commerce: Against Mandeville

'If Dr. Hutchinson could give no lecture without attacking *The Fable of the Bees*, we may be sure that his student Adam Smith very soon turned to it.' So writes F.A. Hayek. Indeed, Hayek proceeds to claim that the central arguments of *The Fable of the Bees* became 'the basis of the approach to social philosophy of David Hume and his successors'.[13] That such statements can be made today is testimony not only to shoddy scholarship, but, more significantly, to the strenuous efforts which have been made for nearly two hundred years to revise Smith in order to transform him into an apostle of self-interest, competition and the market.

Let us start by setting the terms of the discussion. The 'Dr. Hutchinson' in question is Francis Hutcheson (1694–1746), Professor of Moral Philosophy at Glasgow University and teacher of Adam Smith. Modern studies have rightly treated Hutcheson as the key figure in the early Scottish Enlightenment, as 'the personality most responsible for the new spirit of enlightenment in the Scottish universities'.[14] *The Fable of the Bees* was the work of the Dutch doctor Bernard Mandeville. It appeared in 1705 as a poem entitled *The Grumbling Hive, or Knaves Turned Honest*, a satirical effort designed to debunk classical moral theories by showing that selfish passions were the basis of human action and that these, not ostensible virtues, often served the best interests of society, if properly manipulated by a clever statesman. Nine years later Mandeville republished the poem with a prose commentary. Another nine years after that he brought out a second edition under the title *Fable of the Bees, or Private Vices Public Benefits*. Then in 1728 a second volume appeared which elaborated the original argument in greater detail.[15]

Central to the perspective of the *Fable* was the claim that corruption, fraud and deceit were socially and economically beneficial. As the story unfolds, elimination of these three vices, and their replacement by traditional virtues, results in the collapse of industry and trade. Mandeville argues that luxury and extravagance, traditionally considered vices, in fact provide a stimulus to many trades, just as theft provides work for the locksmith. While he did not insist that all vices automatically produce public benefits – this requires the 'dextrous Management of a skillful Politician' – he prided himself on having demonstrated that society is not built on 'the Friendly Qualities and kind Affections that are natural to Man', nor on 'the real Virtues he is capable of acquiring by Reason and Self-Denial'. Rather, he claimed to have proved 'that what we call Evil in this World, Moral as well as Natural, is the grand principle that makes us sociable Creatures, the solid Basis, the Life and Support of all Trades and Employments without exception'.[16]

More than any other theoretical encounter, it was his confrontation with Mandeville which decisively shaped the political thought of Smith's great teacher Francis Hutcheson. Although Hutcheson adduced a number of strictly economic arguments against the author of the *Fable*, his critique hinged on a theory of the human passions. Here, the key line of argument was the claim that human beings possess both selfish and social passions. Among the latter is 'a natural impulse to society with their fellows' and a 'moral sense' (or senses), which predispose individuals to favour the public interest. Social life requires a carefully regulated balance and harmony among these impulses, but it is not simply reducible to any one of them.[17]

Contrary to Hayek's crude effort to collapse Smith into Mandeville's position, it is clear that the author of the *Wealth of Nations* adhered much more closely to the Hutchesonian perspective. In one of his earliest published efforts, a 1756 letter to the short-lived *Edinburgh Review*, Smith took issue with both Mandeville and Rousseau and their shared view that 'there is in man no powerful instinct which necessarily determines him to seek society for its own sake'. Smith rejected this asocial conception of human nature, although he was clearly more sympathetic to Rousseau's overall position. His description of Mandeville's views as 'profligate' and his denunciation of their 'tend-ency to corruption and licentiousness which has disgraced them' go some considerable way toward undermining the notion that Smith was in any sense an adherent of the author of the *Fable*.[18]

Moreover, these criticisms were not isolated events. It was one of the central purposes of Smith's major work in moral philosophy, *The Theory of the Moral Sentiments* (first edition 1759) to refute the claim of 'the selfishness school' that the foundation of all human action is selfish passion. Smith there attacks Mandeville's system as 'wholly pernicious' and as a piece of 'ingenious sophistry'. And he writes that 'It is the great folly of Dr Mandeville's book to represent every passion as wholly vicious, which is so in any degree and in any direction'.

The first sentence of the *Moral Sentiments* directly attacks this position. Smith writes that

> How selfish soever man may be supposed, there are evidently some principles in his nature, which interest him in the fortune of others, and render their happiness necessary to him, though he derives nothing from it, except the pleasure of seeing it.[19]

Smith grounds our capacity for moral behaviour in our ability, via the imagination, to sympathize with the situations of others, and in our desire to act in such a way as to elicit their sympathy in turn. Our impulse for sympathy with others is rooted in the pleasure afforded by communication and conversation. Human beings dislike disharmony and disagreement, Smith believes; this gives rise to 'the naturall inclination every one has to persuade'. In order to produce a convergence and harmony of opinions and sentiments, 'every one is practising oratory on others thro the whole of his life'. 'Nothing pleases us more', he writes, 'than to observe in other men a fellow-feeling with the emotions of our own breast.' Seen in this light, the art of communication is the creation through language of a sympathetic identification between a speaker and his listeners.[20] Smith is quite explicit about the role of sympathy in this process of communication. As he puts it in a passage from his *Lectures on Rhetoric and Belles Lettres*,

> Whenever the sentiment of the speaker is expressed in a neat, clear, plain and clever manner, and the passion or affection he is poss[ess]ed of and intends, *by sympathy*, to communicate to his hearer, is plainly and cleverly hit off, then and then only the expression has all the force and beauty that language can give it.[21]

It follows, then, that sympathy is essential to the fullest possible communication of our sentiments. And sympathy, he argues, 'cannot in any sense be regarded as a selfish principle'.[22] In addition to self-interest, human behaviour is governed by social passions – sympathy and the desire for conversation and communication. Our sentiments thus involve a natural desire for a community of feelings and opinions. 'The great pleasure of conversation and society', he continues towards the end of the *Moral Sentiments*,

> arises from a certain correspondence of sentiments and opinions, from a certain harmony of minds, which, like so many musical instruments, coincide and keep time with another. But this most delightful harmony cannot be obtained unless there is a free communication of sentiments and opinions.[23]

Our desire for sympathy with and from others arises, therefore, from the pleasure we derive from society, understood as a community of language and sentiments. Human beings are thus naturally sociable; yet sympathy involves more than a natural instinct or moral sense: it requires an exercise of the imagination through which we attempt to place ourselves in the shoes of another in order to form an image of their experience, and to imagine how our behaviour in a given situation appears to them. Indeed, Smith maintains that through social interaction we internalize norms of appropriate behaviour (a sort of moral code), and that we attempt to measure our own behaviour against our notion of how it would appear to a disinterested or 'impartial spectator'. Thus, the desire for sympathetic interaction is natural; the moral sentiments, however, are socially constructed through our acceptance of behavioural norms as the necessary condition of sympathy with others.[24]

Smith argues, however, that our imaginary entry into the experience of others is inevitably 'imperfect'; we can never truly experience the full degree of their joy or their grief. For this reason, the fullness of their sympathetic identification with us requires that we moderate and subdue our passions. In so doing, we make our experience more accessible to them, and thereby enhance our 'correspondence of sentiments'. In order that others may enter into his experience, the individual must control his passion; he 'must flatten ... the sharpness of its natural tone, in order to reduce it to harmony and concord with the emotions of those who are about him'.[25] Moderation and self-control are thus prerequisites of communication and conversation; without self-control there will be discord rather than concord of sentiments, and society in the fullest sense of the term will not be possible. Our natural impulse towards society requires, therefore, that we learn to shape our behaviour to conform to prevailing standards and expectations. And this involves 'humbling the arrogance' of our self-love and bringing 'it down to something that other men can go along with'.[26] Thus, however much self-love is part of the natural constitution of human beings, so is the social impulse towards conversation and society, an impulse which underlies learned behaviour through which we control our self-love in the interest of harmony with others.

The psychological underpinnings of Smith's theory of society are thus anything but the sort of self-seeking individualism commonly associated with Hobbes and Mandeville. Following his teacher Francis Hutcheson, Smith starts from the premiss of natural sociability. And he sees the essence of our 'socialization' as involving acquired habits of self-control in order that we might have the pleasures of conversation and society. Moreover, these are the presuppositions of his discussion in the *Wealth of Nations* of the division of labour and exchange.

Sympathy, Communication and Exchange

It seems probable, Smith argues in his treatise on political economy, that the human 'propensity to truck, barter, and exchange one thing for another' is the 'necessary consequence of the faculties of reason and speech'. Indeed, in his *Lectures on Jurisprudence* Smith traces this propensity to our natural inclination to persuade. Moreover, this propensity is uniquely human, 'it is common to all men, and to be found in no other race of animals'. Certainly, 'nobody ever saw a dog make a fair and deliberate exchange of one bone for another with another dog'.[27] Exchange is both a reasonable and a sociable act. It presupposes that, by language, I can communicate the (imagined) benefits that another might derive from something I possess and, similarly, that I might equally conceive of the benefits I would receive from something which they possess in turn. Thus, although I appeal to the self-interest of the butcher, the brewer or the baker, this appeal presupposes that I participate with them in a network of communication and social interaction without which 'deliberate exchange' could not occur.[28] Furthermore, exchange is impossible unless I am able to acquire (via the imagination) a sympathetic understanding of the interests of others.

Division of labour and exchange is thus predicated on co-operation and interaction. Indeed, it is not the anonymous and impersonal character of exchange that appeals to Smith, but the possibility that involvement in an exchange economy or 'commercial society' could have a moralizing impact on the individual. In the *Moral Sentiments* he writes, for example, that

> in the race for wealth, and honours, and preferments, he may run as hard as he can, and strain every nerve and every muscle, in order to outstrip all his competitors. But if he should justle, or throw down any of them, the indulgence of the spectators is entirely at an end. It is a violation of fair play, which they cannot admit of.[29]

However comical this picture may appear in light of the reality of modern capitalist behaviour, there can be little doubt that Smith took it seriously and that he hoped that an exchange economy would provide a context of social interaction which would reinforce the need for self-control and adherence to customary forms of moral behaviour.

Although he appears to have become increasingly pessimistic in later years about the civilizing effects of commerce and exchange, Smith still hoped that commercial society could enforce standards of propriety and prudent behaviour.[30] Indeed, it was central to his view that one of the greatest merits of commercial society – the increase in national wealth it generates – would benefit the 'sober and industrious poor' only if such standards of prudence and propriety were reinforced, not undercut, by the behaviour of people in the market. According to Smith, by interesting others in our economic situation (what we can offer in exchange) and taking an interest in their offerings in turn, human beings construct a network of economic co-operation and transaction – a social economy – in which they can develop unique talents by means of specialization. The result is twofold: first, the development of special talents and professions; and, second, the enormous augmentation of wealth such specialization produces.[31] Smith's praise for the division of labour embraces both of these interrelated consequences. But there can be no doubt that his emphasis is on the latter.

The great achievement of commercial society for Smith is 'that universal opulence which extends itself to the lowest ranks of the people'. Indeed, Smith claims that the gap between the comforts of a European prince and those of 'an industrious and frugal peasant' is not so great as that between the latter and 'many an African king, the absolute master of the lives and liberties' of thousands.[32] While this is the greatest advantage of commercial society over other forms, it is clear that Smith was deeply worried that prevailing prejudices and practices could prevent the poor from enjoying the increased comforts that should rightfully be theirs in modern society. For this reason he endorses the 'liberal reward of labour' and claims, contrary to a long-standing view, that such a reward 'increases' rather than diminishes 'the industry of the common people'. Smith, in fact, defines wealth in terms of consumption which is, he claims, 'the sole end and purpose of production' and he denounces measures to limit wages.[33] In this vein, he defends 'the liberal reward' of labour in terms of straightforward justice and equity:

Is this improvement in the circumstances of the lower ranks of the people to be regarded as an advantage or as an inconveniency to the society? The answer seems at first sight abundantly plain. Servants, labourers and workmen of different kinds, make up the far greater part of every great political society. But what improves the circumstances of the greater part can never be regarded as an inconveniency to the whole. No society can surely be flourishing and happy, of which the greater part of the members are poor and miserable. It is but equity, besides, that they who feed, cloath and lodge the whole body of the people, should have such a share of the produce of their own labour as to be themselves tolerably well fed, cloathed and lodged.[34]

Smith's support for the 'liberal reward of labour' was crucial to his theory of commercial society. Like the other great representatives of 'the Scottish historical School' – Francis Hutcheson, Lord Kames, Adam Ferguson, David Hume and John Millar – and more so than his friend Hume, Smith was acutely aware of the losses that accompanied commercial society. His historical realism, however, coupled with his belief in the importance of personal independence and security, allowed him to construct a cautious – and cautionary – defence of such a social order. Nevertheless, there are important tensions and contradictions in Smith's theory of commercial society as set forth in the *Wealth of Nations*, and these were to be of great significance for the later development of political economy.

Dependence, Independence and Wage-labour

Perhaps the most important of these tensions concerns the problem of personal independence in commercial society. Smith's hostility to feudalism (and the feudal nobility) was fuelled by his belief that the ties of personal 'dependence' which bound the poor to the rich inevitably demeaned and corrupted the former while rendering the latter overbearing and abusive. One of the attractions of commercial society for Smith was that it dissolved these ties: 'Nothing tends so much to corrupt and enervate and debase the mind as dependency, and nothing gives such noble and generous notions of probity as freedom and independency. Commerce is one great preventive of this custom [of dependency].'[35]

Consistent with this view, the early chapters of the *Wealth of Nations* employ a model of commercial society based upon interaction between independent commodity producers like butchers, brewers and bakers. Such individuals are independent not only in the sense that they are not bound to a lord; they are also independent owners of their own means of production and work for themselves, not an employer. It is clear that Smith preferred an economy based on independent commodity producers (including a large number of yeomen farmers). He writes, for example, that

> Nothing can be more absurd, however, than to imagine that men in general should work less when they work for themselves, than when they work for other people. A poor independent workman will generally be more industrious than even a journeyman who works by the piece. The one enjoys the whole produce of his industry; the other shares it with his master. The one, in his separate state, is less liable to the temptations of bad company, which in large manufactories ruin the morals of the other. The superiority of the independent workman over those servants

who are hired by the month or the year, and whose wages and maintenance are the same whether they do much or do little, is likely to be
still greater.[36]

The 'superiority of the independent workman' is thus both economic, because of the greater industry of those who work for
themselves, and moral, as a result of the lack of direct exposure to
the immorality of other (wage-dependent) workmen. But Smith's
idealized independent workman is not economically self-sufficient.
As his strictures against the 'slothful and lazy' country weaver
indicate, Smith envisages independent workmen who are specialized
commodity producers.[37] They operate, therefore, in a network of
market relations with others; but they do so from a position of
independence. It is easy to comprehend the attractions of such an
outlook given Smith's moral philosophy. An economy of independent commodity producers comprises relations between indviduals
who are (at least formally) equal. The butcher, the brewer and the
baker must conduct themselves prudently in order to elicit the
sympathetic understanding of those with whom they exchange, just
as they must be capable of entering into a sympathetic appreciation
of each other's position in turn. A commercial society in which 'every
man is in some measure a merchant' thus constitutes in principle
for Smith a network of equitable relationships between free and
independent individuals.

A model based on independent commodity producers is at the
heart of Smith's *Lectures on Jurisprudence* and the first five chapters
of Book One of the *Wealth of Nations*.[38] Chapter 6 of Book One
introduces a radically different model, however, one based on the
agrarian capitalist triad of landlord, capitalist and wage-labourer.
Smith introduces this triadic model in order to account for natural
price (value) and the distribution of the national income among the
three main social classes. In so doing, his model acquires a much
deeper and richer historical realism.[39] At the same time, however,
the force of his argument that commercial society fosters independence is significantly weakened. Indeed, Smith now acknowledges that
in modern Europe, 'the greater part of the workmen stand in need
of a master' (i.e., they do not own or possess means of production),
and indeed that wage-labourers outnumber independent workmen
by a ratio of 20 to 1.[40] The only way of fitting this reality into Smith's
initial model is to treat those who sell their labour as 'merchants'
just like those who sell commodities produced by their employees.
The notion that both capitalists and wage-labourers represent free

and independent buyers and sellers in the market is, of course, one of the classic apologetic claims of vulgar bourgeois economics. Although Smith's slippage from the one-class model of independent commodity producers to the three-class model opens the door to doing precisely this, it is clear that he does not do so for apologetic purposes. Nevertheless, by treating a tripartite class society as a society of independent 'merchants', Smith developed a line of thought which was to be crucial to the development of political economy as a pure and simple bourgeois ideology.

Exploitation, Equity and the Market

However much the *Wealth of Nations* opened a line towards vulgar economics, Smith's predispositions were clearly on the side of labourers in their relations with their employers. He pointed out, for example, that there were no laws limiting combinations among employers of the sort that prohibit trade union combinations. Indeed, he was openly critical of 'those laws which have been enacted with so much severity against the combinations of servants, labourers and journeymen'. He notes that, although workers' combinations attract enormous public attention, in fact 'masters are always and everywhere in a sort of tacit, but constant and uniform combination, not to raise the wages of labour above their actual rate'. Indeed, so thoroughly does he mistrust the conspiracies of employers that he claims that

> whenever the legislature attempts to regulate the difference between the masters and their workmen, its counsellors are always the masters. When the regulation, therefore, is in favour of the workmen, it is always just and equitable; but it is sometimes otherwise when in favour of the masters.

Finally, he argues against the complaints of masters concerning high wages, that high profits are a greater cause of high prices, and thus more hurtful to the public than high wages.[41]

Smith's emphasis on the public benefits of low prices is worthy of special note. From his *Lectures on Jurisprudence* onwards, he maintained that the best measure of national wealth was the consumption of the average member of society. Consequently, anything that raised the prices of commodities, and thereby made them less accessible to the majority, diminished national wealth or 'public opulence':

> whatever police [*sic*] tends to raise the market price above the natural, tends to diminish public opulence. Dearness and scarceity are in effect

the same thing. When commodities are in abundance, they can be sold to the inferiour ranks of the people ... Whatever therefore keeps goods above their natural price for a permanencey, diminishes [a] nations opulence.[42]

This line of argument provides the theoretical foundation for Smith's critique of merchants and manufacturers, his 'very violent attack' on 'the whole commercial system of Great Britain' as he put it.[43] For Smith believed that the laws of the market which underpin 'natural prices' are consistently violated by policies and practices which produce an upward deviation of market prices from natural prices. In the 'natural progress of opulence', market competition and increases in productivity tend to reduce profits and prices to the benefit of the public. As a result, merchants and manufacturers have a direct interest 'to deceive and even to oppress the public' by conspiring to boost market prices and profits:

> The interest of the dealers ... in any particular branch of trade or manufactures, is always in some respects different from, and even opposite to, that of the publick. To widen the market and to narrow the competition, is always the interest of the dealers. To widen the market may frequently be agreeable enough to the interest of the publick; but to narrow the competition must always be against it, and can only serve to enable the dealers, by raising their profits above what they would normally be, to levy, for their own benefit, an absurd tax upon the rest of their fellow-citizens.[44]

The *Wealth of Nations* rings with an indignant attack on these capitalist groups. Smith denounces 'the mean rapacity, the monopolizing spirit of merchants and manufacturers'; he condemns their 'impertinent jealousy' and their 'interested sophistry'. He compares these groups to 'an overgrown standing army' which attempts to 'intimidate the legislature' into erecting 'the sneaking arts of underlying tradesmen' into 'political maxims for the conduct of a great empire'.[24] Indeed, Smith believed that these groups had managed to construct a set of monopolistic practices – the mercantile system – which depressed wages and rents by boosting profits and prices. On top of this, Smith accuses mercantilism of diverting investment away from those areas where it generates the most employment – agriculture and local manufactures – and into areas such as overseas trade which generate less employment. Mercantilism thus reduces national wealth, defined as it is by Smith in terms of the real level of consumption of the labouring poor.[46]

Smith's theory of natural price thus had explicitly normative concerns. Having defined public opulence (the wealth of the nation) in terms of the level of consumption of the average member of society, and having argued that the natural progress of opulence results in falling prices and rising wages, his theory of natural price invokes notions of justice and equity. Monopolistic practices constitute a form of exploitation – the infliction of an 'absurd tax' on the wealth of others. By raising prices and reducing real wages, they also violate the principle of 'equity' according to which 'they who feed, cloath and lodge the whole body of the people, should have such a share of the produce of their own labour as to be themselves tolerably well fed, cloathed and lodged'. Smith, in fact, held that, by tolerating such monopolies 'for the benefit of the rich and the powerful', the state was complicit in policies which were 'evidently contrary to that justice and equality of treatment which the sovereign owes to all the different orders of his subjects'.[47]

Smith's theory of natural price thus offers a language of moral critique of monopolistic 'exploitation' in the market. This should come as no surprise given that his political economy was deeply rooted in the traditions of natural jurisprudence associated with Grotius and Pufendorf, and transmitted to him by his teacher Francis Hutcheson. As Marian Bowley notes in this regard:

> Adam Smith's reliance on competition to eliminate the divergences [between market prices and natural prices] was wholly consistent with the acceptance by some of the later Schoolmen of the price ruling in a competitive market as the just price. The requirement of competition by such Schoolmen was of course due, as with Adam Smith, to the need to prevent individuals, or groups, from obtaining and taking advantage of favourable bargaining positions to raise prices.[48]

This line of argument was taken up by some popular political economists who employed Smith's theory of natural price in order to attack the 'exploitative' practices of large merchants and master-manufacturers. Smith's idealized notion of the formation of (just) natural prices under conditions of 'perfect liberty' provided a contrast to the exercise of monopolistic powers and privileges. At the same time, however, it confined such 'critiques of political economy' to the sphere of exchange, and in so doing constrained their analytic range and the political perspectives which flowed from them, points to which I shall return.

Moral Economy and the Market

Smith is commonly depicted as a theorist who asserted the superiority of the market economy over a regulated 'moral economy'.[49] There is an important element of truth in this view. Certainly, one finds such a perspective in his treatment of the grain trade in the *Wealth of Nations*. There was a long-standing tradition in England and elsewhere of popular requisitioning of grain and its distribution according to 'just prices' in times of scarcity and high prices. Smith saw popular fears that dealers would engross grain and withhold it from the market in order to await higher prices, and the exercises of *taxation populaire* such fears induced, as entirely irrational, on the same level as 'the popular terrors and suspicions of witchcraft'.[50]

He maintained that inland dealers in grain – independent farmers and bakers – were too numerous to combine effectively; that forcing farmers to market their own grain in order to eliminate middlemen was inefficient as it necessitated tying up capital in the grain trade which could be better employed on the land. Except in rare cases of 'urgent necessity', he held that free trade in grain was the best means of establishing reasonable prices, which would satisfy the subsistence needs of the people while providing a fair profit to the farmer.[51] Clearly, we have here a straightforward case of Smith choosing the market in food over the traditional moral economy.

If the free market in food was one of the intellectual cornerstones of liberal-capitalist thought during this period, so was the argument for the free market in labour. Here again, Smith comes down on the side of 'modernity', which should come as no surprise given his dislike of the dependency and corruption he associated with feudal relations. Yet it is instructive that Smith's discussion of the labour market assumes that restraints on the 'free circulation of labour' usually favour employers, not workers. Thus, when it comes to the poor laws, Smith has nothing to say about the subsidy they provide to labour, or their allegedly deleterious effect on habits of industry – the centrepieces of nineteenth-century attacks on the poor laws. Instead, he focuses his attention upon the laws of settlement, claiming that they are hurtful to the labourers. He maintains that this is so for three main reasons.

First, by requiring a year's settlement to establish eligibility for poor relief, these laws induce employers to hire for periods of less than a year. Second, they establish great inequalities in the price of labour within different areas since they effectively prevent large numbers from migrating to high-wage areas in search of work. Finally, they are 'an evident violation of natural liberty' since they lead to removals from parishes of non-settlement simply because individuals have pursued an opportunity to exercise their labour.[52] I have shown in chapter 1 that the reality was more complex; that the poor often valued the right to parish relief which could be established under the settlement laws. Nevertheless, it is significant that Smith attacks them not for encouraging indolence, but rather for their alleged cruelty. 'There is scarce a poor man in England of forty years of age, I will venture to say, who has not in some part of his life felt himself most cruelly oppressed by this ill-contrived law of settlements', he writes. On balance, then, Himmelfarb appears justified in her judgement that 'Smith tacitly approved of the poor laws'.[53]

Paradoxical as it seems today, Smith's defence of the free market in labour was tied to his conviction that market interference benefits the rich and hurts the poor. 'It is the industry which is carried on for the benefit of the rich and powerful', he asserts, 'that is principally encouraged by our mercantile system. That which is carried on for the poor and indigent, is too often, either neglected, or oppressed.'[54] Thus, Smith's 'language of markets' was meant to break down monopolistic restrictions and thereby boost public opulence. His attack was not directed at the poor; indeed, he sought to improve their position. One of the ironies of capitalist development, however, was that Smith's rhetoric of the market, joined to a moral crusade against the 'indolence' of the poor, was to serve as a powerful ideological weapon against the working class in the age of the industrial revolution.

The Economics and Politics of Social Classes

It should be clear from what we have seen thus far that Smith had deep reservations about the economic and political practices of merchants and manufacturers. He believed that these groups would attempt to build up their political influence to enact legislation directly contrary to the public interest in low profits and prices. This was one reason that merchants and manufacturers 'neither are, nor ought to be the rulers of mankind', and that the state should ensure that their 'mean rapacity' is 'prevented from disturbing the tranquility of anybody but themselves'.[55]

Who then should exercise state power if not these groups? There seems little doubt that Smith hoped that a publicly spirited section of the prosperous and improving landed gentry (including those who may have started out in industry or trade) could rise to their duties to the commonwealth. He maintained that country gentlemen and farmers were 'least subject to the wretched spirit of monopoly', that they were characterized by a 'generosity which is natural to their station', and that 'when the public deliberates concerning any regulation of commerce or police [sic], the proprietors of the land can never mislead it, with a view to promote the interest of their own particular order'.[56] To be sure, Smith was strongly critical of the great proprietors descended from the feudal nobility. But those industrious and improving landowners and farmers who engaged in the market-oriented farming appropriate to a commercial society were a different matter. In their ranks he sought the breeding ground for that 'small party' of 'real and steady admirers of wisdom and virtue' which was essential if commercial society was not to decline towards corruption and abusive domination of the poor by the rich.[57] As Nicholas Philipson writes, 'Smith pinned what hopes he had for the survival of a free society upon the intelligent and commercially-minded gentry' who lived at a distance from the capital.[57]

Thus, while Smith did construct a defence of a society organized along capitalist lines, it was a defence of a transitional form of *agrarian capitalism* in which the most enlightened section of the landed capitalists (many of whom would have come from the ranks of the yeomanry and medium-sized dealers and manufacturers) – the 'natural aristocracy' as Smith called them – would exercise those civic virtues without which corruption and decay were inevitable. Smith's attempt to 'reconcile the old ethics with the new economics' was thus more than a simple 'defence of modernity'; and it was certainly no Mandevillean celebration of the order spontaneously created by the selfish passions in a competitive market. What Smith sought was to delineate those political and social arrangements in which the vigilance of an enlightened section of the landed class aspiring to 'wisdom and virtue' could protect the wealth-creating effects of commercial society from abuse by merchants and manufacturers.

Smith's happy and healthy commercial society was thus intended to further the interests of the poor, while limiting the impact of large merchants and manufacturers on the body politic. To be sure, historical and social realiy proved that such a scenario was naive in the extreme. And when the full impact of capitalist transformation elevated precisely those groups that worried Smith (in alliance with a landed class which eschewed its alleged moral duties), while the poor suffered an intensification of hardship that would have shocked him, it was inevitable that his delicate attempt to balance virtue and commerce, progress and public opulence, would come crashing down. Moreover, because of his idealization of free markets, elements of Smith's political economy could be used to legitimate outcomes that might have troubled him deeply. In this regard, Smith provided at least part of the intellectual armoury for a position (demoralized capitalist apologetics) inconsistent with his own moral predelictions. E.P. Thompson has correctly grasped this point with respect to Smith's arguments concerning the grain trade:

> It is perfectly possible that *laissez-faire* doctrines as to the food trade could have been *both* normative in intent (i.e. Adam Smith believed they would encourage cheap and abundant food) *and* ideological in outcome (i.e. in the result their supposedly de-moralised scientism was used to mask and apologise for other self-interested operations.)[59]

Smith's moral intent was incompatible with the nature of the free markets he often idealized. Those markets embodied a history of force and coercion and a practice of exploitation which his moral theory could not countenance. As a result, his political economy, taken as a totality, was destroyed by the real course of capitalist development. What remained were fragments which would be picked up and carried down roads he might not have imagined. One of these led to the use of political economy against the working class. Another led towards working-class critiques of political economy. The first road ran from Smith to Malthus; the second from Smith to Marx.

The Malthusian Moment: Political Economy versus Popular Radicalism

> Everything rung, or was connected with the Revolution in France; which for twenty years was, or was made, the all in all. Everything, not this or that thing, but literally everything, was soaked in this one event.[1]

Political economy was no exception to this rule. For twenty years or more it too 'was soaked in this one event', or, more precisely, in the popular British reception of, and elite reaction against, the French Revolution. Initially, moderate Whig opinion had embraced the events of 1789 in France. Burke's diatribe of 1790 against the Revolution was, at the time, an isolated undertaking. The majority of moderate Whigs rejected his catastrophism and his vitriolic attack on the French doctrines of 'natural rights' and the right to revolt against arbitrary authority. Many saw the French events as a confirmation of the principles of Britain's Glorious Revolution of 1688. This was the case with the Scottish Whig James Mackintosh, who replied to Burke in 1791 with *Vindiciae Gallicae*, a defence of the French upheaval which was praised by leading Whigs like Fox and Sheridan. Yet if Burke's *Reflections on the Revolution in France* was initially an isolated work, throughout the course of the 1790s ruling-class opinion flowed towards his anti-revolutionary position. Within Whig ranks a noticeable hardening of positions had occurred. By 1796 James Mackintosh was writing to Burke and apologizing for having been 'the dupe of my own enthusiasm'.[2]

This shift in ruling class attitudes towards the Revolution was not dictated principally by events in France. Instead, it was the British adaptation of French revolutionary doctrines – most clearly expressed in Thomas Paine's *Rights of Man* – and the emergence of a radical plebian movement that surged forward during the popular agitation of 1795–1801 against grain shortages, hunger and inflation, which convinced large numbers of Britain's rulers of the need to combat a growing radical threat at home which was deriving sustenance and inspiration from events across the channel. After 1792 – the year of France's 'second revolution', of Part Two of Paine's *Rights of Man*, and of the new radical 'corresponding societies' – the molecular shift in the domain of established ideology became irreversible. The British ruling class in its vast majority took the road of reaction, a reaction which inevitably swept the realm of social and political thought.

Popular Radicalism and the Poverty Debate

The first part of the *Rights of Man* appeared in November of 1791. Paine's clarion call to extend American and French revolutionary principles to Britain, to overturn the monarchy and aristocracy, and to remodel the constitution according to the natural rights of the individual, gave voice to the political grievances of small property owners excluded from the franchise, and of artisans and skilled labourers resisting the proletarianizing effects of the industrial revolution. The *Rights of Man* defined a radical, democratic current which encompassed the aspirations of the excluded. Its politics were plebeian not proletarian. But it was through its language of radical popular democracy that proletarian grievances and aspirations came to be articulated. There is no exaggeration in E.P. Thompson's claim that 'the *Rights of Man* is a foundation-text of the English working class movement'.[3] But it was Part Two of that work, published in February 1792, which brought about a deepening of radical thought.

This second part of the *Rights of Man* fused an economic critique of British government and society to the political theory of natural rights which informed Part One. Poverty and extreme inequality were said to be products of a corrupt political system based on monarchy and aristocracy. Paine had no objection to a commercial, market society; in fact he tended to glorify its natural workings. The problem – and here his argument dovetailed with parts of Smith's *Wealth of Nations*, a work he greatly admired – involved political interference with free exchange and competition. At the heart of such interference was 'excess and inequality of taxation', which were rooted in a corrupt and unrepresentative political system.[4] In Paine's analysis, economic injustice was a product of political monopoly. The abolition of political monopoly would free the market and thereby provide a fair return to all for the exercise of their labour and their property.

Yet this 'free market' argument was joined to a sharp attack on poverty and enormous compassion for the poor. And it was 'this impression of "caring"' which accounts for the book's great resonance among its plebeian readership.[5] This audience could plainly see that Paine's concern for the poor was linked to scorn for the idle rich. 'The peer and the beggar are often of the same family. One extreme produces the other: to make one rich many must be made poor', he wrote. And he offered a perspective in which political reform and massive extension of the suffrage would eliminate poverty:

> When it shall be said in any country in the world, my poor are happy; neither ignorance nor distress is to be found among them; my jails are empty of prisoners, my streets of beggars; the aged are not in want, the taxes are not oppressive; the rational world is my friend, because I am the friend of its happiness: when these things may be said, then may that country boast its constitution and its government.[6]

Part Two of the *Rights of Man* thus politicized the problem of poverty; while accepting the inherent benevolence of the free market, it provided a rhetoric and a programme of political reform for the grievances of those in economic distress. Paine's combination of market principles with a vigorous attack on poverty and excessive taxation represented a radicalization of Smith's ambiguous legacy. But Paine pushed the argument much further than Smith. Although he approached economic issues within a natural rights framework which accepted the free workings of the market, he nevertheless promoted a wide-ranging programme of social services to be provided by government. In place of the existing poor laws, he proposed a system of family allowances, old age pensions, maternity benefits and workshops for immigrants and the unemployed.

Paine held that the poor consisted overwhelmingly of children and the old. If the former were attended to by family allowances and maternity benefits, the latter would be cared for by old age pensions. Once again, the populist edge of Paine's analysis rings through his argument for pensions. 'The persons to be provided for' by the fund for pensions, he writes, will be 'husbandmen, common labourers, journeymen of every trade and their wives, sailors, and disbanded soldiers, worn out servants of both sexes, and poor widows'. Moreover, he insisted that such provision was 'not of the nature of a charity, but of a right', a view which he developed in his *Agrarian Justice* (1795).[7]

The impact of the *Rights of Man* was phenomenal. Most historians accept the estimate that 200,000 copies of Part Two were sold within a year.[8] Such sales were possible largely because the book became the guiding manual of a popular political movement. From late 1791 and early 1792 – as Parts One and Two of the *Rights of Man* came off the press – we can date the emergence of new radical societies organized by artisans. In December 1791, skilled labourers in Sheffield issued the first address of their Constitutional Society. Membership leapt from a handful to 200 within a month; to 600 within two months; and to 2,000 by March 1792. Then London came to life with the formation of the London Corresponding Society (LCS). Beginning with about seventy members when their first public statement was issued in April 1792, the Society appears to have numbered two or three hundred by the summer. Then came September and an enormous burst of recruitment. Years later Thomas Hardy, one of its central leaders, estimated that in November 1792 between 300 and 400 signed up every week. By the end of the year there were 29 divisions of the LCS with a membership probably in excess of 1,000.[9]

Everywhere it was Paine's book which provided the ideological inspiration for the new movement. The Constitutional Society in Sheffield brought out the first cheap edition of Part One. It was said that 'every cutler' in the town had a copy. Weavers, shoemakers, miners, shopkeepers snatched up copies in Norwich, Manchester, Nottingham, Selby, Edinburgh, Oldham and dozens of other localities. One of Paine's opponents complained that 'not less than four thousand per week of Paine's despicable and nonsensical pamphlet have been issued forth, for almost nothing, and dispersed all over the kingdom'.[10]

But if it was Paine who provided the ideological backbone of the movement, it was the second revolution in France – the popular uprising of August 1792, which overthrew monarchy and drove the revolution onto a more radical democratic course – which provided a political model. 'For the British popular movement', notes Gwyn Williams, 'the French revolution which counted was that of 10 August 1792.'[11] The combined impact of events in France and the new popular movement in Britain pushed the British government onto the road of reaction. As early as May of that year, charges of seditious writings were brought against Paine; he was convicted after having fled to France, and outlawed from ever returning to Britain. In November the anti-revolutionary Association for the Preservation of Liberty and Property against Republicans and Levellers was formed by John Reeves, a government officer. Groups such as this organized effigy burnings of Tom Paine; indeed twenty-six such burnings were reported within 20 miles of Manchester in March 1793 alone.[12] At the same time, the crackdown began in Scotland, with trials for sedition of a number of prominent radicals, two of whom were sentenced to lengthy terms of transportation.

Fear of the growing popular movement and intimidation by the government combined virtually to eliminate open opposition within the 'political nation' represented within parliament. Denied a point of entry into 'legitimate' political debate, the radical societies were thrown back on their own resources. And these resources proved adequate to the task of organizing and mobilizing political dissent. New popular societies appeared throughout 1793 and 1794 in spite of the loyalist demonstrations. In London the LCS grew to some five thousand members in forty-eight divisions. Its first attempts at repression having failed, the government now raised the stakes. Habeas corpus was suspended in May 1794. Radicals were imprisoned throughout the kingdom; in October the LCS leaders Thomas Hardy and John Thelwall were arrested along with ten others and all charged with high treason. The LCS and other radical societies were quickly thrown into disarray. Then came the dearth and hunger of 1795, and the radical movement surged forward again – this time tightly binding its political demands with mass economic grievances. A deeper and more proletarian radicalism now asserted itself.

Since late 1794 wheat prices had been rising steadily. By August of the next year, they were more than double the level of a year earlier; although prices fell somewhat thereafter, they remained exceptionally high until 1797. For most workers the situation was devastating. Indeed, average wages throughout much of this period were inadequate to purchase even ordinary amounts of wheat, let alone other commodities.[13] The dearth of 1795 produced a rising tide of grain seizures, food riots and popular price-setting. What distinguished these efforts in popular 'moral economy' from earlier protests, however, was the leading role often played by an increasingly articulate radical minority. The ideas of Thomas Paine and British Jacobinism provided a language of protest, a framework of analysis, and a set of demands which shaped this upsurge of *taxation populaire*. The result was that the right of subsistence now loomed large in radical discourse.

The LCS in particular became the focus for much of this upheaval.

Francis Place believed that by May of 1795 perhaps 2,000 men were attending as many as sixty-five divisions; total membership may have been as high as ten thousand. Equally significant, large numbers of poor wage-labourers now made their way to meetings. Discourse on political reform increasingly gave way to talk of revolution. And the revolutionary current quickly spread as the popular movement outside London also revived. A demonstration of ten thousand was claimed for Sheffield in August 1795; nineteen divisions of the Patriotic Society were active in Norwich. In the second half of the year demonstrations as large as two hundred thousand were claimed in London by the LCS. Increasingly the weathervane of ruling class hysteria, Burke railed against these 'pure Jacobins; utterly incapable of amendment' and called for the 'critical terrors of the cautery and the knife' to cure the diseases of the body politic.[14]

At the head of these 'pure Jacobins' throughout this tumultuous year was John Thelwall of the LCS, who now emerged as the leading agitator and theorist of popular radicalism. The son of a silk mercer, Thelwall went beyond Paine to proclaim that subsistence was a natural right of all human beings. He did so within the framework of Paine's natural rights position and thus accepted the legitimacy of the small manufacturing employer; but he pushed this perspective as far as could be done without shifting to an explicitly anti-capitalist and proletarian stance. As Thompson writes, 'Thelwall took Jacobinism to the borders of Socialism; he also took it to the borders of revolutionism'.[15]

Thelwall delivered lectures twice a week during much of 1795–6, which were published in *The Tribune*. While Paine's social programmes for the unemployed, children and the elderly implied a right to subsistence, the author of the *Rights of Man* rarely addressed this issue explicitly, assuming, following Smith, that the natural workings of the market would generate demand for the labour and services of the overwhelming majority; the unfettered free market was thus the key to subsistence. But the hunger of 1795–6 forced popular radicals to address an immediate subsistence crisis which could not await the removal of monopolistic economic and political powers. What was implicit in Paine had to be rendered explicit. This required affirming an irreducible right of subsistence, and thus entailed a more radical attitude towards property than Paine had adopted. For rather than assuming that one simply needed to free the market and let its mechanisms distribute the wealth fairly, Thelwall's position affirmed the moral priority of a just distribution which guaranteed not simply bare subsistence, but 'comfort and enjoyment'. Although he did not reject Paineite assumptions with respect to the market, Thelwall asserted that the right to labour and subsistence had a priority over the right to property ownership. His vigorous affirmation of the right to a decent standard of living pushed certain elements to be found in Part Two of the *Rights of Man* towards conclusions which opened in the direction of a new, more socialistic perspective:

> I affirm that *every* man, and *every* woman, and *every* child, ought to obtain something more, in the general distribution of the fruits of labour, than food, and rags, and a wretched hammock with a poor rug to cover it; and that, without working twelve or fourteen hours a day ... from six to sixty. – They have a claim, a sacred and inviolable claim ... to some comfort and enjoyment.[16]

The tenor of the popular movement of 1795–6 thus involved a twofold radicalization. On the practical level, talk of revolution now vied with traditional commitments to mass pressure for reform. On the theoretical plane, powerful assertions of a right to comfort and subsistence encouraged sharper and more critical attitudes towards property. The result was that the political argument inspired by the French Revolution became in the British context a debate over property. As Arthur Young put it in 1792, the real contest was not between liberty and tyranny; instead, it was 'a question of property. It is a trial of arms, whether those who have *nothing* shall not seize and possess the property of those who have something.'[17] In this context, anti-revolutionary theorists and pamphleteers consistently – and incorrectly – attributed 'levelling' attitudes to Paine and his adherents.[18] Yet, the reality was that by the mid 1790s many of the English Jacobins inspired by the *Rights of Man* were moving towards radical perspectives on the property question. In the forefront of this trend were Thomas Spence and his followers.

Spence was a utopian radical from Newcastle who in 1775 delivered a lecture to the local Philosophical Society entitled 'The Real Rights of Man'. This lecture, which earned him instant notoriety and expulsion from the Society, was republished on numerous occasions. Indeed, all of Spence's later writings represent a series of elaborations of the basic position adopted in this lecture: that private property in land is the root of all social ills. Spence developed this argument within a straightforward natural rights framework. Granted that we have a right to life, he argued, and that life is impossible without the products of the land, it follows that we have an inherent right to property in land. This right to land is a simple extension of our right to property in ourselves. Thus, 'mankind have as equal and just a property in land as they have in liberty, air, or the light and heat of the sun'.[19] Just as no one has the right to deprive us of those things necessary to life, such as air, light and liberty, so no one can deprive us of land or its products.

Spence's critique of existing property arrangements thus focused on private ownership of land; as a result it blended quite easily with Paine's attack on aristocracy and monarchy. As with Paine, manufacturing and commercial capital tended to be immune from criticism in his writings. Indeed, he adhered to the Jacobin model of a republic of small independent producers: in the new society all 'would be little farmers and little Mastermen'.[20] Despite the obvious shortcomings of such a model – and its obvious appeal – for a radical movement experiencing the proletarianization of petty producers and the early phases of industrial revolution, Spence's writings nevertheless deepened popular radicalism: to the overwhelmingly political doctrine of natural rights set forth by Paine, he added a theory of economic rights (to land and subsistence) and a critique of the social distribution of property. Writing of 'the professed Reformers of the World' in *The Restorer of Society to its Natural State* (1803) he states that 'instead of striking at the Root, they aim only at the Branches'. And he argues that it is of more importance to determine 'which System of Society is most favourable to existence' than to engage in the typical radical endeavour of debating 'which form of Government is most favourable to Liberty'.[21]

But Spence's importance to the popular movement was not confined to the propagation of ideas such as these; in addition, he made crucial contributions to the practice of the movement. Having moved to London, probably in 1787 or early 1788, just prior to the upsurge of plebeian radicalism, he was by the early 1790s in the thick of things, republishing *The Real Rights of Man*, and launching *Pig's Meat*, a weekly periodical which popularized democratic ideas and his version of agrarian socialism. During the three-year period from 1792 to 1794, he was arrested four times, and thrice imprisoned. After the vicious repression of 1798–1803, Spence and his followers provided perhaps the most important organizational and political focus for the surviving elements of the radical Jacobin movement. Much of this movement did not survive the wave of repression that followed the notorious Two Bills of 1795 – which extended the law of high treason to cover criticism of the king, the constitution, and the

government, and outlawed meetings of over fifty people – a wave
which included the erection of the spy system, the Irish Insurrection
Act 1796, and the civil war launched against the United Irishmen
and their supporters.[22]

Spence became an outspoken advocate of revolution during this
period. He argued for a well-armed organization of 'a few
thousands of hearty and determined fellows' who would lead an
insurrection and establish a provisional government. In the event
that the aristocracy resisted, he advocated 'destroying them root and
branch' and confiscating their wealth. Moreover, he recommended
a 'Mutiny on the Land' – a euphemism for strikes and riots – along
the lines of the 1791 naval mutinies in which the United Irishmen
and their British supporters had participated.[23] During this period,
Spence also became one of the sharpest proponents of self-activity
on the part of the lower classes as an alternative to deferential support
for upper-class 'reformers'. Real change would be achieved, he
insisted, through action designed to transform the constitution and
the government 'not by addressing ourselves to the Religion,
Generosity, and Feelings of the Rich and Powerful, for their
humiliating Charity'. This position became a hallmark of
Spenceanism; in 1818, for example, Dr Watson claimed that 'the
working People are become fully competent to manage for themselves' and cautioned against alliances with 'persons of Property'.[24]

Deserted by upper-class reformers during the period of intense
repression, plebeian radicals had little option but to fall back on their
own resources, 'to discover means of independent quasi-legal or
underground organization', and 'to nourish traditions and forms of
organization of their own'.[25] During these trying years of repression
and self-reliance, Spence remained on the side and in the midst of
these radical English Jacobins; indeed, the society he formed in
London 'gradually rallied the survivors of the Jacobin revolutionary
cadres smashed in the government repression of 1798–1803' and
maintained 'a small but *continuous* revolutionary-republican 'underground' which runs from the mid-1790s to early Chartism'.[26] Equally
significant, Spence and his followers introduced notions of female
equality into their revolutionary-democratic perspective, signifying
an important step in the deepening of the radical thought of the
period.[27]

At the centre of the Spencean movement was the former secretary
of the LCS, Thomas Evans. Despite his central role in London
radicalism during the years 1790–1820, Evans has generally remained

a shadowy figure in histories of the period. There are a number of reasons for this, not the least of which was his strong concern for security given his periodic involvement in insurrectionary plots. Equally important, however, has been the tendency of many historians to assume, incorrectly, that Spenceans were utopian cranks with little connection to or impact on the plebeian radicalism of their time. Fortunately, recent studies have disproved this picture. We now know that the Spenceans constituted one of the most important radical currents of their time, and that their legacy was carried forward into the Chartist period.[28] Moreover, it is clear – contrary to a recent simplistic interpretation of radical thought – that the Spenceans kept alive a tradition of thought which saw *economic* inequalities as the root of political injustice and corruption, in contrast to the more orthodox Paineite view, which focused overwhelmingly on political monopoly as the source of economic oppression.[29]

In a typically Spencean statement, for example, Evans argued that 'it is property and property alone that gives power and influence'.[30] Nor, as I have insisted, was this a marginal view within the spectrum of radical thought. For much of the period 1790–1820, Spenceanism was at the heart of the politics of the more revolutionary elements of the popular-democratic movement; indeed it is no overstatement to insist that 'it was Spencean agrarianism that was to inform theory and practice in the labour movement wherever gradualism was rejected'.[31] To be sure, the agrarian focus of Spence's analysis handicapped radical economic thought, a point to which I shall return in the next chapter. For present purposes, however, this much should be clear: the popular movement of the 1790s had pushed radicals towards affirming a right of subsistence – an implicit challenge to existing property arrangements given the conditions of the period – and towards analyses which made 'property and property alone' the heart of the problem of improving human society. In so doing, it had defined the agenda of political debate that would dominate the period 1792–1834.

Alternatives to Radicalism: 'Humanitarianism' and the Poverty Debate

The rise of agrarian and industrial capitalism in England was, after 1688, carried through within political arrangements which appeared traditional, indeed immemorial. The English ruling class clearly promoted this appearance of tradition, permanence and stability.

Inevitably, however, tensions developed in the relation between revolutionary socio-economic changes and their organization within apparently traditional political forms. As Hobsbawm and Rudé put it,

> A fundamental contradiction lay at the heart of English agrarian society in the period of the Industrial Revolution. Its rulers wanted it to be both capitalist and stable, traditionalist and hierarchical. In other words they wanted it to be governed by the universal free market of the liberal economist (which was inevitably a market for land and men as well as for goods), but only to the extent that suited nobles, squires and farmers.[32]

Yet, Hobsbawm and Rudé go too far when they describe this balance as 'a fundamental contradiction'. On the contrary, as Marx argued, the rise of capitalism in Britain could be accomplished within the political form of constitutional monarchy and its attendant aristocratic trappings precisely because, from the time of Henry VIII, the landed estates of the great landowners 'were not feudal but bourgeois property', and thus a 'permanent alliance' based on a genuine commonality of interests could be constructed 'between the bourgeoisie and the greater part of the big landlords'.[33] Nevertheless, Hobsbawm and Rudé are right to see a real tension running through the attempts to accomplish, unconsciously to be sure, a genuine socio-economic revolution within political forms which, although they had been revolutionized between 1640 and 1688, nevertheless projected an ethos of traditional aristocratic values. It is not overstating the case to claim that political debate within the ruling class during this period often revolved around the viability of such an ethos, moving between those who sought to buttress traditional 'obligations' to the poor as a means of circumventing mass upheaval, and those who advocated jettisoning such 'sentimental' and 'self-defeating' strategies in favour of a campaign to eliminate traditional rights of the poor to land or to relief from hunger and want.

If the dearth of 1795–6 brought to the fore radical arguments on behalf of a right of subsistence, so it produced forms of 'bourgeois humanitarianism', which tacitly granted such a right, albeit one subject to its administration by traditional rulers conditional on due respect and deference from its recipients. Many of these arguments became doubly insistent when the radical upsurge of 1795–6 was followed by the naval mutinies of 1797, the Irish insurrection of the following year, and the terrible subsistence crisis of 1800 which produced an enormous wave of rioting.[34]

Historians have often focused on the so-called 'Speenhamland system' in discussing upper-class initiatives to relieve the distress caused by the dearth of 1795–6. It is now generally accepted that this system, drawn up by Berkshire magistrates meeting at Speenhamland in May 1795, was not widely followed throughout England. Nevertheless, it should be noted that the Berkshire magistrates' establishment of a minimum wage tied to the price of bread *did* reflect one important current of ruling-class opinion at the time.[35] Indeed, the Berkshire approach was largely supported at the national level by Samuel Whitbread who put forward an unsuccessful minimum wage Bill in the House of Commons in both 1795 and 1800.[36]

Whitbread's scheme, and by implication the Speenhamland approach, was actively opposed by Prime Minister Pitt on the grounds that it represented 'legislative interference into that which ought to be allowed to take its natural course'.[37] Pitt deliberately employed the language of political economy in his attack on Whitbread's proposal. Moreover, his opposition was strengthened by a memorandum he received from Edmund Burke in which the vitriolic opponent of the French Revolution turned his fire on the principle of public relief from distress. Burke's document, 'Thoughts and Details on Scarcity', written in November 1795, is an indispensable text for deciphering its author's intellectual world-view. For here was the anti-revolutionary exponent of custom and tradition attacking two hundred years of customary relief for the poor by employing the same sort of abstract philosophical principles – in this case those of the free market espoused by political economy – which he had condemned when used by the French *philosophes* in their critique of absolute monarchy. Some customs and traditions, it appears, were for Burke less sacred than others.[38]

'Thoughts and Details on Scarcity' commences with a defence of free trade in provisions and proceeds to a direct attack on the Speenhamland system.[39] Burke employs the rhetoric of custom and tradition to describe the 'chain of subordination' which binds the labourer (as well as beasts and implements) to the farmer, and to argue that the relation between labourer and farmer should be left to 'convention'. But Burke is engaged here in a subtle manoeuvre: it is the wage established by free competition that he identifies with convention, ignoring centuries of wage regulation and relief. 'I premise', he writes, 'that labor is, as I have already intimated, a commodity, and, as such, an article of trade.' It follows that 'labor must be subject to all the laws and principles of trade'. And he extends the same argument to means of subsistence, arguing that their prices too must be free from government regulation.[40]

Burke's memorandum includes a predictable diatribe against Jacobinism. It is instructive, however, that he attempts to paint those advocating poor relief as dangerous speculators.[41] Yet, as I have noted, custom came down on the side of regulation and relief, not free competition; in this sense, it is Burke who adopts new-found 'speculative' principles – those of political economy. Despite its specious reasoning, Burke's linking of the right to subsistence with radicalism is historically significant in that he instinctively grasped what was new in relations between upper and lower classes in the epoch of the French Revolution: the emergence of an *independent* plebeian radicalism which did not function as mere cannon-fodder for political manoeuvring at the top. As the solicitor-general noted in a reply to Samuel Romilly (when the latter retrospectively criticized the suspension of habeas corpus on the grounds that such a move had not been necessary during the Gordon riots of 1780), there was a profound difference between 1780 and the years after 1789; unlike the latter period, formerly 'there was no plan to disorganise the state … no plans for revolutionary reforms were on foot'.[42] In the era of lower-class self-organization, the argument for a right of subsistence, however much it might have been rooted in tradition, was part of an armoury of radical natural rights arguments which threatened to undermine the established order. Given this context, Burke's attempt to draw a line against radicalism compelled him to reject any right of subsistence. It may seem ironic that this philosopher of conservative anti-revolutionism should have hinged his arguments on the new doctrines of political economy; but this should merely alert us to the degree to which 'liberal' economics was often joined to conservative politics in the age of popular radicalism and the French Revolution.

Indeed, so doctrinaire had become much of ruling-class opinion about poor relief that Pitt was roundly attacked in 1797 when he put forward an alternative to Whitbread's minimum wage Bill, one which would have provided poor relief via schools of industry. This proposal was vigorously denounced by Bentham and soundly defeated in debate in the House of Commons. An attempt to revive Pitt's scheme in 1800 was then attacked by Malthus in his *An Investigation of the Cause of the Present High Price of Provisions*. Seven years later, Malthus directly took on Whitbread when the latter proposed a liberal amendment of the poor laws.[43] By this point Whitbread was overwhelmingly isolated. Christian humanitarianism had now been defeated by, or had consciously capitulated to, Malthus's critique of the poor laws. In the twenty years after the French Revolution, a new orthodoxy with respect to the poverty question had been constructed; and as Poynter notes, this 'orthodox view of poverty was Burke's as refined and extended by Malthus'.[44]

Against the Right of Subsistence: Malthus's First *Essay on Population*

It was Malthus, rather than Burke, who set the public agenda and defined the terms for the early nineteenth-century debate on poverty. This had nothing to do with the greater theoretical depth or cogency of Malthus's argument. On the contrary, Malthus offered a meandering, second-rate performance, full of self-contradiction, which scarcely deserves mention alongside Smith or Ricardo. Nevertheless, he cut with the grain of the intellectual and political prejudices of ruling-class opinion. While sharing Burke's opposition to the right of subsistence, Malthus developed his version in naturalistic terms, eschewing the strident political voluntarism which leapt from the pages of Burke's *Reflections*. Burke had campaigned for a political, ideological and religious crusade against radicalism; the direction of social development thus depended on *choice*, most notably that exercised by the landed gentry. Ironically, however, such a position implied that nothing necessarily blocked the road towards radicalism; it came down to a clash of political wills, a choice between competing visions of society. While sharing Burke's hostility to the principles of the French Revolution – that 'fermentation of disgusting passions, of fear, cruelty, malice, revenge, ambition, madness, and folly', as he put it[45] – Malthus maintained that radical dreams of social improvement were incompatible with fundamental laws of nature. Whereas for Burke radicalism was undesirable, for Malthus it was impossible.

Such an argument offered intellectual and political advantages. Most important, Malthus's *Essay* shifted the debate over social improvement from the terrain of politics to that of nature. In addition, in Malthus's hands the intellectual contest appeared to involve nothing but disinterested scientific investigation. As Donald Winch notes, 'whereas Burke appeared in the guise of an enraged critic, Malthus presented himself as a calm and dispassionate seeker after scientific truth in the Newtonian manner'.[46] Yet however dispassionate he might strive to appear, there could be little doubt that Malthus's *Essay* was intended as an attack on radicalism and the doctrine of improvement. Indeed, the author consistently acknowledged the origins of the *Essay* in the disputes related to the French Revolution: in 1798 the targets were Condorcet and Godwin; later editions attacked Robert Owen and the Spenceans. Moreover, what Malthus attempted to refute – although in an increasingly inconsistent fashion, as we shall see – was the notion that there could be any significant improvement in the conditions of the poor. He claimed, for example, that his argument was

> conclusive, not only against the perfectibility of man ... but against any very marked and striking change for the better, in the form and structure of general society; by which I mean any great and decided amelioration of the condition of the lower classes of mankind.[47]

Malthus drew this conclusion from his law of population, according to which population growth inevitably exceeds the growth of the food supply, the former increasing geometrically, the latter arithmetically. The tortoise of food supply being unable to keep up with the hare of population growth, human society must inevitably tend towards overpopulation, hunger and misery. The law of population thus 'constantly tends to subject the lower classes of the society to distress and to prevent any great permanent amelioration of their condition'. This is a natural law which 'no possible form of society could prevent'.[48]

The anti-radical attractions of such a position are obvious. Where Burke had treated radicalism as largely sinister, Malthus depicts it as unscientific. The radicals' preoccupation with human institutions, he argues, belies a failure to understand the deeper causes of social phenomena. Against Godwin, for example, he writes that 'human institutions ... are mere feathers that float on the surface, in comparison with those deeper seated causes of impurity that corrupt the springs and render turbid the whole stream of human life'.[49] It should be clear, however, that it is not just the radicals who are impugned in Malthus's argument; so are all those who adhere to doctrines of social improvement, not the least of whom is Adam Smith.

It is curious that Malthus's critique of Smith in the *Essay* has received so little attention from commentators.[50] Certainly the focus of the *Essay* was its attack on radicalism. But having come from a Dissenting background, Malthus could not have been unaware of the degree to which much non-radical thought of the eighteenth century subscribed to notions of societal improvement. Moreover, such a view was, as we have seen, central to the whole thrust of the *Wealth of Nations*. If any significant improvement in the circumstances of the poor was impossible, as Malthus maintained, then Smith's political economy was crucially flawed. Chapter 16 of the *First Essay* was devoted to demonstrating Smith's error.

Malthus's critique of Smith presents us with another example of a rambling, inconsistent argument, which so shifted over time that the author clearly ended up abandoning his essential position (and in so doing subverting much of his original doctrine). Nevertheless, at the heart of the *First Essay* is the claim that Smith erred in believing that all accumulation involves an expansion in the supply of wage goods – and corresponding increases in employment and living standards – since much accumulation is devoted to manufacturing, not to agriculture (only the latter representing a sector in which accumulation expands the food supply). As a result, Malthus claims, it is possible to have capital accumulation, which draws labour out of agriculture and into manufacturing and thus results in a diminution of the food supply and a decline in real levels of consumption.[51] It is clear that Malthus believed such a pattern of growth had characterized the British economy throughout the eighteenth century, and that he favoured a return to a more agriculturally-based course of development. Yet, in the Malthusian view, even a decided bias of investment towards agriculture would not enable society to evade the pressures of excessive population growth. Smith was thus wrong on all counts with respect to improvement for the poor. While an agriculturally-based pattern of accumulation might delay the onset of subsistence crises, such crises were nevertheless inevitable.

Having disposed of Smith's doctrine of improvement – on the basis of a thoroughly primitive piece of reasoning – and having rejected radicalism, Malthus had little to offer the poor by way of any reasonable prospect of a better life. Yet there was one institution which could be changed, he argued, so as to eliminate a debilitating effect of human contrivance: England's poor law system. Whereas Smith had criticized the restrictions on personal mobility caused by the settlements laws, Malthus turned his fire on efforts to protect the poor from hunger and starvation. The poor laws, he argued, maintain hungry mouths without increasing the supply of food, thereby exacerbating crises of subsistence. Worse, they unjustly divert food away from those who are 'more industrious and more worthy'. Finally, they shield the poor from the full consequences of their own 'carelessness and want of frugality'.[52] Malthus thus advocates 'the total abolition of all the present parish laws', along with all other apprenticeship and employment regulations in order to free 'the market in labour'. Such policies involve rejecting every 'vain endeavour to attain what in the nature of things is impossible', a lasting improvement in the conditions of the poor.

Poor Laws Under Attack: Later Editions of the *Essay on Population*

The second edition of Malthus's *Essay* appeared in 1803. Not only was this a massive expansion of the version of 1798; it also signified a thoroughgoing revision of Malthus's views. As Robert Southey wrote in the *Analytic Review*, by the end of the second edition Malthus 'admits everything which he controverted in the beginning, and is clearly and confessedly a convert to the doctrine of the perfectibility of man!'[53] Indeed, as we shall see, so sweeping were the changes introduced in the second edition that it is difficult to see in what theoretical respects it remained merely another edition of the previous work; in substance it represented a new and different book. Ironically, Malthus's theoretical inconsistencies did nothing to diminish his influence – in fact, his population principle became more influential in the years after 1803. Here we have a case of support for a theory because of its ideological import, regardless of its theoretical shortcomings.[54]

Before turning to the changes introduced into the Malthusian doctrine in 1803 and after, it is worth noting its two constant themes: first, the attack on radicalism; and second, the assault on the poor laws. It is not overstating the case to suggest that these were the only significant elements of the *First Essay* that remained untouched, however much the theoretical arguments designed to sustain them changed.

As radicalism developed, Malthus added material intended as responses to new weapons in the radical armoury. Paine, who was not mentioned in the *Essay* of 1798, for example, came in for specific rebuke in later editions. Moreover, the fifth edition of 1817 included a whole section in refutation of Owen, as well as arguments against the followers of Thomas Spence.[55] Furthermore, the author made no effort to disguise his hostility to the growing militancy of the popular movement. 'A mob', he argued 'is of all monsters the most fatal to freedom'. And he went on to denounce the fact that events had transpired in which 'political discontents were blended with the cries of hunger', the result of which would have been 'a revolution' and 'unceasing carnage' had the government not resorted to the use of force. Given this prospect, Malthus had no difficulty accepting incursions on civil liberties in the name of social order, proclaiming that he would 'submit to very great oppression rather than give the slightest countenance to a popular tumult'. In this spirit, later editions of the *Essay* continued a frontal assault on 'the delusive arguments on equality which were circulated among the lower classes'.[56]

Coming to the second constant in the different versions of the *Essay*, Malthus left little doubt as to which 'delusive argument' he considered most dangerous: the notion that the individual possesses 'a right to subsistence when his labour will not fairly purchase it', a proposition which, along with most anti-radical writers, he attributed to Paine.[57] The second edition of the *Essay* thus registered Malthus's perception of the decisive shift within radical thought represented by Thelwall, Spence and Evans: the fusing of a right to subsistence to the Paineite theory of natural rights. Once again, Malthus was concerned to combat concessions to radicalism within the theory and practice to be found in the ruling circles. Just as the *First Essay* had challenged notions of improvement in Adam Smith and Dissenting thought, the second edition attacked the acceptance of a right of subsistence implicit in the English poor laws. For this reason, as Malthus shifted his emphasis to a critique of the right of subsistence, 'the attack on the poor laws, which was secondary in the *Essay* of 1798, usurped the position of the attack on perfectibility'.[58] To this end, the second edition argued that the poor laws should be outrightly abolished, following a government declaration that children born to the poor two years after the date of declaration would not be eligible for public relief. The limited support for workhouses for the poor to be found in the *Essay* of 1798 was henceforth dropped.

Eclectic work that the *Essay* was, the attack on perfectibility remained in later editions, as did the original population principle. Yet, as we shall see, these were so diluted as to become almost meaningless. Nevertheless, beneath the weight of ponderous 'evidence', meandering argument and *ad hoc* qualifications, the *Essay* retained its central attack on radicalism and the poor laws. Before tracing the structure of the argument Malthus offered in this area, it is worth noting the four most important changes to be found in the post-1798 editions of the *Essay*.[59]

At the heart of the *First Essay* was a theodicy designed to show how the evil effects of the population principle (hunger, misery and starvation) conformed to a Christian view of the world and the place of the human species within it. Hunger and the difficulty of procuring subsistence – since the species increases much more rapidly than its food supply – are necessary to prompt humans to labour and to awaken their intellects. 'The original sin of man is the torpor and corruption of the chaotic matter in which he may be said to be born.' The supreme being seeks to stimulate human beings to develop their reason, since 'God is constantly occupied in forming mind out of matter', and this, says Malthus, requires the whip of hunger and the threat of starvation since the species is by nature 'inert, sluggish, and averse from labour, unless compelled by necessity'. It follows therefore, that 'moral evil is absolutely necessary to the production of moral excellence'. Without the evil of hunger and starvation caused by the law of population, industry, reason and moral behaviour would not develop.[60]

These views were out of step with the principal trends of Anglican social thought at the time. In particular, the harsh fatalism according to which, by divine plan, the excess poor would have to starve in order to contribute to the moral good of the formation of mind ran against the grain of religious orthodoxy. In order to conform better, Malthus dropped from later editions chapters 18 and 19 of the *First Essay*, which sketched out this theodicy. In the appendix to the fifth edition, he claimed that he had expunged these passages in deference to the judgement of 'a competent tribunal'.[61] It is not the case, however, that Malthus completely abandoned his earlier views. What he did was to introduce one added element – albeit one which radically changed his overall argument – to bring his views closer to orthodoxy. This addition involved the notion that individuals, cognizant of the evil effects of reproducing beyond their means of subsistence, could affect their destiny through rational control of their behaviour, a position which modified the fatalism of the *First Essay*.

Nevertheless, Malthus still maintained that a state of inequality which

> offers the natural rewards of good conduct, and inspires widely and generally the hopes of rising and fears of falling in society is unquestionably the best calculated to develop the energies and faculties of man, and the best suited to the exercise and improvement of human virtue.

He also claimed that 'natural and moral evil seem to be instruments employed by the Deity' in order to shape human conduct; and he insisted that if we could procure subsistence as easily as we can procreate, then it would be impossible to overcome the 'indolence of man, and make him proceed in the cultivation of the soil'.[62] And the conclusion Malthus draws from this argument retains 'the fundamental meanness' which Marx attributed to Malthusianism. For, argues Malthus, the individual who reproduces without the means to maintain children violates his or her duty to society. 'To the punishment therefore of nature he should be left, the punishment of want.' As for the fact that the children have no responsibility for their birth (and the conditions of their hunger), this need not be of great concern since 'the infant is, comparatively speaking, of little value to society, as others will immediately supply its place'.[63]

The 'fundamental meanness' revealed in such passages is a constant throughout all versions of the *Essay*. Nevertheless, Malthus's concessions to his 'competent tribunal' weakened the theoretical argument he offered in support of such harsh conclusions. In contrast to the fatalism of the 1798 edition, he now claimed that 'it is in the power of each individual to avoid all the evil consequences to himself and society resulting from the principle of population'; as a result, 'we can have no reason to impeach the justice of the Deity'.[64]

The element of individual agency introduced into the second edition borrowed explicitly from the social and theological writings of William Paley, and later of John Bird Sumner, who was to become the Archbishop of Canterbury. However, this introduction of individual agency into Malthus's argument – the first great change in the second edition of the *Essay* – undermined the theoretical foundation of the original argument. After all, if the majority of individuals could direct their behaviour so as to 'avoid all the evil consequences' of the population principle, then it followed that society could evade its general effects. But, didn't this mean that improvement, possibly even radical improvement, was in principle possible? That Malthus's answer should have been in the affirmative is clear once we examine the second, and interrelated, change introduced into the second edition: the concept of moral restraint.

In the 1798 *Essay*, Malthus had argued that all checks to population growth came under the heading of misery or vice, i.e. starvation, or 'irregular' sexual practices (in which category he included the use of contraceptives). In tune with the idea that individuals could regulate their behaviour in such a way as to avoid both misery and vice, Malthus was forced to accept that they were capable of rationally choosing to postpone marriage (but not childbirth, since this would entail the vice of birth control) until their economic situation was adequate to support a family. Such a course of action – moral restraint – was now considered a virtue.[65]

This argument enabled Malthus to escape the bitter fatalism of the *First Essay*, and to make the impoverished individual responsible for his or her own plight. Acceptance of some notion of individual improvement, in other words, served the anti-radical purpose of claiming that individuals are responsible for their own well-being. Writing of the poor man, he argues: 'The last person he would think of accusing is himself, on whom in fact the principal blame lies.' And he proclaims that his doctrine 'attributes the greatest part of the sufferings of the lower classes of society exclusively to themselves'.[66]

Notwithstanding the anti-radical thrust of this position, it rests on a theoretical claim quite foreign to the *Essay* of 1798: the idea that individuals can, through moral restraint, 'improve' their behaviour and escape the effects of the law of population. This implies a possibility of social improvement as well, should society be capable of 'enlightening' and directing individual conduct. Indeed, Malthus at times lapses into an 'optimism' entirely at odds with his earlier views, as when he writes:

> I can easily conceive that this country, with a proper direction of the national industry, might, in the course of some centuries, contain two or three times its present population, and yet every man in the kingdom be much better fed and clothed than he is at present.[67]

Such formulations lend credence to Southey's claim, cited at the outset of this section, that in the *Essay* of 1803 Malthus had become a convert to the doctrine of perfectibility. Apparently uneasy about such an interpretation, Malthus regularly pulled back from the full implications of his new position. 'Few of my readers', he wrote, 'can be less sanguine than I am in their expectations of any great change in the general conduct of men'; and he claimed to be 'very cautious' in his 'expectations of probable improvement'. Such refusals to entertain prospects of improvement fit with the mood of Malthus's work; but they were essentially arbitrary estimations, which did not flow logically from the theoretical core of the *Essay* once individual agency and moral restaint had been taken on board.

Having undermined the theoretical foundations of his original position, Malthus's 1803 work attempts to buttress the principle of population with a plethora of empirical detail, the third main change introduced into the *Essay*. The result is a series of tedious chapters which, drawing on data from a host of countries, claim to provide evidence for the 'law' of the *First Essay*. What immediately strikes the reader about these empirical demonstrations, however, is the complete arbitrariness with which Malthus marshalls and interprets the data. As Thomas Sowell puts it, 'Malthus showed no awareness of the distinction between facts with a topical connection and facts with an analytic relevance'.[68] Indeed, the census of 1801 obliged Malthus to acknowledge that, contrary to his earlier claims, the British population was increasing quite rapidly, an acknowledgement which finds its way into the second edition. Moreover, in an essay of 1807, Malthus conceded that in England, despite the alleged effects of the poor laws, the 'proportion of births and marriages to the whole population is less than in most of the other countries of Europe' – in other words, that social, cultural and institutional factors could have a determining effect, a conclusion which defied both his general law and his specific analysis of the poor laws.[69] Of course, such exceptions could be accounted for by way of *ad hoc* explanation. But either the population law was an essential and unalterable fact of human existence, as Malthus never tired of repeating, or it was one highly malleable tendency among others, in which case its practical import for social policy was minimal. Clearly Malthus could not accept the latter conclusion. Yet, once individual agency and moral restraint were introduced into the corpus of the doctrine, no specific direction to population growth and food supply could be specified. The result was that from the second edition on, '*any* empirical consequence of increased prosperity was consistent with the new population principle. It was emptied of meaning as a theory, though it retained some significance as an exhortation.'[70]

The result of these three 'modifications' of the *Essay* was to transform the work from a naturalistic claim that social improvement, particularly in the form of better conditions for the poor, was impossible, to the much weaker, although still anti-radical, argument that there was one means alone of advancement for the poor: the individual practice of moral restraint, the need for which was undermined by the poor laws. Yet, as if these three alterations did not do enough damage to the theory advanced in 1798, Malthus proceeded to reverse himself on matters of economic analysis, and in so doing, unwittingly again, he drove the last nail into the coffin of his earlier position.[71]

Malthus's agrarianism became increasingly muted throughout the revisions which entered into the various editions of the *Essay*. 'Commerce and manufactures are necessary to agriculture', he soon conceded; and he proceeded to assert that 'a country in which manufactures and commerce flourish' will be 'peculiarly favourable to the progressive increase of capital'.[72] Moreover, he now acknowledged that 'the comforts of the lower classes of society do not depend solely upon food, nor even upon strict necessaries'.[73] This concession destroyed his original argument against Adam Smith's theory of improvement. Previously, Malthus had claimed that accumulation in manufacturing did nothing to improve the conditions of life for workers – indeed, it could make them worse – since it did not contribute to an augmentation of the food supply. In later editions, however, he accepted that growth of manufacturing and commerce were essential to investment in agriculture; that workers consumed more than food; and, therefore, that workers' conditions *could* improve (should they practice moral restraint) with the expansion of national wealth:

> the effects of increasing wealth on the condition of the poor ... brings with it advantages to the lower classes which may fully counterbalance the disadvantages with which it is attended; and, strictly speaking, the good or bad condition of the poor is not *necessarily* connected with any particular stage in the progress of society to its full complement of wealth.[74]

In other words, the direction of real wages is indeterminate. Even under conditions of industrially biased growth, working-class living standards might rise. This represented the total collapse of Malthus's case against Smith. Improvement for the working class was now entirely possible. Moreover, by the time he brought out his *Principles of Political Economy* in 1820, Malthus had completely abandoned the economic analysis of the *Essay*, although there is no evidence that he understood this fact.

One of the central concerns of Malthus's *Principles* was to refute the position of the 'Ricardo school', first formulated by Jean-Baptiste Say, according to which production, by generating wealth and incomes, creates its own demand. Say's Law thus holds that general overproduction is impossible in a free market economy. One of the few interesting features of Malthus's *Principles* is his rejection of this argument; yet his rejection rests on an argument completely at odds with the theory of the *Essay on Population*.

The theoretical structure of Malthus's *Principles* is thoroughly eclectic, revolving as it does around his effort to balance a costs of production theory of value with a supply and demand model. Nevertheless, this eclectic enterprise enables him to recognize that demand and supply need not automatically balance. Moreover, Malthus contends that the process of saving which is essential to capital accumulation poses a problem on the demand side. At times Malthus seems headed towards the argument that what is withdrawn from the revenue stream as savings for accumulation may not immediately translate into investment and production. Yet his simple-minded doctrine of 'proportions' – according to which all extremes must be avoided – leads him to claim that it is excessive savings and accumulation which are the danger (although he is incapable of specifying what levels are problematic). Nevertheless, Malthus sees that without 'an effectual and unchecked demand for all that is produced', accumulation will slow down or come to a halt. Recognizing the necessity of effective demand, he then jumps to the principle (which does not logically follow) that it is demand which drives growth: 'general wealth ... will always follow the effectual demand.'[75]

Malthus claims that workers and capitalists cannot make up for the deficit in demand caused by capitalist saving. These two groups produce more than they consume; demand and supply will thus be brought into balance only if there is a group which consumes more than it produces. It is the great economic virtue of the landed class that they perform this function, particularly by employing 'non-productive' labourers who perform personal services. The luxury consumption of the landlords is thus the key to stable economic growth.[76]

The whole of this argument is completely at odds with the economic analysis of the *Essay*. According to the population principle, the chronic – and 'immediate' – danger which confronts society is *underproduction* of food relative to people. In the *Principles*, however, we are thrust into a world threatened by *overproduction*. Rather than there being too little supply relative to demand, there is now too little demand relative to supply. In the place of a world struggling against scarcity, we now encounter a world drowning in abundance. Moreover, we are now informed that the unproductive employment of a part of the population – one of the evils railed against in the *Essay* – is crucial to economic well-being. Indeed, the *Principles* advocates 'the employment of the poor in roads and public works' as one of the solutions to crises of overproduction![77]

As Malthus's biographer notes in something of an understatment, 'it was surely inconsistent of Economist Malthus to say there were too few demanders for the products available, when Population Malthus had insisted that there were too many.'[78] To be sure, theorists often commit various inconsistencies; it is the scale of these inconsistencies which is staggering in the case of Malthus. As Morton Paglin puts it,

> the Malthus of the *Principles* speaks with a different voice: Instead of conceiving population as pressing relentlessly on the means of subsistence, he sees vast powers of production lying fallow, with existing resources adequate for ten times the present population. In place of exhortations to the working class to save and establish banks to encourage thrift, he declaims against those who declare thrift and parsimony to be a virtue and national benefit, and suggests devices to encourage consumption. In place of the condescension shown in the *Essay* to those who advocate employing the poor productively, he sees in the *Principles* the need for public works programs. Yet no formal retraction of the *Essay* was made.[79]

Examination of the revisions introduced into the economic analysis of the *Essay*, and the completely different theory which underpins the *Principles*, makes it difficult to dissent from the view of Robert Torrens, expressed in 1815, five years before the publications of Malthus's *Principles*, that 'in the leading questions of economical science, Mr. Malthus scarcely ever embraced a principle which he did not subsequently abandon'. However, this observation did not prevent Torrens from proceeding to praise Malthus as a theorist.[80] Indeed, Torrens's attitude reflects the general view one finds throughout political economy circles during this period – enormous praise for Malthus coupled with disdain for his analytic abilities. Unravelling this apparent paradox is crucial to understanding the development of bourgeois political economy in the first part of the nineteenth century.

For a period of about twenty-five years Malthus's *Essay* occupied a position second only to the *Wealth of Nations* in shaping the theoretical structure of classical political economy. The *Essay* was, as Bernard Semmel puts it, 'the most significant and most widely read work in political economy to appear in the quarter-century after the publication of the *Wealth of Nations*'. J.R. Poynter concurs: 'the *Essay* was second in importance only to *The Wealth of Nations* as a formative influence on that school of economics loosely called classical.' In the same vein, Patricia James claims that during the first decade of the nineteenth century, 'Adam Smith's mantle had fallen upon' Malthus; 'he was regarded as the country's foremost living political economist'.

James goes on to note that the currency of the word 'Malthusian' at this time 'could be compared with the word "Freudian" about a century later', a view which is echoed by Robert Young, who notes that 'Malthus' ideas were as commonplace in the first half of the nineteenth century as Freud's were in the twentieth'.[81]

It seems fair to say that no nineteenth-century political economist – and this includes Ricardo – had the public impact of Malthus. However, all the leading economic theorists of the period – James Mill, Ricardo, Nassau Senior, Robert Torrens, John Stuart Mill – had disdain for his theoretical achievements in political economy. Their attitude towards Malthus is nicely captured in a statement by Nassau Senior: 'Although Mr. Malthus has perhaps fallen into the exaggeration which is natural to a discoverer', he wrote, 'his error, if it be one, does not affect the practical conclusions which place him, as a benefactor to mankind, on a level with Adam Smith.'[82] Malthus's theoretical principles may have been suspect, but his 'practical conclusions' were worth defending.

This attitude explains the praise for Malthus's population theory which ran through publications as diverse as the *Edinburgh Review*, the *Quarterly Review*, the *Analytic Review* and the *Monthly Review* and accounts for Henry Brougham's effusive claim during the debate on the New Poor Law Bill that Malthus was one of the greatest 'political philosophers' of the age.[83] For it was Malthus's 'practical conclusion' with respect to the poor law and the right of subsistence which was taken over and integrated into classical political economy during this period. It was Population Malthus, not Economist Malthus, on whom the political economists built. This is why 'Ricardo and Mill supported the Malthus of the *Essay* while they vigorously opposed the Malthus of the *Principles*'.[84]

What, then, was Malthus's achievement? Put simply, it was to have constructed a 'discourse of poverty' which challenged head-on the views of the radical Paineites, such as Thelwall, Spence and Evans, who ranked subsistence among the natural rights of human beings. It was Malthus the 'scientific' theorist of anti-radicalism to whom Mill, Ricardo, Senior, Bougham and the rest turned. Too often it is forgotten that Malthus's most infamous attacks on the right of subsistence in the second edition of his *Essay* (1803) were specifically directed against Paine and his followers. It is in the course of a diatribe against 'the mischiefs occasioned by Mr Paine's *Rights of man*', particularly the notion that an individual has 'a right to subsistence when his labour will not fairly purchase it', that Malthus introduced his notorious 'nature's feast' metaphor. This passage is worth citing in full in order to transmit the temper of Malthus's argument during the period when the radical movement of 1792–1803 had risen to heights of militancy:

> A man who is born into a world already possessed, if he cannot get subsistence from his parents on whom he had a just demand, and if the society do not want his labour, has no claim of *right* to the smallest portion of food, and, in fact, has no business to be where he is. At nature's mighty feast there is no cover for him. She tells him to be gone and will quickly execute her own orders, if he do not work upon the compassion of some of her guests. If these guests get up and make room for him, other intruders immediately appear demanding the same favour. The report of a provision for all that come, fills the hall with numerous claimants. The order and harmony of the feast is disturbed, the plenty that before reigned is changed into scarcity; and the happiness of the guests is destroyed by the spectacle of misery and dependence in every part of the hall, and by the clamorous importunity of those, who are justly enraged at not finding the provision which they had been taught to expect. The guests learn too late their error, in countering those strict orders to all intruders, issued by the great mistress of the feast, who, wishing that all her guests should have plenty, and knowing that she could not provide for all, humanely refused to admit fresh comers when her table was already full.[85]

The message could not be clearer: starvation is the just lot of those who cannot procure their own means of subsistence or, in the case of children, of those whose parents cannot provide for them. These should be left to 'the punishment of nature ... the punishment of want'. The impoverished individual

> should be taught to know, that the laws of nature, which are the laws of God, had doomed him and his family to suffer for disobeying their repeated admonitions; that he had no claim of *right* on society for the smallest portion of food, beyond that which his labour would fairly purchase.

As to the children who starve due to the poverty of their parents, they are, as we have seen, 'of little value to the society, as others will immediately supply [their] place'. And in tune with this argument, Malthus made his famous proposal that 'no child born from any marriage, taking place after the expiration of a year from the date of the law, and no illegitimate child born after two years from the same date, should ever be entitled to parish assistance'.[86]

This harsh argument against a right of subsistence, even for children, elevated Malthus to the status of prophet of the labour market. In attacking the right of subsistence, he challenged the idea that 'the market price of labour ought always to be sufficient decently to support a family ... a conclusion which contradicts the plainest and most obvious principles of supply and demand'.[87] Moreover, this insistence that labour should earn only what the market dictates was wedded to the argument that food supply would always tend to be inadequate to provide subsistence for the whole population, a law which it was 'utterly beyond the power of any revolution or change of government' to affect. The poor would thus have to be made to understand that 'a revolution would not alter in their favour the proportion of the supply of labour to the demand'.[88]

Malthus thus laid down those elements of 'social conservatism' which were indispensable to the construction of economic liberalism. And, as I have suggested above, by defining these in terms of laws of nature, he avoided the problem of political voluntarism which pervades Burke's attempt to render bourgeois thought socially conservative. By claiming that the tendency of population growth to outstrip growth of food supply creates an ever-present threat of starvation, Malthus depicted social inequality as inevitable – and useful. If all human beings were equal, he suggested, then hunger and distress would 'be constantly pressing on all mankind'. The result would be a failure of any members of human society to rise above hunger and want, to cultivate reason and to achieve higher forms of moral behaviour. Clearly, Malthus argued, such could not have been God's will. Fortunately, human beings respond *unequally* to the law of population and the threat of hunger. The result is that while some starve (which is in any case inevitable), others exercise their industry and reason to advance the moral status of humankind:

> A state, in which inequality of conditions offers the natural rewards of good conduct, and inspires widely and generally the hopes of rising and the fears of falling in society, is unquestionably the best calculated to develop the energies and faculties of man, and the best suited to the exercise and improvement of human virtue.[89]

The law of population, harsh though it may be, is thus providential: it forces humanity to elevate itself through industry, reason and moral improvement. In so doing, it generates inequality, as some fail to keep up with the pace of virtuous improvement. Moreover, the unequal gains of improvement must be protected; they constitute 'the foundation of the laws relating to property'.[90]

This line of argument, extolling the necessity of social inequality and private property, moves entirely to the forefront of Malthus's last significant restatement of the population principle, *A Summary View of the Principle of Population* (1830). Humanity stagnates under systems of common property, Malthus claims, once more directing his argument against radicalism. Only under a system of private property can there be any 'hope of obtaining a large produce from the soil', since only security of possessions provides an inducement to labour. A system of private property can maintain the largest number of people at the same time as it provides a stimulus to virtue and improvement. Yet concede a right of subsistence and you undermine private property by granting the poor a right (in principle unlimited) to help themselves to the property of others. The right to subsistence and the right to private property are two diametrically opposed principles; they are 'absolutely incompatible, and cannot exist together'.[91]

From the necessity of social inequality and private property, Malthus then moves on to the necessity of wage-labour. The growth of social inequality tends to produce propertied and propertyless classes, the latter subsisting through the employ of the former. This is the natural structure of any society founded on the principle of private property. It follows, Malthus contends, that 'the structure of society, in its great features, will probably always remain unchanged. We have every reason to believe that it will always consist of a class of proprietors and a class of labourers.'[92] We have here the complete 'naturalization' of capitalist social relations. From the laws of nature, Malthus claims to have deduced the structure of a capitalist society with a completely 'free' labour market, i.e. one which recognizes no inherent right to subsistence.

And this was Malthus's central achievement as a theorist of bourgeois society: to have used 'scientific' laws of nature and political economy to refute the radical claim to a right of subsistence by demonstrating that any concession to such a right merely aggravated the problem of hunger and poverty; to have 'demonstrated' the superiority of private over common property; and to have shown the necessity of wage-labour. In so doing he did not reject modern categories of analysis, as Burke periodically did; instead, he harnessed these categories to the anti-radical cause. That he did so in an intellectually feeble and thoroughly contradictory fashion did not affect his influence.

What Malthus achieved was a fundamental shift in the argument for the market. Whereas Smith had conceptualized the market as a means to improve the material conditions of the labouring poor, the Malthusian defence posited the free market in labour as a mechanism which reproduced the poverty of the labourers in order to assist the moral and intellectual improvement of a minority. The labour market was depicted as an institution which disciplined the poor, breaking their laziness and dependence on the rich while eliminating policies, like the poor law, which bred overpopulation. Poverty and inequality were said to be inherent in human society. By encouraging private property and social inequality, however, the Malthusian market ensured that a few would be elevated and not dragged down to the level of the majority. Thus, while poverty was inevitable, private property and the market were desirable – for moral and intellectual reasons – but depended upon correct social policy. Any attempt to prevent poverty by providing for the subsistence of the poor would subvert private property and moral improvement. In these terms Malthus defined the discourse of poverty which dominated political economy for fifty years. He constructed a pessimistic market economics which jettisoned Smith's hopes for material improvement for the majority. And in so doing, he made classical economics an open enemy of the working class.

The Malthusian Legacy, 1: Anglican Social Thought

One key index of the impact of Malthus's discourse of poverty was its substantial incorporation into religious orthodoxy. Given the traditional role of the Church of England as a bastion of conservatism, it is not surprising that its hierarchy should have thrown itself into the battle against radicalism. What is interesting is the degree to which in so doing it drew upon the theoretical armoury of political economy as reshaped by Malthus.

By the mid-1790s, Anglican bishops were portraying the struggle against Revolutionary France as a holy war to save Christian civilization. In 1798 Bishop Samuel Horsley demanded, for example, that the clergy should be organized into an armed militia in preparation for the ultimate defence of Christianity.[93] Inspired by such talk, Church leaders determined to combat Paineism. In this vein, Beilby Porteus, bishop of Chester, denounced Paine's writings as *irreligion made easy* to the great bulk of mainkind and rendered intelligible to every capacity'.[94]

As with Malthus, the Anglican prelates linked their attack on

Paineite radicals to a sharp defence of inequality and private property. According to Bishop Pretyman, it was obvious that 'private
property is essential to the very existence of civil society'. George
Hone agreed, announcing in a sermon that 'if none were poor, none
would labour, and if some did not labour, none could eat'.[95] This
argument was also used to attack radical claims for a right of
subsistence. Charity might be bestowed on the supplicant, but militant
protesters for bread or relief should never be satisfied. 'While you
demand ... we refuse', explained the vicar Thomas Whitaker. 'When
you begin to supplicate, from that moment we bestow ... We crush
the stubborn; we spare the vanquished.'[96]

Increasingly, then, Anglican social thought merged with the
doctrines of bourgeois political economy. This was most clear in the
writings of John Bird Sumner, the future Evangelical Bishop of
Chester (1828–48) and Archbishop of Canterbury (1848–62). Sumner
was centrally involved in that great historic document in which
clerical conservatism and political economy came together to recast
social policy – the Poor Law Report of 1834. His achievement was
to graft aspects of Adam Smith's discussion of division of labour and
economic improvement to Malthus's theory of population and to
fit these into an orthodox theological perspective. In so doing,
Sumner's *Treatise on the Records of Creation* (1816) portrayed laws of
nature laid down by God which required private property and social
inequality. Moreover, like many bourgeois commentators of the time,
he was to insist upon the distinction between poverty, which 'is often
both honourable and comfortable' and indigence, which 'can only
be pitiable and is usually contemptible'. Inevitably, this position led
him by the early 1820s to declare that he was 'a decided enemy'
of the poor relief system.[97]

The hardening of Sumner's attitude towards poor relief reflected
the general trend in orthodox religious circles at the time. Edward
Copleston, Bishop of Llandaff, for example, openly praised
Malthus's *Essay* as 'that blazing beacon ... the rock upon which all
former projects, and all legislative measures split', and he attacked
the poor laws because they embodied the 'false assumption of a *right*
to support'.[98] An even more vociferous Malthusian was the Scottish
prelate Thomas Chalmers, who published two lengthy articles in the
Edinburgh Review in 1817–18 on the 'Causes and Cure of Pauperism'.
A hardcore abolitionist, Chalmers attacked charity and poor relief
as practices which destroyed self-reliance, overpopulated society, and
demolished respect for industry and property.[99]

Although it is likely that few prelates read Malthus directly, by the 1820s, if not earlier, Malthusianism had become part of the arsenal of anti-radical doctrine employed by Anglican propagandists. It should come as no surprise then that two bishops were named as Poor Law Commissioners in 1832 when Parliament struck its Royal Commission on the Poor Laws. Joined with them were a number of prominent figures in political economy circles, that other milieu in which Malthus made a decisive impact.

The Malthusian Legacy, 2:
Classical Political Economy

Conventional histories of economic thought have looked at early nineteenth-century political economy largely in terms of the dispute between Malthus and Ricardo over Say's Law and the possibility of general crises of overproduction. To be sure, in terms of economic theory *per se*, this analytic debate is of much significance. Furthermore, the controversy between Malthus and the Ricardians over the Corn Laws is of no little import. It remains the case, however, that in terms of the dominant debates over social policy Malthus and Ricardo were of one mind. Indeed, as I have noted above, for all their theoretical differences with Malthus, Ricardo and his followers continued to profess their allegiance to Malthus's theory of population and his attack on the poor laws. For this reason, 'it was not as leaders of rival schools, but as theoretical brothers in arms, that a large part of the generation of Ricardo, and of the decade after his death, regarded Malthus and Ricardo'.[100]

Certainly this was the signal Ricardo gave in his *Principles of Political Economy and Taxation* (1817) where, in his chapter on Wages, he attacked 'the pernicious tendency' of the poor laws, which had been fully explained 'by the able hand of Mr. Malthus,' and proceeded to call for the abolition of these laws in a series of 'gradual steps'.[101] Ricardo's gradualism on this occasion contrasts with his more extreme abolitionism at other times. Indeed, during parliamentary debates on this and related questions, Ricardo generally appeared as a hard-line Malthusian. In 1819, for example, he was nominated to the parliamentary committee of inquiry into the poor laws headed by William Sturges-Bourne, who proposed to eliminate all poor relief to destitute parents of large families, but advocated providing relief to hungry children on condition that they be taken from their parents and placed in workhouses. Yet Ricardo found even this harsh proposal too liberal. It would encourage population growth, he claimed, by assuring poor adults 'that an asylum would be provided for their children, in which they would be treated with humanity and tenderness'. Indeed, Ricardo maintained that the proposal 'was only the plan of Mr. Owen, in a worse shape and carried to a greater extent'.[102]

The same doctrinaire opposition to any public support for wages and living standards appears in Ricardo's response to the plight of unemployed and impoverished cotton and silk weavers. In an effort to relieve suffering cotton workers, MP John Maxwell, in June 1820, moved that a select committee be appointed to examine their plight. Maxwell suggested that the government consider taxing machinery; that it subsidize travel by workers in search of employment; that it repeal the combination laws, and sponsor land settlement schemes for workers. Ricardo objected to these proposals claiming they ignored the principles of free trade and class distinction, and that they 'would likewise violate the sacredness of property, which constituted the great security of society'.[103]

Three years later, Ricardo threw his energies behind the campaign 'to destroy the industrial relations system of the silk industry at Spitalfields in London'.[104] Long-standing legislation governing the Spitalfields industry provided that London and area magistrates could set wage levels in cases of labour disputes. When London silk manufacturers petitioned for repeal of this legislation, Ricardo immediately took their side, denouncing the existing Act as 'an interference with the freedom of trade'. In particular, he attacked the notion that legislators should treat labour differently from any other commodity: 'Why should he have the power to fix the price of labour, more than the price of bread, meat, or beer?'[105]

The older moral economy had an answer: because labour was more than a mere commodity; it was a power which pertained to living human beings who had a moral right to preserve themselves. But such a notion was entirely foreign to bourgeois political economy. The price of labour – wages – was to be governed by the same laws of supply and demand that regulated all commodity prices. Any attempt at extra-economic regulation of wages was an interference with 'freedom' of trade; the fund for human subsistence should be determined by market demand. As Ricardo put it, 'if the demand was great, the number of persons employed would be in proportion'.[106] Conversely, as Malthus had persistently emphasized, if demand were lacking, the surplus of labourers would have to suffer and/or die. Any interference with that law of nature was a violation of free trade.

Ricardo's *Principles* openly adopted Malthus's position on the poor laws. Indeed, Ricardo told Francis Place, in words that could have come right from Malthus (or Bentham), that he completely rejected all talk of a 'right' to relief. Moreover, in Parliament in 1821 he threw his support behind a proposal to abolish immediately all relief payments in aid of poverty-level wages, claiming that such a move was necessary 'to regulate the price of labour by the demand'.[107] So hard-line was Ricardo's opposition to poor relief, especially for children of the poor, that in December 1818 he refused to send James Mill a donation towards the Westminster Infant School because the children were to be given some dinner.

> If it is part of the plan of the establishment ... to feed as well as take care of and educate the children of three years of age, and upwards, belonging to the poor, I see the most serious objections to the plan, and I should be exceedingly inconsistent if I gave my countenance to it. I have invariably objected to the poor laws, and to every system which should give encouragement to excess of population.[108]

If Ricardo played a central role in advancing Malthusian policies within the House of Commons, it was the *Edinburgh Review* – unquestionably the most important publication in the dissemination of bourgeois political economy to 'educated' opinion – which did the most to elevate Malthus's law of population (and his opposition to the poor laws) to the status of scientific principles of political economy. It is no secret that 'the *Review* from the beginning supported Malthusian doctrine'.[109] In fact, the *Review*'s first year saw a vigorous application of Malthusian principles by one of its editors, Sydney Smith, in a sharp attack on poor relief.[110] The tendency of the *Review*'s editors was to treat Malthus as a contributor to political economy of the status of Adam Smith. Jeffrey Horner, for example, described Malthus as 'the discoverer of a new world'; while Henry Brougham lauded him as one of the greatest 'political philosophers' of the age.[111] In 1808 Malthus became a contributor to the *Review*, a position he was to enjoy until he came out in support of the Corn Laws in 1815; even then, his views on population were upheld by the Edinburgh reviewers.

The editors of the *Edinburgh Review* often recognized that by adopting Malthus's law of population they were significantly modifying Smithian political economy. Nevertheless, they were loath to acknowledge this since they believed, as Francis Horner put it, that 'we owe much at present to the superstitious worship of Smith's name; and we must not impair that feeling, till the victory is more complete'.[112] As a result, they tended to advocate an eclectic amalgam of Smith, Malthus and Ricardo dressed up as a unified 'science' of political economy. Creating this amalgam was very much the work of J.R. McCulloch, who emerged as the main popularizer of the Mill–Ricardo tradition upheld by the *Edinburgh Review*. McCulloch, who had by 1824 'established himself as the major exponent of political economy and a fierce foe of the Poor Laws', sought to advance a Smithian economics modified by Malthus, Say and Ricardo. Yet there can be little doubt that 'the retention of Smith's approach disguised the fact that the actual content of the arguments had changed profoundly' – and this was especially so with respect to the issues of wages, poverty, and poor relief.[113]

The new, post-Smithian framework of political economy is best revealed in the 1834 Report of the Poor Law Commission, and in the attitude of its chief inspiration, the economist Nassau Senior. A vicious opponent of trade unions and all restrictions on the rights of employers, Senior advocated the criminalization of all combinations by workers, opposed the Ten Hours Bill, and, as head of a Royal Commission on the plight of handloom weavers, vigorously attacked all relief measures for the impoverished and the unemployed.[114] But he was most outspoken in his assault on the principle of poor relief. Following the great uprising of agricultural labourers in 1830 (to be discussed in the next section), Senior wrote a Preface to his *Three Lectures on the Rate of Wages* in which he blamed the riots on the fact that the poor laws encouraged workers to believe that subsistence is a political right, as opposed to a fortuitous result of the blind working of the economic laws of supply and demand. Echoing Malthus, he argued that 'nature has decreed that the road to good shall be through evil – that no improvement shall take place in which the general advantage shall not be accompanied by partial suffering'.[115]

This view – that hunger and starvation were inevitable aspects of the 'partial suffering' which accompanies that 'general advantage' of the capitalist economy – was echoed endlessly in that crucial document in the history of nineteenth century social policy and political economy, the *Poor Law Report of 1834*. And with the *Poor Law Report*, what Marx called the 'vulgarization' of political economy was complete. Those elements of genuinely disinterested scientific analysis developed by Smith and Ricardo receded; and Smith's attempt to define political economy in terms of a commitment to rising wages and working-class living standards was openly abandoned. With the *Poor Law Report of 1834*, mainstream political economy became an openly bourgeois ideology.

The Malthusian Legacy, 3: The Poor Law Debate

As we have seen, the Malthusian discourse of political economy was constructed as a direct reply to radicalism. Moreover, from the second edition of Malthus's *Essay* onward, the argument pivoted on an attack on the alleged right of subsistence. By the early 1820s, as poor relief costs declined and popular radicalism receded, the British ruling class became less preoccupied with the poor law debate. The agrarian riots of 1830 changed all that. Once more, ruling-class opinion sought to combat those popular notions which sustained radical thought; once more, the poor law system and its implicit acceptance of a right to subsistence came under siege. The renewal of the poor law debate from 1830 to 1834 was, in other words, a direct response to a perceived crisis in social control and class relations. In the forefront of this renewed debate were political and ideological concerns, not in the first instance financial ones. The issue was not so much that poor relief costs were rising, as it was the view that the relief system sustained attitudes and beliefs that encourged the poor to stand up for (and revolt on behalf of) the subversive notion that the rich owed them their subsistence.

Whereas poor relief costs had soared between 1795 and 1803, they declined during the boom that accompanied the Napoleonic wars. With the end of the wars, the demobilization of soldiers, and the decline in demand for military goods, a depression set in. By 1818, poor relief expenditure almost equalled the total spending of all other civil departments combined. Indeed, it has been suggested that between 1817 and 1821 as many as 20 per cent of the entire English population may have received some relief.[116] Yet, the peak of relief expenditure was reached in 1818; there was a steady decline thereafter until the late 1820s. By 1830–5, average spending per head on relief was almost a third lower than it had been for 1815–20; as a percentage of national income it had declined by almost half.[117]

What renewed the poor law debate at the beginning of the 1830s was not, therefore, a dramatic surge in relief costs. On the contrary, it was the new rebelliousness of the agricultural labourer, especially in the south and east of England – a rebelliousness which burst forth in 1830. Behind this rise of class protest in the agricultural regions of southern and eastern England was the acceleration after 1760 of pressures towards market specialization and proletarianization. Increasing reliance on production of wheat coupled with the labour-intensive techniques of the new husbandry created a demand for a regular supply of wage-labourers (as opposed to casual labour from domestic workers and cottagers). The result was the emergence of larger and increasingly proletarian work teams, a concomitant decline in perquisites, and a weakening of traditional ties between farmer and labourer as the wage-form came to dominate the relations between agrarian classes. When the agricultural depression hit after 1815, these more fully capitalist relations on the land provided the foundation for widespread agitation over wages by farm labourers.[118]

The first symptom of the emerging crisis in agrarian class relations in the period after the Napoleonic Wars was the wave of protests in East Anglia in 1816, which was followed by similar protests in 1822.[119] Equally indicative was the rise in rural crime, especially a directly socio-economic 'crime' such as poaching.[120] But, as I have suggested, it was the massive uprising of 1830 – the Swing riots, known as such because of the use of the name 'Captain Swing' on anonymous letters of protest to farmers, magistrates and overseers of the poor – which reflected the enormous tensions involved in the transition to agrarian capitalism in these parts of England.

The story of Captain Swing has been told admirably and in great detail.[121] Beginning in east Kent in late August 1830, there developed an enormous wave of rural protest, which swept across southern and eastern England, and included arson, threatening letters, rent and tithe revolts, the destruction of threshing machines, wage protests, attacks on overseers, magistrates, and prisons, mass assemblies, and so on. The ruling class was thrown into an utter panic over the breadth and the militancy of these actions. A magistrate writing to Sir Robert Peel urged the government to 'sanction the arming of the Bourgeois classes' in order to suppress the uprisings, claiming that 'if this state of things should continue the Peasantry will learn *the secret of their own physical strength*'.[122]

This was no isolated case. The Swing riots drove the bulk of the ruling class towards an increasingly hard-line attitude to the poor laws. Rural protest could only be halted, went the argument, if a concerted effort was made to break the political assumption that the rich had an obligation to guarantee the subsistence of the poor. This subversive notion was said to be the root of those popular attitudes which fomented riot and rebellion. By creating the expectation that subsistence was a matter of political will – and not of the inexorable laws of the market – relief encouraged the poor to rebel when the supply of food was precarious.

There can be little doubt that large numbers of England's rulers believed that 1830 represented a turning point for class relations in the countryside. William Day, a Sussex squire who became an assistant poor law commissioner, told the Poor Law Commission of 1834 that when he went to the parish of Mayfield in order to examine the poor rates,

> on the door of the first vestry I attended I found a notice that they intended washing their hands in my blood. In 1826, a threat of that kind was readily disregarded; at present it would be consummated in a riot or fire.

This situation made it necessary, he claimed, that the central government take over the poor law system. After all, 'the complaining pauper ... may hope to intimidate a vestry, but he cannot dare to oppose a government'.[123] Similarly, explaining his support for the New Poor Law bill of 1834, R.A. Slaney, the Liberal M.P. for Shrewsbury, reminded his audience of the panic of 1830. The Bill was necessary, he argued, because 'no village, hamlet or parish was safe from the work of the incendiary; and when the flames were raging at the highest, the labourers, instead of helping to extinguish them, were seen silently looking on'.[124]

The uprisings of 1830 drove the gentry of England to launch a further attack on the traditional rights of the poor. Having seen the face of incendiary working-class protest in the villages, they resolved to move decisively.[125] And they had chosen their solution well in advance of the *Report* of the Poor Law Commission. As William Day, who has been quoted above, put it in 1833, the answer was to centre poor relief in a workhouse which 'joins the discipline of a prison to the incontamination of a manufactory', i.e. a workhouse which 'is, in short, a barrack'.[126] Poverty, in other words, would have to be punished; only in this way could the expectation of a right to subsistence be thoroughly demolished.

The composition of the Poor Law Commission, established in 1832, reflected the importance of the two ideological groups upon which Malthusianism made its greatest impact: Anglican social theorists and mainstream political economists. Representing the former were John Bird Sumner, Bishop of Chester, and Charles

James Blomfield, Bishop of London. Representing organized political economy circles were Nassau Senior, Walter Coulson, like Senior a member of the Political Economy Club, and Edwin Chadwick, one of the most important of Jeremy Bentham's disciples. Among the four remaining commissioners was William Sturges Bourne, the leading Tory opponent of the poor laws in the House of Commons.

There can be little doubt that it was the outlook of leading members of the Political Economy Club which most indelibly put its stamp on the Commission. As Cowherd notes,

> during the years of the Poor Law inquiry, the Political Economy Club stood as a shadow government for economic policy. Members of the Whig Government, with primary responsibility for economic affairs, were also members of the Political Economy Club.[127]

Not surprisingly, the *Report* which the Commission produced dogmatically reasserted the orthodox preconceptions of vulgar political economy – in particular, the notion that the old poor law encouraged widespread indigence among the able-bodied who chose the luxury of outdoor relief over 'a hard day's work'. J.R. Poynter, not a particularly harsh critic of the *Report*, notes that the Commission produced 'a dogmatic document, unhistorical and unstatistical'.[128]

From the outset the poor law commissioners adopted the assumption that the existing poor relief system was 'destructive to the morals of the most numerous class' and that 'the greatest source of abuse is the out-door relief afforded to the able-bodied on their own account, or on that of their families'.[129] This choice of focus was both deliberate and misleading. In reality, the vast majority of recipients of outdoor relief were elderly people. Women with illegitimate children formed another substantial group. One examination of outdoor relief in Halifax for 1802 indicates that 80 per cent of those who received such relief were widows, elderly women and men, women with illegitimate children, and those with physical and mental disabilities.[130] The commissioners, however, were not interested in such facts. Their concern was not an accurate profile of the poor relief system; rather, it was to prosecute the ideological conviction that only a labour market freed from traditional forms of protection against hunger and poverty could produce the disciplined workforce appropriate to a capitalist economy. For this reason, they focused their attack on what was in statistical terms a marginal group: the able-bodied poor.

At the heart of their argument was the claim that conditions of relief should be made decidedly inferior to those of the independent labourer. They argued that a strong line of demarcation had to be drawn 'between pauperism and independence' and that this could best be done 'by making relief in all cases less agreeable than wages'. To this end, the commissioners proposed that relief of the able-bodied should take place only in workhouses in which recipients would be separated from their families and receive a diet inferior to that available to the poorest wage-labourer.[131]

One of the interesting features of the 'analysis' by which the commissioners upheld this proposal is that they rested their case not on the apparent encouragement to overpopulation which poor relief provided, but, rather, on the alleged corrupting effects of relief to the able-bodied. In this they followed the shifting emphasis of Malthus's argument from 1803 onward. Yet, whereas Malthus tried to combine the two anti-poor law arguments, the *Poor Law Report* almost entirely ignored the overpopulation thesis.[132] Instead, it built its case against relief on the damage done by poor relief to personal morality and labour discipline (much the same thing in the eyes of the commissioners).

Among the countless quotations from farmers, overseers and country gentlemen with which the *Report* is liberally sprinkled, one endlessly finds phrases to the effect that those whose wages are subsidized (through the allowance system) 'will not work'; that the provision of an allowance 'makes them idle, lazy, fraudulent, and worthless'; that as a result 'the labourers are not as industrious as formerly'; that recipients 'have become callous to their own degradation'; that with the liberalization of relief 'all habits of prudence, of self-respect, and of self-restraint, vanished'; and that 'the greatest evil' of the system 'is the spirit of laziness and insubordination that it creates'.[133] The most insidious and subversive consequence of these many evils was said to be that the poor labourer comes to see subsistence as a right. The able-bodied recipient of relief

> receives a certain sum, not because it is the fair value of his labour, but because it is what the vestry has ordered to be paid. Good conduct, diligence, skill, all become valueless. Can it be supposed that they will be preserved? We deplore the misconception of the labourers in thinking that wages are not a matter of contract but of right.[134]

Worse, it is this notion of 'right' which fosters riot and rebellion. As one magistrate told the Commission, the relief system will keep producing labourers who believe that society owes them a livelihood until a generation of superfluous labourers has risen up, all demanding work or pay from the scale. If this system continues, in ten years more another generation will be hastening on. The present race, which this illegal perversion of the Poor Laws has created, are playing the game of cunning with the magistrates and the overseers; give them ten years, and they will convert it into a dreadful game of force. My humble opinion is that if some measure be not adopted to arrest the progress of the evil, a fearful and bloody contest *must* ensue.[135]

Indeed, the commissioners held that such a point had been reached in 1830; that during the agricultural riots 'the violence of most of the mobs seems to have arisen from an idea that all their privations arose from the cupidity or fraud of those entrusted with the management of the funds provided for the poor'; and that the main lesson the poor had learned from 1830 was that their 'rates can be effected by intimidation'.[136] Until the expectation of relief to the able-bodied could be broken, violence, riot and intimidation would haunt rural England.

The commissioners followed the dogmas of bourgeois economics in insisting that the old poor law violated 'the ordinary laws of nature' (i.e. the laws of the market). Thus, they depicted their draconian reforms as efforts designed merely to return to the natural laws of human society: 'one of the objects attempted by the present administration of the Poor Laws is to repeal *pro tanto* that law of nature by which the effects of each man's providence or misconduct are borne by himself and his family.'[137] To this end, they adopted the 'Benthamite' notion that poor relief should be subject to a 'self-acting test': given the provision of relief at inferior levels and subject to the punitive constraints of the workhouse, one could safely assume that labourers would do everything within their powers to avoid turning to poor relief. Indeed, the spectre of the workhouse being sufficiently terrifying, the New Poor Law might be expected to heighten labour discipline and instill a new willingness to work for less.

It is important to note, however, that both the *Report* and the implementation of the New Poor Law failed to conform to Benthamite prescription. In reality, massive resistance to the new law and its officials, especially in the north of England, produced a series of concessions, some of them supported by local gentry, which limited the scope of the workhouse, continued some outdoor relief to the able-bodied and provided ample powers of discretion for overseers and magistrates to make judgements about the character of recipients. All of these compromises diluted much of the intent of Senior and others; moreover, their plans for a radical centralization of poor law administration were largely stillborn. Even at the time of the *Report*, the Benthamite Francis Place bemoaned the fact that the government 'had castrated the Poor Law Bill'.[138] Popular resistance was to force the government to restrict its plans further.

However much the *Poor Law Report* may have departed from specific Malthusian positions (often positions Malthus himself later revised), there can be little doubt that 'the abrasive class character of the New Poor Law was ... rooted in the moral sentiments of Malthus'.[139] To be sure, Bentham had played some role in shaping the attitude toward poverty which permeated the *Report*. But this attitude had largely been defined in public debate by Malthus, not Bentham. This is what Malthus's long-time friend Bishop Otter grasped when he wrote, 'The Essay on Population and the Poor Law Amendment Bill will stand or fall together'.[140] More than any other work, it was Malthus's *Essay* which had defined the anti-radical opposition to poor relief in the age of the French Revolution.

And this fact was clearly grasped by the popular opponents of the New Poor Law. In May 1837 a massive demonstration of between 200,000 and 260,000 against the New Poor Law was organized on Peep Green. The banner leading the Huddersfield contingent announced boldly: 'The Huddersfield division swears destruction to all Malthusian bastiles.'[141] Working-class radicals saw clearly the connection between Malthusian doctrine, the attack on poor relief and the new 'bastiles' (workhouses). They saw as well that Malthusianism was now a cornerstone of mainstream political economy. Inevitably, their confrontation with Malthusianism and the New Poor Law embroiled them in a confrontation with bourgeois political economy. And out of this confrontation there emerged a new popular political economy, a political economy of the working class.

4

Exploitation, Inequality and the Market: the Making of Popular Political Economy

Hostility to Malthus was at the heart of the critique of political economy which developed within popular radicalism during the early nineteenth century. William Cobbett's vilification of the author of the principle of population – particularly in his 'Letter to Parson Malthus' (1819), 'The Sin of Forbidding Marriage' (1822), and his three-act comedy *Surplus Population* (1831) – had alerted a growing popular audience to Malthusianism and the doctrines of political economy.[1] Advanced at a time when employers and politicians were using political economy to justify deregulation of wages, Cobbett's polemics helped make Malthusianism 'perhaps the central social issue preoccupying radicalism in these decades', so much so that the epithet 'Malthusian' had become, by the 1820s, 'one of the dirty words of popular radicalism'.[2]

Yet treating Malthusianism as a dirty word was not enough. As the offensive of political economy against the working class became more aggressive during this period, popular radicalism was forced to shift from mere diatribe and vilification of the sort fashioned by Cobbett towards a more systematic and theoretically informed critique of political economy. One sees the evidence of such a move in the *Trades' Newspaper*, an organ of London artisan radicalism during the 1820s, and in that celebrated voice of articulate radicalism, *The Poor Man's Guardian* of the early 1830s.[3] This developing critique was urgently needed as political economy became *the* 'scientific' justification for legislative attacks on wage regulation and trade union rights. But this was only one level on which the offensive of political economy operated. Perhaps more important were attempts to popularize political economy, to advance its doctrines via school, pulpit, popular journalism, and working-class institutions.

The launching in 1802 of the *Edinburgh Review* was the first significant step in the popularization of political economy. By 1814, sales
of the *Review* had risen to 13,000 from a mere 750 at its launch. Equally
important, by 1826 all the major representatives of mainstream
political economy (except Ricardo whose ideas and disciples dominated the publication) were contributors to the *Review* – Malthus,
James Mill, Thomas Chalmers, Robert Torrens and J.R. McCulloch.[4]
The appointment of Malthus in 1805 as Professor of History and
Political Economy at the East India Company's College in Hertfordshire is indicative of the new respect accorded the 'science' of
political economy (and of Malthus as its chief disseminator). Twenty
years later Nassau Senior, a chief architect of the New Poor Law
Report, was to take the newly established Chair of Political Economy
at Oxford.

Significant as these moves were for establishing a veneer of
intellectual respectability for political economy and, in the case of
the *Edinbugh Review*, for broadening its middle-class audience, they
were still a far cry from a genuine popularization of its doctrines.
By the second decade of the nineteenth century, however, Francis
Place emerged as probably the earliest proponent of a truly popular
dissemination of political economy. His voice was soon joined by
many others. By the 1820s, Henry Brougham was calling, in his
Practical Observations on the Education of the People (1825), for works on
political economy that would 'be more extensively circulated for the
good of the working classes, as well as their superiors'; the following
year Thomas Chalmers proposed using political economy as a means
of 'tranquilizing the popular mind and removing from it all those
delusions which are the main cause of popular disaffection'; and in
1827 Nassau Senior could be read advocating the diffusion of political
economy in order to 'attract the notice of the mechanic and the
artisan' and to 'penetrate into the cottage of the labourer'.[5]

What we observe by the 1820s, then, is a quite conscious attempt
to employ political economy not simply as an ideological justification
for the ruling class, but also as a means of legitimating capital's
assault on the moral economy of the labourers. Such a popular
legitimation required blunting the edge of the vitriolic anti-radicalism
which pervaded Malthus's *First Essay* (a task Malthus himself had
partially carried through in subsequent editions), and presenting
political economy as a science which delineated rational and respectable – as opposed to fantastic and delusionary – means of working-
class advancement. Among the efforts at doing so were the crude

Conversations on Political Economy published by J. Marcet in 1816 (which went through five editions by 1824) and Harriet Martineau's fictional work *The Rioters* (1827), which aimed to expose the deluded and corrupt nature of machine-breaking. But the site of the real fight to establish the hegemony of political economy within the working-class movement was the Mechanic's Institutes of the 1820s.

The first 'Mechanical Institution' was founded in London in 1817. Although that effort collapsed after three years, the editors of the *Mechanics Magazine*, Thomas Hodgskin and J.C. Robertson, revived the idea in 1823. In short order, a battle ensued for control and direction of the Institute between those, like Hodgskin and Robertson, who favoured a democratic organization run by working-class subscribers, and Francis Place, who solicited wealthy benefactors and fought for an orientation dominated by Benthamism and middle-class political economy. Place and his supporters ultimately prevailed, consolidated middle class control over the Institute, put a stop to Hodgskin's critical lectures on political economy and remodelled the institutes into 'self-conscious disseminators of the entrepreneurial ideal'.[6]

The conflict over the Mechanic's Institutes illustrates the divide that was taking place within radical politics over the doctrines of political economy. Those with an orientation towards middle-class reform embraced Malthusianism and the doctrines of Ricardo, while popular radicals who rejected both found themselves under an increasingly systematic theoretical barrage from orthodox political economy. Radical critics were regularly dismissed for 'ignoring Political Economy', as Place wrote of Godwin. A similar line of argument was adopted as early as 1817 by political economists who opposed the reforms advocated by Robert Owen.[7] Arguments for trade union rights, wage regulation, poor relief, popular education, and so on were now invariably conducted on the terrain of political economy. The result was that, as radicalism split into two camps, 'the dividing line came to be, increasingly, not alternative "reform" strategies ... but alternative notions of political economy'.[8] From these alternative notions there emerged in the 1820s a new popular political economy.

Popular Political Economy – the Forerunners

Historians of popular protest and the making of the working class have long recognized the importance of a loose set of customary values and beliefs which sustained the moral economy of the English poor.[9] At the heart of this moral economy, as we have seen, was the notion of a right to subsistence. During the period of the agrarian and industrial revolutions of the eighteenth and early nineteenth centuries, however, the right of subsistence argument shaded into the idea of a right to secure employment at a living wage. To be sure, such an idea was ultimately implicit in the argument for a right of subsistence. But given the experiences of wage-cutting, enclosure, mechanization and industrial reorganization, the emphasis on the right to work at a living wage came increasingly to the fore. Moreover, this inevitably involved the assertion that labour was not a commodity like soap, lace or beer.

The attack on the commodity status of labour became the centrepiece of opposition to the doctrines of Malthus, Ricardo, and the Benthamites. As Thomas Single put it in the *Trades' Newspaper* in the mid-1820s:

> The great evil with men who have written on what they term political economy is, that they never take into consideration the habits and customs, and all the natural passions and propensities belonging to human nature … They also have in general this radical evil at the bottom of their systems. They consider man as a machine, and the labourer as a commodity.

Yet, he continued,

> To call labour a commodity that is to be brought to the market like wheat or any other article, is sheer nonsense – the one is a shadow, the other a substance. Before you can order Englishmen to be worked like cattle, you must first deprive them of all the natural passions and feeling which are implanted by God.[10]

At the heart of this argument is the moral elevation of human labour above the status of a commodity. This dignifying of labour – and most crucially of *the labourer* – owed an important debt to the dissident journalism of William Cobbett. Notwithstanding the severe limits of his radicalism, Cobbett gave voice to the moral and political claims of the labouring poor. This is perhaps nowhere clearer than in his 'Address to the Journeymen and Labourers' (1816) where he asserted that 'the real strength and all the resources of a country, ever have sprung, and ever must spring from the *labour* of its people'. It followed from this that labourers possessed an inalienable 'right to have a living out of the land of our birth in exchange for our labour duly and honestly performed'.[11]

What Cobbett developed from the traditional moral economy of the poor, then, was the notion that the right to a decent living from honest labour took precedence over the laws of supply and demand. Yet his was a *market utopianism*; like Paine he believed that constitutional reform (or, in his case, constitutional renewal) would allow each – landlord, farmer, master and labourer – to receive their fair share of the national wealth. Just as he did not object to property or class, but merely to their perversion and distortion by unpatriotic innovators, so he entirely accepted the principle of market exchange while criticizing its manipulation. As Raymond Williams puts it, Cobbett sought not the overthrow of 'the supposed principles of bourgeois society', but rather, their 'extension to all men, rather than just the proprietors and entrepreneurs'. The result, notes E.P. Thompson, was that he 'reduced economic analysis to a polemic against the *parasitism* of certain vested interests. He could not allow a critique which centred on ownership.'[12]

It was the achievement of Thomas Spence and the radical agrarians to have introduced such a 'critique centered on ownership' into popular radicalism. The agrarian programme developed by the Spenceans represented one of the main solutions advanced to counter the commodification of human labour power. By establishing common ownership of the land, Spenceanism offered a way of eliminating the need for the poor to rely on the labour market for their subsistence. Reunite labourers with the land, went the argument, and you will either eliminate wage-labour or so reduce the supply of labour as to force up wages and eliminate poverty.

The Spenceans' attack on private ownership of land brought the property question increasingly to the fore of radical discourse. Thomas Evans's claim that 'it is property and property alone that gives power and influence, and wherever the people are wholly deprived of property they are slaves' signifies this crucial shift within the parameters of radical thought.[13] Yet although they took a more vigorous line towards the property question and were more thoroughgoing egalitarians, the Spenceans shared with Cobbett an idealized image of a community of small producers. Common ownership of the land would enable all to be 'little Farmers and little Mastermen', Spence claimed. His supporter Thomas Evans similarly 'idealised small-scale individual enterprise'.[14] Changes in property arrangements were thus seen as ways to eliminate exploitation by allowing the market to operate naturally and equitably.

This, then, was the aspect of the Paineite tradition which even the most left-wing of the popular radicals tended to maintain: the dream of a utopia of independent proprietor-producers equitably exchanging in free markets. Common ownership of the land was not designed to create communal conditions of life and work, but was envisaged, rather, as a means of establishing equal relations between free and independent commodity producers. Although there would be a degree of economic self-sufficiency involved, Spence envisaged a fairly developed level of economic specialization, production and exchange of manufactures, and employment of wage-labour.[15] Spencean socialism, in other words, rested on acceptance of individualized production and market exchange in the context of communal ownership of land. This vision of socialism (or a new social order) as the true society of free trade and independent commodity exchange was to become of increasing importance within the British working-class movement. Before turning to the popular political economists of the 1820s and 1830s, however, there are two other elements of the legacy bequeathed to them by their forerunners which deserve mention: the radical theory of exploitation and the critique of paper money.

Theories of exploitation themselves were not new in the 1820s; throughout many epochs of society one finds prayers, poems, songs and writings which condemn the domination of the rich over the poor. What was unique about the notions of exploitation that developed within British radicalism from the 1780s onwards is that they joined to the moral condemnation of inequality a search for a clear measure of economic exploitation (i.e. the amount of wealth expropriated by the rich from the labour of the poor) and that they sought to anatomize the social classes which interacted in the economic process that created this exploitation. By the beginning of the nineteenth century, in other words, elements of a *theory* of exploitation were being sketched in terms of categories other than those of moral economy, and increasingly in the language of political economy – and in that of its predecessors, political anatomy and political arithmetic, in particular.[16]

One glimpses something of the older approach in William Ogilvie's *Essay on the Right of Property in Land* (1782) where he states that 'whoever enjoys any revenue, not proportioned to such industry or exertion of his own, or of his ancestors, is a freebooter'.[17] Yet already by the second and third editions of William Godwin's *Enquiry Concerning Political Justice* (1796, 1798), one observes an increasing specification of the economic processes of exploitation. By the time of the second edition, a rudimentary analysis of the 'capitalist' was entering radical discourse; Godwin consequently replaces the term 'middleman' by 'capitalist' and describes the latter as 'an idle and useless monopolizer'. Moreover, in the third edition of two years later, he begins to disaggregate the surplus product taken from the labourers in terms of rent, profit and taxes: 'The landed proprietor first takes a very disproportionate share of the produce to himself; the capitalist follows and shows himself equally voracious ... Taxation comes in next.'[18]

Godwin's argument involves a rudimentary specification of the component parts of the economic surplus taken from the labourers, and of the appropriating classes which enjoy this surplus. Nevertheless, it did not attempt to employ the categories of political economy; indeed, as I have noted, it was dismissed by Francis Place for its ignorance of them. By 1805, however, radicalism had found a critic of exploitation whose work did utilize the concepts of political economy, particularly those of Adam Smith: Charles Hall and his book *The Effects of Civilization on the People in European States*.

Hall was a London doctor whose work made at least a minor impact in radical circles.[19] Most influential initially was the appendix to his work, which attacked Malthus's theory of population. But at least as important as time went by was his analysis of poverty and exploitation. Using government statistics, he attempted to quantify the degree of exploitation of the working class. The top 20 per cent of the population, he suggested, consumes seven-eighths of the national wealth; a mere one-eighth remains for the 80 per cent who produce that wealth. Employing the concepts of productive and unproductive labour used by the Physiocrats and Adam Smith, albeit in a confused fashion, he undertakes to explain how it is that the rich appropriate for themselves the bulk of society's output.

The root cause of the problem, he maintains, is the monopoly of land maintained by the landowning class. Yet he also attempts to delineate the processes of capitalist exploitation. 'The means enabling tradesmen to share a part of the product of the labour of the poor', he writes, 'is their capital.' But the exchange of capital for labour is not a fair exchange. In truth, the capitalist simply gives the labourer some of the product of his past labour in exchange for labour in the here-and-now: 'The rich man has truly nothing to give the poor man; the money, as well as the bread that was bought with it, the poor man's hands had before produced.' The result is that society is divided into a consuming class which buys, and a producing class which sells, labour.[20]

In analytic terms, there is much that is deficient in Hall's explanation. He has a physiocratic theory of value and exploitation in which capitalist profit is seen as a deduction from the rent of land; and he conceives of the capitalist as an intermediary in the sphere of exchange, not as an employer of labour.[21] Notwithstanding these shortcomings, his work represented a significant step forward in the economic analysis of exploitation precisely because it engaged this discussion on the terrain of, and in terms of, the categories of political economy. As one historian notes, 'without classical political economy, Hall's book would have been impossible ... there can be little doubt that Hall owes to classical economy his ability to perceive – and hence criticize – an economic and social *system*'.[22]

There is one further aspect of radical economic criticism of which we must take note at this point: the analysis of money. Here Cobbett's view exercised perhaps the greatest influence. After reading Paine's *Decline and Fall of the English System of Finance* in 1804 his eyes were opened, Cobbett told his readers, to the evils of taxation, the national debt and paper money. Yet Paine himself had not attacked the latter; indeed, he had earlier emerged as a defender of paper money.[23] Cobbett's innovation on Paine was twofold: first, to link the public debt to paper money; and, second, having done so, to launch a generalized attack on 'the monied interest'. By the latter term, he explained,

> I mean an interest hostile alike to the land-holder and to the stock-holder, to the colonist, to the real merchant, and to the manufacturer, to the clergy, to the nobility, and to the throne; I mean the numerous and powerful body of loan-jobbers, directors, brokers, contractors, and farmers-general, which has been engendered by the excessive amount of public debt, and the almost boundless extension of the issues of paper-money.[24]

Cobbett's attack on paper money was tied to his celebration of the virtues of labour as the true source of wealth. In contrast to the artificial, the fanciful and the speculative, he extolled the natural, the sturdy, the substantial:

> That paper-money, and, indeed, that money of no sort, can *create* any thing valuable, is evident; and that it cannot *cause* it to be created on a *general* scale, is also evident; for all valuable things arise from *labour*. ... Nothing is *created* by [money]. It is not value *in itself*, but merely the *measure of value*, and the means of *removing valuable things from one possessor to another*. But a *paper-money*, while it removes things from one place to another, *is a false measure of value*.[25]

This analysis betrays all Cobbett's strengths as a popular propagandist and his weaknesses as a theorist. The argument is sharp and clear, it is free of pretentious rhetoric, it can be easily grasped and disseminated: only labour creates value; money is artificial and sterile, a mere means of circulation. Yet it eschews rigorous theorizing, echoes its readers' known biases and fails to fuse to their grievances a genuine analysis of the social phenomena involved. There is no real theory of value, nor of money in metallic or paper form. As a result, Cobbett can set forth no clear economic alternative; rid the system of corruption, the national debt and paper money, he implies, and life will revert to the tried and true patterns of the past. Where analysis is needed, one finds a populist nostalgia.

When the first major working-class critics of political economy emerged in the 1820s, then, they took up and developed a number of strands of thought which had come to the fore during the previous quarter-century or so. Ready to hand were: a rudimentary theory of labour as the source of value; a critique of the existing distribution of property; a design for a system of free and equal exchanges among independent producers; a primitive theory of the exploitation of labour; and a critique of paper money. Most of these elements were to enter in different ways into the arguments of the working-class critics of political economy. But first, they were filtered through the writings of Britain's first important modern socialist – Robert Owen.

Owenism and Political Economy

One of the great achievements of Owenism was that it taught many working-class radicals 'to see capitalism, not as a collection of discrete events, but as a *system*'.[26] A key reason for this was Owen's choice in around 1820 to confront his critics on the terrain of political economy, a choice which was to be of lasting significance for the British working-class movement.

This achievement, which I will discuss more closely in a moment, was offset by Owen's elitism and paternalism. For the bulk of his public career Owen appealed directly to segments of the ruling class to undertake a general reform of society. Of the four essays which comprised his *A New View of Society* (1813), for example, one was originally dedicated to the Prince Regent, another to the philanthropic reformer William Wilberforce, and a third to his fellow manufacturers. Indeed, in the latter work, Owen described workers to his 'fellow manufacturers' as 'your vital machines'. With the partial exception of the early 1830s, Owen addresed himself to 'men of influence' and sought social reform *from above*. He was obsessed with the reception of his proposals, for example, by the ultra-Tories Sidmouth and Liverpool. Moreover, Owen always presented his reform package as a means of avoiding class conflict, violent protest and revolution. He railed against those evils which threatened to 'forcibly dissolve all existing Governments and institutions', and took the side of reaction in the aftermath of the June 1848 uprising of the Paris workers, welcoming 'the military force of the government', which 'must overwhelm the deluded mass opposed to them'. The workers, he stated in his *Address to the Chartists*, were 'too ignorant and inexperienced to find a remedy to the existing evils'. They would have to rely on the paternal benevolence of people like himself.[27]

As Marx and Engels were to write in the *Communist Manifesto*, socialism of the sort espoused by Owen originally developed at a time when some contradictions of emerging capitalism were clear – like the coexistence of new productive powers and widespread poverty – but when the working class had not yet come forward as a class with 'historical initiative' and an 'independent political movement'. Seeing the workers as merely 'the most suffering class', not as a force capable of reorganizing society, such utopian socialists 'habitually appeal to society at large, without distinction of class; nay, by preference, to the ruling class'. Despite these limitations, early socialism of this sort was progressive, they argued, because it contained 'a critical element', and because its theorists set out to 'attack every principle of existing society'.[28]

Owen played just such a role in the British working-class movement. His move towards a critique of capitalism which confronted the categories of political economy signified a crucial turn in radical thought. Moreover, when he was drawn directly into the working-class movement, during the years 1829–34, his thought underwent significant shifts in emphasis. Equally important was the way in which many radicals of the working-class movement borrowed from, added to, deepened and developed Owen's insights. The result was a new brand of Owenism, a tougher, more proletarian approach, which looked to working-class self-activity, not benevolence from above, as the means to social transformation.

Throughout the 1820s, a growing group of labour radicals embraced Owen's critique of competition and his views on co-operation. Only at the end of the decade, however, did Owen himself grasp the significance of the upsurge of working-class co-operativism as a possible means for his objectives. For the next five years, notes one historian, 'the British working-class movement was saturated with Owenism'. Comments another: at this time 'Owenism seemed to have captured organised labour'.[29] There were a number of key phases in Owen's five-year immersion in the workers' movement. Although each overlapped and intersected, it is possible to identify a co-operative store phase, one based on labour exchanges and another dominated by general trade unionism. Taken together, these years witnessed a remarkable burst of activity, which produced hundreds of co-operative stores and societies, scores of Owenite newspapers and magazines, institutes, conferences and trade unions. The launching of the Grand National Consolidated Trade Union represented the highest achievement of this period. At its peak in 1833, it allegedly signed up a million members in a matter of weeks; throughout that year Owen toured the country speaking to union meetings and propagating his vision of 'a new moral world'. Yet by the end of 1834, the GNCTU was in a shambles, defeated by a vicious campaign of lockouts and repression by the government and the employers. Dismayed by such intense social conflict, Owen resigned from the movement; never again was he to play such a role in a working-class organization. Nevertheless, his activities during this period left a lasting 'influence of Owenite socialism on a whole generation of trade union leaders'.[30]

But this influence was not a passive inheritance from Owen; it involved an active appropriation of a set of doctrines and practices which were modified in light of the direct experience of working-class co-operativism and trade unionism. Owenite radicals can fairly be said to have both proletarianized and democratized the originator's doctrine, by making mass mobilization and democratic organization of workers central to the achievement of a new society. Owenite groupings in Manchester, for example, consciously ignored their teacher's paternalism and cultivated a strong democratic culture and organization.[31] Working-class Owenism, then, was precisely that: a theory and a practice which owed as much to workers' self-activity as to Owen himself. As E.P. Thompson comments, 'from the writings of the Owenites, artisans, weavers and skilled workers selected those parts which most closely related to their own predicament and modified them through discussion and practice'. Owenite thought was thus an 'ideological raw material diffused among working people, and worked up by them into different products'.[32]

We can see the nature of this adaptation of Owenism in the claim by one artisan that it was Owen 'who impressed upon our minds a conviction of our importance; who convinced us, working men, that we were the pillars of the political edifice; that we sustained the whole superstructure of society'.[33] The political conclusions drawn from this impression were often not those intended by Owen. Yet the idea that labourers were the most important group in society did find a point of departure in Owen's critique of political economy, a critique that first appeared in his most important work, the *Report to the County of Lanark* (1820).

The *Report* represents a crucial turning-point in Owen's writings. Moral criticism of poverty and suffering now took a back seat to economic criticism. If Owen had previously operated on the terrain of a certain strain in Scottish moral thought, he now set his sights on the political economy of the classical school. It was a shift of enormous import. Within the first few pages of its Introduction, the *Report* confronts political economy on its own ground. Owen claims that the prevailing economic distress of the time is a result of the ignorance 'connected with the science of political economy', and he sets out to show how only his system corresponds to the true principles of that science.[34] Much of this argument was to have a deep and abiding impact on the socialist movement, especially his criticism of the division of labour in industry, and his attack on the principles of individual interest and competition, the root causes, he maintained, of poverty and economic crisis.[35] These views composed the ethical foundation of socialist thought throughout the period. Yet at the level of economic analysis, Owen's concepts of value and money were to be most influential.

The central economic problem of society, Owen argues, is that gold and silver represent artificial standards of value. The natural standard of value is labour; the use of gold and silver, however, has 'altered the *intrinsic* values of all things into *artificial* values'. Were labour made the standard of value, the 'artificial system of wages' would disappear, markets would expand (since wages based on the intrinic value of labour would result in increased demand by workers) and 'poverty and ignorance' would disappear.[36] All these benefits would be reaped by creating a system in which goods exchange on the basis of their labour values. Change the standard of value and the unit of exchange, Owen suggests, and it will be possible to create an economy based on 'exchanging all articles with each other at prime cost, or with reference to the amount of labour in each', an amount which he suggests can easily be determined.[37]

Owen's analysis had great powers of attraction for the working-class radicals of the day. It extolled the productive powers of labour as the basis of all wealth; it condemned the artificial system of wages and the poverty it creates; and it reinforced the widespread sentiment that mere movers and accumulators of monetary wealth enjoyed artificial fortunes, which could be eliminated through a change in the monetary system. The *Report to the County of Lanark* is a landmark text in the English labour movement because it attempted to make the case for socialism in terms of an economic analysis; an analysis that employed the lexicon of classical political economy. Notwithstanding this achievement, however, the *Report*, like Owen's later writings, failed to address clearly some of the analytical problems that a rival theory of value and money needed to confront.

The first major difficulty with Owen's economic analysis is his failure to clarify the problem of exploitation and productive labour. If we proceed from the principle that everyone should be remunerated in proportion to the productive labour they expend, we soon confront the issue of profit on industrial capital. Is profit a pure surplus, or does the capitalist manufacturer contribute some productive labour of his own? Owen never directly answered this question. His acceptance of a rate of profit of around 5 per cent, however, implies that he believed – or should have believed according to his value theory – that the manufacturer is a productive labourer.[38] This immediately raises the problem of exploitation. If workers are not paid the full value of the labour they perform, as Owen insisted, yet capitalist profit does not derive in principle from the appropriation by an unproductive class (the capitalists) of a share of the labour of the productive class (workers), then what is the process by which such exploitation occurs? Owen's suggestion (and it is little more than that) is that the price mechanism, based on an artificial standard of value, undervalues labour and thereby enables capitalists to appropriate a share of the national wealth greater than their productive contribution. It is not capitalist ownership, or the social organization of production, that is at the root of exploitation; it is the monetary standard.

We thus return to one of the central economic issues of the *Report*: how to construct a true standard of value which could eliminate exploitation by remunerating labour at its natural rate. Owen, of course, always insisted that this was no problem. All we need do, he claimed, is calculate 'the average physical power of men' in order to find a measure for calculating the input of average labour into a given commodity. Once we have this average measure, we can then read off the amount embodied in any commodity simply from those quantities called 'prime costs' in most business operations.[39] Needless to say, both of these assumptions – that we can determine the value of an input of average labour, and that we can then ascertain the amount embodied in any commodity – enable Owen to skirt the crucial problems in the classical theory of value, problems whose solution eluded a theorist as astute as Ricardo. The result is that Owen does not construct a theory of value so much as he puts forward a series of first principles which he asserts to be true. As I show below with respect to the problem of labour exchanges, this failure at theoretical elaboration was to have serious consequences for the practice of the labour and co-operative movements Owen inspired.

What these movements inherited from Owen, in sum, was an economic analysis which asserted that labour was the basis of value, but which also accepted the legitimate claim of capital to a 'fair' profit, and which challenged not the capitalist ownership and organization of production, but the monetary, exchange and distributive relationships which prevailed. This Owenite bias towards analysis of money and exchange was to dominate the labour movement during the great flowering of popular political economy in the 1820s and 1830s.

Popular Political Economy: Labour, Exchange, Money, Co-operation

The years 1824–7 saw a remarkable outpouring of critical works on political economy from the standpoint of the working class: William Thompson's *Inquiry into the Principles of the Distribution of Wealth* (1824) and *Labor Rewarded* (1827), Thomas Hodgskin's *Labour Defended Against the Claims of Capital* (1825) and *Popular Political Economy* (1827), and John Gray's *Lecture on Human Happiness* (1825).[40] While Gray continued to publish such works until 1848, and John Francis Bray's *Labour's Wrongs and Labour's Remedies*, an important addition to the literature of popular political economy, did not appear until 1839, the peak of labour's developing critique of political economy was the decade 1824–34.[41]

Of these works, it was Hodgskin's *Labour Defended* which had the greatest and most immediate impact. Written to strengthen the intellectual case for a repeal of the Combination Laws, which severely restricted trade union rights, its arguments were soon taken up in the radical artisan press. The *Trades' Newspaper* published extracts from the book, along with letters from its author, and Francis Place complained that its views 'were carefully and continually propagated' by working-class publications. In 1832, James Mill believed that 'the mad nonsense of our friend Hodgkin' with respect to 'the right of the labourer to the whole produce of the country' was finding a mass audience through publications that 'are superseding the Sunday newspapers'.[42]

There is a certain irony in Hodgskin's influence within the labour movement, as he was the most removed of the popular political economists from co-operativism and the closest to the intellectual outlook of Bentham, Mill and their school, remaining an ardent advocate of the principles of free trade throughout his life.[43] Nevertheless, his passionate anti-authoritarianism, and his commitment to the principle that rights should be equally applied, drew him into the workers' movement of the 1820s. We have already seen his involvement in launching the Mechanic's Institute in London in 1823; it was there that he delivered lectures on economics, later published as *Popular Political Economy* (1827), which did much to provoke the battle in which he and the artisans lost control of the Institute to Francis Place and his middle-class allies. But it was his first treatise on political economy, *Labour Defended*, which made the greatest impact by giving intellectual expression to a sentiment for far-reaching reform which had started to grip large numbers of British workers. Many of the book's basic ideas were 'in the air' in artisan circles. But Hodgskin brought them together and gave them a sharp, theoretical formulation. For this reason, Max Beer was not far from the mark when he wrote that *Labour Defended* 'may be said to have been the Manifesto of British Labour in the memorable year 1825, the commencement of the organized and systematic struggle of the British working class'.[44]

At the heart of Hodgskin's book is the assertion that capital exercises an undeserved claim to a share of labour's produce. This was nothing new to readers of Owen. But Hodgskin took his readers further than had the author of the *Report to the County of Lanark*. His book, unlike Owen's works, exhibits a deep familiarity with political economy. Ricardo, McCulloch, James Mill and Adam Smith are all cited in the text. Equally important, Hodgskin attempts to counter the classical economists directly on the ground of one of their major innovations: the theory of capital. He does this by denying claims for the productivity of capital. In fact, he asserts that capital is a sort of cabalistic word, like Church or State which are invented by those who fleece the rest of mankind to conceal the hand that shears them. It is a sort of idol before which men are called upon to prostrate themselves.

In truth, he argues, it is labour which does all. The capitalist merely intervenes between labourers as a 'middleman', charging for his parasitic 'service', and appropriating to himself a share of the value created by these producers. It is an 'extraordinary perversion of thought' which has led economists to attribute to capital the productive achievements of labour.[45]

Hodgskin's argument thus possesses a cutting edge absent in Owen: a sharp critique of the claims of capital to a share of national wealth. Yet, like Owen, Hodsgkin remains remarkably imprecise about the processes of exploitation itself. While insisting that capital appropriates wealth it does not deserve, he does little to explain how this appropriation occurs. To the degree to which he does provide such an explanation, he develops a market-based approach derived from Adam Smith's theory of price. Whereas the 'real price' of a commodity 'is a certain quantity of labour', he states, its market price is comprised of labour costs plus the profits added on by all the capitalists through whose hands the commodity passes. Hodgskin thus employs Adam Smith's 'adding up' theory of value, discussed in chapter 2. But he does so with a subversive twist: Hodgskin treats labour as the only *real* determinate of value, and profit on capital as an *artificial* cost deriving from the unequal political power of capitalists which allows them to monopolize market transactions which could, and should, be left in the hands of the producers. Given the power of capitalists to make laws which favour their economic interests, the market is not truly free; the result is artificially inflated prices which include an unearned profit, and 'poverty and misery' for the labouring majority.[46]

The theoretical underpinnings of this explanation of value and profit – and its debt to Adam Smith – are spelled out more clearly in a letter of 28 May 1820 from Hodgskin to Francis Place. This letter followed from Hodgskin's reading of Ricardo's *Principles of Political Economy*. Hodgskin informs Place that 'Adam Smith was much more just' than Ricardo. He goes on to argue that Ricardo errs by equating natural price (which is determined by labour) with exchangeable value (or market price), an error that Smith did not commit. He then uses this distinction in a way foreign to Smith: to delegitimate capital's claim to a share of value and national wealth.

'Profits do not increase the labour necessary to bring a commodity to the market', he writes, 'but they enhance its price to the labourer and its exchangeable value to any person not a capitalist'.[47]

In this view, profit and exploitation are exchange-based phenomena. Profit follows from the monopolistic power of capitalists, their ability to advance materials to workers and then appropriate and sell the workers' product. Exploitation, if it should be called such, is based on the gap between wages, which remunerate workers for their productive hours, and prices, which exceed real value (or natural price). Profit is thus seen to derive from an add-on or mark-up operation, not from the appropriation of unpaid labour. Nowhere in this account do we find a theorization of exploitation in the process of production. In fact, Hodgskin treats master employers as productive labourers and argues that they 'deserve the respect of the labourer'; it is only the capitalist in the sphere of circulation that stands condemned.[48] Thus, for all the harshness of its attack on capital, *Labour Defended* remains at the level of a condemnation of exchange-based inequalities; as with Owen, there is no critique of capitalist relations of production, nor is there the sort of value theory such a critique would entail.

The popularity of *Labour Defended* underlines a crucial ambiguity in the working class radicalism of early nineteenth-century Britain. Alongside virulent attacks on 'capitalist monopolizers' went praise for competition, the division of labour and genuinely free trade. The last was not usually as pronounced as it was in Hodgskin's case. As the years went by, in fact, Hodgskin became more outspoken in his embrace of free trade, and his opposition to socialism and trade unions.

To be sure, few radicals were prepared to follow him in his advocacy of the Anti-Corn Law League as an alternative to Chartism, or to go so far as his statements of the 1850s that 'competition … is the soul of excellence, and gives to every man his fair reward', and that 'the interferences between capital and labour by Communists, Socialists, and combinations … are all evil'.[49] Yet there can be no denying that the liberal-individualist position that he set out in *The Natural and Artificial Right of Property Contrasted* (1832), drawing as it did on Locke, echoed a deeply held attitude towards the sanctity of individual property, which informed popular radicalism throughout this period. Drawing from Locke a labour theory of property according to which the individual had a right to the property of his own physical labour, popular radicals could attack private ownership of land, incomes accruing to the idle or 'excessive' exactions by industrial capitalists. They could not, however, attack capitalist private property *per se*. If this popular Lockeanism on the property question limited radical criticism, a sort of popular Smithianism on economic issues vitiated its critique of competition and the market. As a result, it was often not private property and the market which were condemned, merely their deformation under the prevailing system of political and economic monopoly.[50] For this reason, there can be little disagreement with C.H. Driver's assessment that Hodgskin's 'is really, after all, a *bourgeois* Utopia' – one in which the free working of the liberal principles of individual property and market exchange would produce justice for all.[51] As we shall see, this attachment to a form of bourgeois – or, more precisely, petty bourgeois – utopianism was to remain one of the crucial problems of radicalism and popular political economy throughout this period.

If any one popular political economist could be said to have moved significantly outside the orbit of the categories of liberal economics it would be William Thompson; even in his case, however, important tensions and ambiguities persist. An Irish landowner by birth, Thompson became a central figure in the Owenite and co-operative movements of the period, an ardent advocate of women's emancipation, the most thorough critic of competition, and the most consistent proponent of 'co-operative political economy'. The large shadow cast by Owen has often obscured Thompson's importance to early nineteenth-century British socialism. Yet while never rivalling that of Owen, Thompson's impact was substantial. In theoretical terms, in fact, he was the dominant figure in that section of the London co-operative movement which staked out a position to the left of Owen. As his biographer notes, 'though Thompson was Owen's first important disciple, he soon became the outstanding theoretician of the Co-operative Movement'.[52] While his analysis certainly did not displace that which accepted liberal precepts with respect to competition and private property, it did win the favour of the Belfast co-operators, who drank a toast to this 'enlightened author', and of the American Owenites who gathered to hear his 'lessons' read out; and it influenced certain of the arguments taken up by Chartists like William Lovett and James Bronterre O'Brien.[53]

Thompson's *Inquiry into the Principles of the Distribution of Wealth* (1824) was the first significant work of popular political economy. It did not, however, exercise an influence remotely similar to that of Hodgskin's first book, published the following year. There are two main reasons for this. First, the *Inquiry* is a long, and at times a tedious and repetitive work, occupying fully 600 pages. Although Mechanic's Institutes and co-operative societies did purchase the book, it was not as easily read or as quickly absorbed as *Labour Defended*. Second, Thompson's *Inquiry* was written at a more abstract level of discussion than Hodgskin's tract. Whereas Hodgskin was intervening directly in the debate generated by the movement to repeal the Combination Laws, Thompson was engaged in a more general reflection on the principles of distribution which governed society and which could regulate a new moral order.

Notwithstanding these considerations, the *Inquiry* did reach hundreds of artisans and co-operators, and its arguments spread wider as they were taken up by small publications and in Owenite and trade union meetings. In attending to Thompson's influence, one should not overstate the distance between his co-operativism and those strands of radicalism that grew more directly out of liberalism. After all, Thompson's starting point was that of Bentham's utilitarianism, according to which the purpose of law and human institutions is to maximize human pleasures, to achieve the greatest good of the greatest number. It follows that every social practice and institution, be it government or private property, should be subordinate to this principle. But where Bentham had given this potentially radical argument a strongly conservative twist by insisting that security of property was of more importance than the increase in human satisfaction which might be derived from greater equality (and common ownership), Thompson sharpened its radical edge by arguing that 'as *near an approach as possible* to equality' should be made, 'as near as is consistent with the greatest production'. And he went on to argue that 'the strongest stimulus to production' would be provided be securing 'the *entire use* of the products of labour, to those who produce them'.[54] Thus, Bentham's stress on security (which had justified a conservatism towards existing property arangements) was transformed into an argument on behalf of workers' rights to the whole product of their labour. With this twist, Benthamite utilitarianism could be employed as the theoretical support for a radical critique of established political economy.

Much of the first half of the *Inquiry* proceeds in this way, as an attempt to justify the claims of popular political economy in terms derived from a current of liberal thought (in this case Benthamite utilitarianism). So much does Thompson appear immersed in the categories of liberal economics that he accepts the necessity of economic exchange and praises its moral effects, asserting that it is 'at the basis of social virtue'. But exchange, he argues, must be voluntary not forced. On this basis, he goes so far as to suggest that Owen's co-operative communities represent 'the perfection of voluntary exchanges', in this case an exchange of benefits but not of goods.[55] The problem with modern society, according to Thompson, is that exchanges are not genuinely equal and voluntary. Capitalists, he claims, 'abstract' a proportion of the labour performed by the producers, an unearned 'surplus value'. The result is an immoral and unjust system of inequality. Thompson's solution to these social ills is one which would be almost endlessly repeated in radical and co-operative literature: 'unite capitalist and laborer' in one person. This could be done by forming 'joint associations' of small producer-capitalists, or 'voluntary associations of small capitalists', so that 'every laborer would become a capitalist'. Once such associations were in place, 'the natural laws of distribution' would 'cause capital to be accumulated in the hands of *all*, instead of those merely of a few capitalists'.[56]

Thus far, Thompson's argument captures clearly one of the essential features of petty bourgeois socialism: the belief that poverty can be eradicated and human association developed to a higher level in an exchange economy based on small independent producers who experience the 'invigorating' effects of competition in truly free markets. There is nothing especially co-operativist about this; in fact, Thompson's attempt to depict Owen's plan for co-operative communities as an example of an economy based upon voluntary exchange is implausible.[57] Moreover, it is clear that he too had serious misgivings about this perspective. For halfway through the *Inquiry*, Thompson stops trying to squeeze co-operative socialism into the categories of bourgeois political economy and proceeds to produce one of the boldest critiques of those categories that had yet been offered.

While 'it is true', he offers, 'that the undeviating adherence to free competition under equal security, would wonderfully increase useful activity', there are 'limits in the very nature of the principle of individual competition itself'. He identifies five such limits of the competitive principle: the retention of selfishness as a basic motivation of social action; the oppression of women in the family structure inherent in the competitive system; the waste of some social labour through unprofitable pursuits; lack of insurance for those who as a result of sickness, old age, disability or injury cannot provide for their own well-being; inhibition of education and the progress of knowledge.[58] For these reasons, Thompson proposes a superior alternative to the establishment of voluntary exchanges within a competitive framework: a co-operative system of voluntary equality. Here he seems to envisage a transcendence of exchange and the market in the context of co-operative production. 'Wants being supplied in common', he maintains, 'there would be nothing to retail' – except, perhaps, 'a few superfluities'.[59]

This second alternative, the system of voluntary equality, was to move to the forefront of Thompson's second tract on political economy, *Labor Rewarded* (1827), a work written in large measure as a reply to Hodgskin's *Labour Defended*. Thompson maintains that Hodgskin's goal – to deprive the capitalist middleman of a share in the product of labour – cannot be achieved within the framework of the system of 'labor by individual competition' which the latter advocates. 'The possession by Labor of the whole products of its exertions', Thompson writes, 'is incompatible with individual competition'.[60] To this end, he breaks radically from 'competitive political economy,' and projects the system of voluntary co-operation as its only real alternative.

Thompson now makes three major charges against the system of competition and market exchange. First, he argues that competition is incompatible with equality; that the 'higgling of the market' embraced by Hodgskin 'will never effect a just remuneration to all'. Second, and clearly connected to the first point, he maintains that a competitive market framework invariably generates 'unjust exchanges' and that the beneficiaries of these will inevitably become capitalists; there can be no 'just exchange' within a competitive system. Third, Thompson moves beyond the whole doctrine of the right of the labourer to his whole product by pointing out, as Engels would do sixteen years later, that this doctrine condemns children, childbearing women, the sick and the injured to starvation. Such a position clearly does not correspond to the maximization of human happiness.[61] With this critique in mind, Thompson then proceeds to develop his case for co-operative production and economic planning.

Arguing that 'the wretched and eternal "higgling of the market"' can never produce justice and prosperity, Thompson advocates 'other arrangements and institutions ... which will look forward *before production*, into a wise and benevolent distribution of the products of labor, and will so regulate its distribution as to ensure the greatest happiness to all'.[62] This remarkable argument breaks radically with the market as the mechanism of economic distribution, and intimates that it will be replaced by social planning based on a determination of that distribution of the products of labour which maximizes human happiness. Although Thompson does not set forth a model for such planning, the argument in *Labor Rewarded*, placed alongside his other contributions to the co-operative movement, suggests he envisioned a network of co-operative communities which would afford 'an unfailing market to each other'. But the 'market' envisaged here is not society's mechanism of resource allocation, or of price formation, but merely a societal arrangement for economic interchange between co-operative communities.[63]

Labor Rewarded thus represents that work of popular political economy which broke most radically with commodity production and the market – and in so doing developed a perspective centred on the notion of socialized labour. Indeed, much of the book's importance derives from the degree to which its vision of a co-operative society transcended the horizon of petty bourgeois socialism. Yet in two important respects, Thompson's approach was still connected to this petty bourgeois outlook. First, he continued to argue that in order for the co-operative system to be created, 'laborers must become capitalists' and must accumulate capital 'out of the savings from the wages of well remunerated labor'. Although he treated this as one step towards the union of many 'capitalist-laborers' into co-operative communities, it could easily be treated as an exhortation to form associations of petty capitalist producers. Second, he persisted in depicting the process of capitalist exploitation as based on 'unjust exchanges', which derived from the 'additions to price' enacted by 'the never-ending charges of intermediate agents'.[64] As a result, exploitation was conceptualized in terms of unfair or unnatural market exchanges, and the analysis could be taken to imply a Smithian ideal society based on true natural or voluntary exchanges, much as he had portrayed Owenite co-operativism in the *Inquiry*.

Thus, although Thompson increasingly moved beyond the idealization of a free and harmonious market system which was at the heart of much radical criticism, he continued to use many of the discursive categories of just such an approach. The result was a fundamental ambiguity, despite the general direction of his thought, as to whether socialism involved a perfection of commodity production (i.e. production for an unplanned market by independent producers) or its transcendence. Given the practical difficulties caused by co-operative experiments – in particular their persistent financial collapse as they attempted to construct cooperative islands in a sea of capitalism – it was almost inevitable that many working-class radicals would come to de-emphasize grand schemes for the transcendence of the capitalist market and treat Thompson as another proponent of the equalization of market exchanges within the parameters of the capitalist economy. Although the drift of his analysis was in another direction, its theoretical ambiguities allowed for such an interpretation.

While Thompson never made the shift from co-operativism to a perspective centred on the purification of market exchange, such was the trajectory of his contemporary John Gray, whom he defended from attacks by Owen at the third Co-operative Congress held in April 1832. Gray's *Lecture on Human Happiness* (1825) has been described as 'probably the best-known single Owenite text on economic ideas'.[65] Certainly it represented the most serious attempt to develop and systematize the economic analysis of Owen's *Report to the County of Lanark*. And like that work, it attempted to employ the lexicon of political economy on behalf of co-operation.

Gray's *Lecture* is clearly of Smithian inspiration. Human sociability, he claims, is based on our capacity for economic exchange; in fact, he argues that it is 'the propensity to exchange labour for labour' which differentiates humanity from 'brute creation', and that 'barter, *and barter alone*, is the basis of society'. To this essentially Smithian view of society he adds a Lockean theory of property: individuals are entitled to that property which arises from their labour.[66] Any property which derives from sources other than individual labour violates the principle that all economic transactions should consist of equal exchanges of labour. In fact, at the heart of Gray's critical analysis is the claim that there is a huge layer of unproductive labourers – landlords, retailers, moneylenders and so on – who give no equivalent in exchange for a share of the productive labour of society.

Gray's treatment of productive and unproductive labour, categories taken from Smith, draws directly upon Patrick Colquhoun's *Treatise on the Wealth, Power and Resources of the British Empire* (1814). Following Colquhoun's statistical analysis, Gray maintains that four-fifths of the output of productive labourers is appropriated by unproductive classes, and that this is the secret of the poverty that plagues the British working class. This argument serves an important polemical purpose, depicting the plight of society in terms of a monstrous level of exploitation of those who produce its wealth. Yet it must be said that Gray has difficulty analytically defining the categories of productive and unproductive labour. He does not define these by the nature of the labour expended, but rather by the nature of the product which labour creates. Thus, manual labourers who produce lace dress are unproductive, despite the physical labour they perform, because lace dress is socially useless, a mere extravagance.[67] Gray's argument immediately confronts the problem we have encountered in Owen, Hodgskin and Thompson: that of specifying the mechanisms by which the exploitation of productive labour occurs. In company with these writers, he locates the problem in 'the commercial arrangements of society'. And in line with such an analysis, he suggests that unjust market exactions are at the root of the problem:

> the real income of the country, which consists in the quantity of wealth annually created by the labour of the people, is taken from its producers, chiefly, by the rent of land, by the rent of houses, by the interest of money, and by the profit obtained by persons who buy their labour at one price, and sell it at another.[68]

Here again we encounter an 'adding on' theory of exploitation. The monopolization of land (and with it of housing) allows landowners to exact a rent, the monopolization of money sustains lenders who live on interest, and the inability of labourers to organize the production and marketing of their own ouput enables interlopers to intervene and add on costs for socially useless services such as retailing. It is instructive with respect to this last point that Gray rails against 'the present system of retail trade'.[69] It was, after all, precisely such a view of retailing and related market exchanges which underpinned much of the drive to create co-operative stores in the 1820s and 1830s in the belief that if producers could market their products they would receive their full value and could purchase at real, not artificially inflated, prices. This was a central aspect of the case Gray made for co-operation. Owenite communities would embody economic relations in which 'the useful labourer' could 'keep for his own use the property he creates' and enter into exchanges only 'for something else of *equal value*'. This would be a true state of justice since 'all just contracts have for their foundation *equal quantities of labour*'.[70] Once more, we find co-operativism depicted as the rationalization and equalization of exchange.

There is one other aspect of the *Lecture* which deserves notice before we turn to Gray's later work: its explanation of economic crisis.

Drawing again on Owen, Gray claimed that the competitive system creates 'an unnatural limit to production'. Competition between capitals, he suggests, sustains a superstructure of unproductive members of society who, while consuming the bulk of its output, do not contribute to its expansion. Create a framework in which capitals co-operate with each other, he implies, and the number of unproductive labourers will be radically reduced, total output will expand, as will employment opportunities.[71] While this is far from a theoretically satisfying analysis, it is important to see the significance of this effort to show that underproduction and unemployment – and not simply unjust or unfair exchanges – were inherent defects of the competitive system. The result was a direct refutation of bourgeois political economy's claim that competitive market society formed a self-regulating and crisis-free economic system.

The *Lecture* was Gray's only true Owenite tract. The same year that it appeared, he and his brother undertook the business of publishing an advertising newspaper. This was followed by a series of other, generally successful, publishing ventures, which made him a reasonably wealthy man. These business successes probably account for his move away from co-operativism.[72] Yet, while abandoning Owenism and the co-operative movement, Gray continued to adhere to the idea that there were profound defects in the 'commercial arrangements' of society. These were seen no longer as originating in competition, but, rather in 'the principle of exchange' and its monetary basis. This growing preoccupation with money and exchange is clearly evident in his next work, *The Social System: A Treatise on the Principle of Exchange* (1831).

Gray maintains in this tract that 'there has never existed a rational system of exchange, or a proper instrument for effecting exchanges'. The reform of society requires 'merely a conventional plan of exchange, and a rational species of money'. He continues to extoll the virtues of exchange as 'the bond and principle of society', but argues that 'a defective system of exchange … is *the* evil – *the* disease – *the* stumbling block of the whole society'.[73] *The Social System* exemplifies the ease with which a concern for rationalizing exchange could slide into acceptance of the basic relations of a capitalist market society. Gray makes it clear that he opposes equal distribution of wealth as 'a premium on idleness', that he supports privatized production since 'it is both desirable and customary … for each to live by exchanging that which he produces for innumerable portions of the labour of others' (a clear rejection of co-operative production), and that his plan for reform is 'consistent with individual competition in bodily and mental occupations, with private accumulation to any amount'. Not surprisingly, given his acceptance of competition, individualized production, and private accumulation, he claims that the principles of his system 'are embodied in the sentence, *Freedom of Exchange*'.[74]

If *The Social System* signifies an abandonment of co-operative principles, it also represents a more developed theory of economic crisis. The root cause of crisis, Gray states, is that money takes a commodity form and thus possesses an 'intrinsic value'. Developing Owen's distinction between natural and artificial media of exchange, he argues that the rate of expansion in the supply of a money-commodity such as gold cannot keep pace with the rate of increase in the national wealth. 'Hence arises a powerful check on production'; in anticipation of the inevitable shortage of money (and its deflationary effects), manufacturers invariably cut back their production, creating a drop in employment and a contraction of 'effectual demand'. The solution to poverty and economic crisis is thus remarkably simple: money 'must be a *symbol*, not a commodity', it must possess 'no intrinsic value'. Given the right arrangements, the adoption of such a purely symbolic form of money would guarantee that condition sought by political economists: 'that production would become the uniform and never failing cause of demand', thereby eliminating economic crises.[75]

In outlining the arrangements necessary to a rational system of exchange, Gray was prepared to countenance a high degree of economic regulation. He called for the establishment of a National Chamber of Commerce, which would be responsible for pricing, distribution (via national warehouses), regulation of wage and salary levels, national investment and maintenance of a national bank.[76] While this involved a relatively high level of centralized economic decision-making, it is important to realize that Gray did not envisage economic regulation extending to public ownership of the principal means of production; as already indicated, he happily accepted individual ownership, competition and private accumulation. Gray intended a regulated system of pricing, distribution and banking to underpin a truly free system of competition and exchange. Regulation would free the market, not eliminate it.[77]

Economic regulation would proceed, therefore, according to 'equitable principles'. This was especially so with respect to wages. Gray believed it was possible to determine an 'average price of labour', which would then form the basis of '*an immutable standard of value*. This was a return to something approximating Owen's labour-money; once the average price of labour was determined, 'a pound note from that time forth would be just another name for a *week* of reasonable exertion'. Gray recognized the difficulty posed by labours of different skill, productivity and intensity, and suggested some sort of 'fixed scale of payment for different employments'.[78] But nowhere does he begin to come to terms with the real problems this poses – especially that of translating particular (concrete) labours into units of average (abstract) labour, a point to which I shall return.

Gray's two final economic works, *An Efficient Remedy for the Distress of Nations* (1842) and his *Lectures on the Nature and Use of Money* (1848) add nothing of theoretical value to the analysis of *The Social System*. Their significance lies chiefly in registering his break from co-operative socialism and his increasingly 'degenerate and enervating monetary crankiness'.[79] *An Efficient Remedy* restates the theory of rational exchange and his explanation of crisis in terms of inadequate growth in the supply of gold or of any money with an intrinsic value. He again argues for a labour standard of value and skirts the attendant problems this involves. Indeed, these problems take on greater significance in that he now wishes to combine regulation of 'the average rate of wages' with a system in which 'individual wages would be as much open to competition as ever'.[80] Nowhere does he manage to square this theoretical circle, nor could he; if individual wages are to be arrived at by competition so, ultimately, must be the average level around which they revolve. This means, of course, that regulation would have little impact upon the labour market; and an unregulated and competitive labour market would make it impossible to regulate prices if these are to be arrived at in terms of labour values. Gray's inability to recognize this problem, never mind resolve it, would appear to have been a function of his increasing obsession with monetary reform, an obsession which dominates his last economic work, the *Lectures on Money*.

Gray's *Lectures* represent his most open embrace of the doctrines of Adam Smith and his most explicit rejection of socialism. He ridicules 'the injustice, impracticality, and, in a word futility' of 'projects for the establishment of co-operative communities, hives for wingless bees, and the like', and he claims that his earlier use of the term 'social system' was in no way intended to connote 'socialism'.[81] Nevertheless, he apparently retained some contact with the Owenites, for in the *Lectures* he reprints a letter from Owen's follower William Pare urging him to assist the new French government in reform of its monetary system.[82] That someone who had moved so far from Owenite socialism could be held in such esteem by members of that movement indicates the persistent attraction of the idea that social justice could be achieved through the purification of market relations.

One sees this especially in the case of John Francis Bray, whose book, *Labour's Wrongs and Labour's Remedy* (1839) has rightly been described as 'the last and most powerful manifesto of Owenism'.[83] The ambiguities of Owenite political economy appear particularly acute in Bray's case because his attack on competition did not skirt the property question. Bray maintained that existing property arangements 'must be totally subverted' – therein adopting a tone which earned the praise of Marx – and he maintained that 'the land, buildings, machinery, vessels, and every other description of reproducible wealth' should be the property of society as a whole.[84] At the same time, however, like William Thompson in his *Inquiry*, Bray continued to project co-operative society as the realization of a genuine system of 'equal exchanges'. Indeed, social ownership of the means of production was for him the essential precondition of 'personal property of individuals' in the products of their own labour. At no point did Bray confront the dilemma inherent in support for public ownership of the principal means of production and private ownership of the products of labour: that some of the products of labour – buildings, machinery, vessels, etc. – must themselves be means of production. Bray's failure to recognize this contradiction between social ownership and private appropriation, despite his radicalism on the property question and his life-long commitment to the labour and socialist movements, illustrates the degree to which acceptance of some key categories of bourgeois economy – equal exchange, and private ownership of labour's products – limited the theoretical and political range of the popular critique of political economy during this period.[85]

Labour's Wrongs commences with the argument that the labour movement has restricted itself to the campaign for 'a merely political equality' which would simply 'modify the position of the working class *as a working class*', instead of organizing for 'a general remedy' which could provide 'a remedy for their poverty'. Having claimed that the property question is the key to any 'general remedy', Bray proceeds to argue for common ownership of the land and most means of production, and for equal rewards for equal labour.[86] Central to his critique of the competitive order is the claim that it violates the latter principle – that equal contributions of labour are not equally rewarded, that the existing structure of inequality rests on 'a fraudulent system of unequal exchanges'. There are two essential features of this system: first, the capitalist practice of 'buying at one price and selling at another'; and second, the fact that there is no real exchange between capitalists and labourers, since the former 'give the working man, for his labour of one week, a part of the wealth which they obtained from him the week before! – which just amounts to giving him *nothing* for something'. It follows that 'the whole transaction, therefore, between the producer and the capitalist, is a palpable deception, a mere farce'. On its own capital is nothing; it is merely the offspring of land and labour, the product of labour appropriated by alien hands through unequal exchange: 'When the workman has produced a thing, it is his no longer – it belongs to the capitalist – it has been conveyed from the one to the other by the unseen magic of unequal exchanges.' It follows from this analysis that taxes are less the problem for workers than the unjust appropriations of capital.[87]

There is much that is suggestive about this analysis, so much so that at least one commentator has claimed that Bray anticipated some of the main tenets of Marx's critique of political economy.[88] Yet the suggestiveness of Bray's work should not blind us to some of its analytic shortcomings. Four stand out in especially sharp relief, two of them analytical, two practical. First, Bray adheres to the radical convention of describing the capitalist as an intermediary in the sphere of commodity circulation, rather than as an employer of wage-labour. The result is that he depicts capitalist profit not as a result of surplus labour, but, rather, of market manipulations: 'The vocation of such men', he writes, 'is to buy cheap and sell dear'. Second, like Owen and Gray, he sees the commodity-form of money as at the heart of these market manipulations (or unequal exchanges) to the point where he claims that 'the system of banking, or the creation and issue of money ... constitutes the great armoury from whence the capitalists derive all their weapons to fight and conquer the working class'. It follows from this, third, that he continues to see a co-operative society as embodying the perfection of an exchange economy, as necessitating 'nothing but a total change of system – an equalizing of labour and exchanges'. Finally, this involves Bray in an argument for monetary reform, the conversion of the existing currency into notes denominated in terms of 'amount of labour'.[89]

Here we encounter once more the slide into reformist efforts to bolster small-scale capitalism of the sort we saw in William Thompson's *Inquiry*. Despite his support for a co-operative society based upon 'community of possessions', Bray feels compelled to formulate an 'intermediate' solution, which would constitute a bridge between the existing order of competition and that 'most perfect form of society' to which he aspires. To this end he advocates the formation of 'joint stock companies', which would unite labour and capital in their own hands, and would exchange with each other according to equal labour times via some kind of labour-money.[90] At this point his radical co-operative socialism starts to buttress a perspective for petty bourgeois socialism. He envisages a 'joint stock movement', which accumulates savings adequate to purchase the principal means of production of society from their owners, and which initiates a system of equal exchanges between small common stock associations via a new 'circulating medium' and according to 'one uniform scale, in regard both to time of labour and amount of wages', all articles being 'valued according to the labour bestowed upon them'. He then proceeds for fourteen pages to show that such an arrangement would be entirely consistent with the principles of 'the leading political economists'.[91]

In spite of his radical rejection of competition, and his support for communal property arrangements, Bray's work ends by outlining a reform programme which promises to realize the idealized market arrangements of bourgeois political economy through the equalization of exchange and reform of the currency. Thus, as much as his book, like Thompson's *Inquiry*, offered a critique of the system of market competition, it also provided a theoretical rationale for efforts to purify that system rather than replace it. It should come as no surprise, then, that the co-operative movement gave birth to an extraordinary array of plans for co-operative stores, joint-stock companies, labour exchanges, and currency reforms, all designed to produce an internal metamorphosis of the system without its radical or revolutionary transformation.

From Theory to Practice: The Labour Exchange Experiment

It is impossible to understand the changing practice of the radical movement, especially during the years 1829–34, without acknowledging the way in which it was affected by popular political economy. The idealist and ahistorical thesis of Gareth Stedman Jones –

according to which working-class radicalism of the 1830s failed to pass beyond the horizons of the radical thought of the 1770s, which offered a critique of political corruption but failed to attack existing property arrangements via an economic analysis of society – irreparably distorts the experience and practice of the radicalism of the 1830s. This ought to be clear from even a cursory examination of that crucial publication of the period, the *Poor Man's Guardian*, and the writings of its editor throughout most of its life, James Bronterre O'Brien.[92]

O'Brien was decisively influenced by Owen and the popular political economists, but he rejected Owen's opposition to political action. At the same time, he transformed the traditional rhetoric of radicalism by treating parliamentary reform as meaningless on its own. Reform of parliament could only address the ills of the working classes, he argued, if it led to social and economic transformation. As he put it in a speech to the Second Co-operative Congress in Birmingham in October 1831: 'A Reform of Parliament can effect little good except in so far as it may conduce to a reform in the construction of society.' Winning the vote should be seen as a means for workers to organize co-operatively in order to escape their oppression by that 'tyrant called Capital'. Only through co-operation, he argued, can workers do '*collectively* what it is impossible for them to do *individually*. They can become capitalists, and thus intercept the profits of trade in addition to the wages of labour.'[93]

Here we encounter a remarkably clear example of the incorporation into radical discourse of the arguments of popular political economy. Moreover, this was no isolated utterance. Such an analysis was to be central to O'Brien's political thought, arguably the most important influence on the activists of the Chartist movement. Nearly three years after the Birmingham conference, O'Brien again argued that

> universal suffrage can be of little use, if applied only to political purposes. In fact, it is only as an auxiliary to social reform, or as a means of protecting the multitude in the establishment of new institutions for the production and distribution of wealth, that universal suffrage would develop its virtues.

At first, O'Brien put little stock in efforts at establishing co-operative institutions prior to the conquest of parliamentary reform. However, the labour exchange movement which grew out of a plethora of co-operative experiments did capture his enthusiasm.

The labour exchange movement emerged during the years

1829–34, when the workers' movement teemed with schemes for the co-operative reorganization of society. Three of these stand out as especially important: co-operative stores; co-operative communities; and labour exchanges. But it is the last of these, which has rightly been described as 'the most interesting experiment in the whole movement', which is especialy deserving of attention in any evaluation of popular political economy.[95]

Co-operative stores pre-dated Owen's enthusiasm of the early 1830s. In fact, Owen's embrace of co-operative experiments reflected *his* adaptation to the working-class movement, not vice versa. It was the First Western Co-operative Union in London, for example, which took the initiative in establishing a labour exchange – a mart where workers could directly exchange the products of their labour based on a common standard of valuation – by adding a labour bank in early 1832.[96] The idea had been in the air for some time, as is evidenced by one co-operator's exhortation in a pamphlet of 1831: 'let us open labour banks ... make arrangements for exchanging your labour with each other, as by doing so you will become self-producers, self-employers, self-consumers.'[97] In by-passing the 'artificial market', it was claimed, workers could construct their own natural and equitable system of exchange which would allow them to procure the full value of their labour (as there would be no deduction of profits by a capitalist 'middleman').

By July 1832, Owen was converted to the idea that he could bring about a peaceful transition to cooperation through a system of labour exchanges. At a meeting at his Institution on Gray's Inn Road he read out a resolution declaring

> that the monetary system, as at present established, was the chief cause of all existing evils; that gold, silver, and ordinary bank notes, are inadequate to exchange the wealth that may be produced by the industry of the United Kingdom; that the time had arrived for the introduction of a natural medium of exchange, by means of notes representing the average labour or time necessary to produce the wealth which each note should be made to represent.

He told his audience that

> Bazaars and markets would be established in this metropolis, and throughout the country, where everything would be sold according to its labour value ... These banks would be the means of relieving the people from the evils of poverty and misery.[98]

Fired with enthusiasm for this project, Owen established a labour exchange at Gray's Inn Road in September 1832. The exchange quickly captured the attention of thousands of co-operators and trade unionists. In March of the next year, an artisan group organized the London United Trades Association to co-ordinate craftsmen who were using the exchange. Four months later a Depositors' Association was created for small masters and independent craftsmen. These two groups then fused with the Owenite Missionary Society to form the National Equitable Labour Exchange Association of the Industrious Classes.[99] Artisan response to the labour exchange was tremendous. A full-scale experiment was launched in Birmingham, and plans drawn up in Manchester and Worcester among other centres. As the Spencean socialist Allen Davenport recounted of the London Exchange's first week:

> the public mind was completely electrified by this new and extraordinary movement ... every avenue to the Exchange, during the whole week, was literally blocked up by the crowds of people that constantly assembled – some attracted by the novelty of the institution; some to watch its progress; some to make deposits and exchanges.

Even Bronterre O'Brien was swept up in the excitement; he reversed his earlier scepticism regarding the prospect for equalizing exchanges without first winning a parliament elected by labour, exhorting his readers 'as far as possible [to] promote mutual exchanges of labour for labour'.[100]

Despite its tremendous impact on the imaginations of thousands of artisans, despite the participation of Sheffield cutlers, Huddersfield clothiers, Leicester laceworkers, shoemakers from Kendal, artisans of every description in London and Birmingham, the labour exchange movement soon collapsed. By the early summer of 1834 not one exchange continued to operate.[101] The failure of this remarkable experiment is one of the major indicators of the theoretical and practical weaknesses of popular political economy's drive to implement a system of equal exchanges, a purified commodity market. Five fundamental problems with the theory and practice of the labour exchange movement stand out in especially sharp relief.

First, the exchanges confronted the problem of procuring an adequate supply of all those commodities for which there was a demand. Otherwise, those workers who brought in goods and received labour-notes in return would not be able to carry through a satisfactory exchange. Given the circumstances of the time, it was virtually inevitable that they should have insufficient quantities of foodstuffs, the basic staple of workers' lives. As one co-operator put it in a letter to the *Poor Man's Guardian*, the problem for the exchanges was that 'it is impossible that they can ever have *provisions* in sufficient quantity, without purchasing them, which is not exchanging'. But this inadequacy undermined the very principle of the exchanges since, 'before "Labour Notes" will pass you must have *every thing* at the Bazaar, which, as far as I can see, is impossible'.[102] Put simply, without social ownership of the means of production (including land), and social planning of production prior to exchange (to guarantee an adequate supply of all goods desired), the exchanges would be forced to purchase on the competitive market or else watch many workers fail to realize any exchange at all – which in the event is precisely what happened.

The second problem which faced the exchanges was their irrelevance to the fully proletarianized wage-labourer. Such workers did not, after all, produce on their own any commodity which they could later bring to the exchange. This meant that 'the movement was likely to attract few except those who produced finished goods in small workshops'. And since many basic staples, like food and clothing, were produced in fully proletarianized settings, these never entered the system.[103] It was this that determined the third problem that plagued the exchanges: that labour-notes had to remain tied to existing prices and monetary values. After all, if the exchanges were not self-sufficient in all goods, then they would have to enter the capitalist commodity market in order to make 'exchanges' based on market prices. For this reason, as one enthusiast explained,

> the labour-note must, in the first instance, bear a relative *money-value* ... for until we can produce the raw material, or, in other words, so long as we are compelled to buy it for money we must have a *relative money value* expressed on our labour-note.[104]

But this was to admit that labour-notes were nothing other than reflections of the very 'artificial values' co-operators had sought to escape by forming exchanges in the first place.

This difficulty is related to the fourth problem encountered by the movement: that of assigning value to the labour of those who brought their goods to the exchange. A committee was established which assumed responsibility for determining the average time necessary for an artisan of average skill to produce a given commodity. But how were such average times to be determined? Moreover, how was the committee to determine the relative value of different skills? Were some labour processes not more detailed or complex than others? This problem was 'solved' by adopting an average market wage of sixpence an hour and then allowing for differences in skill according to differentials prevailing in the capitalist labour market. Yet this was a tacit admission that they needed that 'artificial' market and its monetary values in order to equate particular (concrete) labours to an average (abstract) standard. As G.D.H. Cole put it, 'this was, in effect, accepting the market valuation of the different grades and kinds of labour and to all intents and purposes making the labour notes mere translations into labour time of money amounts arrived at in an ordinary commercial way'.[105] Rather than providing an escape from the competitive market, the exchanges essentially duplicated their price relations.

These shortcomings encouraged a fifth error: increasing obsession with currency reform. For, if the exchanges were forced to refer back to the 'artificial values' created by use of a money-commodity, it appeared that one way to circumvent this would be to move immediately towards a reformed currency based on labour. As early as November 1832, Owen was emphasizing 'the connection between the exchange movement and schemes for a reformed currency' and soliciting the support of currency cranks such as Thomas Attwood.[106] Thus, the growing monetary preoccupation of men like John Gray and Bronterre O'Brien was no personal quirk; it reflected instead a theoretical flaw in popular political economy's location of exploitation at the level of exchange and price formation. As the Operative Builders' Union put it in their *Manifesto*, 'the present artifical, inaccurate and therefore injurious circulating mechanism for the exchange of our riches, may be superseded by an equitable, accurate and therefore rational representation of real wealth'.[107] British socialism thus became characterized by a penchant for currency reform schemes as the key to eliminating market-based exploitation. The result was a 'market socialism', which accepted commodities, prices and money while attempting to evade their inevitable effects. To get out of this dead end, socialism needed radically different theories of exploitation and of money. To provide these was one of the burdens of Marx's critical theory of capitalism.

5

'Proudhon did Enormous Mischief': Marx's Critique of the First Market Socialists

Marx's direct engagment with petty bourgeois socialism came via his encounter with the thought of the French anarcho-socialist Pierre-Joseph Proudhon. Criticism of Proudhon was a persistent theme running through all of Marx's writings on political economy. 'It is no exaggeration to say', observes Rubel, 'that an important part of what Marx published was "in answer" to Proudhon.'[1] In Marx's view, Proudhon was the paradigmatic theorist of petty bourgeois socialism, a socialism constructed from the standpoint of small commodity producers which sought to improve society not by abolishing commodity production but, rather, by purifying commodity exchange. Because Proudhon's thought exercised a major influence within the French workers' movement from the 1840s through to the 1880s, Marx believed it necessary to confront a theoretical perspective which was, he maintained, diverting and disorienting the social and political energies of the French working class. The battle against Proudhonism was thus of pressing theoretical and practical import. But in combating Proudhonian socialism, Marx rarely lost sight of the general significance of this theoretical contest; indeed, he saw this fight as part of a wider effort to liberate the working-class movement from attachment to commodity relations and the capitalist market.

Proudhon, Property and Political Economy

From the mid-1840s onwards, Marx waged an unrelenting battle against Proudhon. Yet he never lost a certain sympathy and respect for his adversary's first major work, *What is Property?* That book, Marx wrote in an obituary letter about his rival, 'is undoubtedly his best. It is epoch-making.' Marx was most taken with the work's 'provocative defiance' of the ruling ideas of liberal economics – in particular the latter's justification of capitalist property. Although its critique of property was 'from the standpoint and with the eyes of a French small peasant (later petty bourgeois)', Marx heralded the achievements of *What is Property?* as one of the earliest and boldest radical assaults on political economy.[2]

At the heart of Proudhon's first book is the claim that 'property is robbery', a claim that pivots on its distinction between property and possession. Labour, Proudhon asserts, is the basis of wealth, and its performance entitles the producer to possession of its product. But labour does not entitle anyone to own means of production – and here he has the land principally in mind – or to appropriate the product of others. In fact, Proudhon uses the term 'property' to refer to wealth used in employing the labour of others. He accepts the liberal principle according to which performance of labour confers a right to its product; but he distinguishes this right to 'possession' from property right.[3]

Just as Proudhon attempts to turn this premiss of political economy against one of its (illegitimate) conclusions, so he accepts the theory of exchange developed by the classical economists and tries to use it against the claims of capital. Commerce, he maintains, is the exchange of equivalents, a view which is expressed in the maxim that 'products exchange only for products'. But property violates this maxim, he claims, by justifying an exchange of non-equivalents (money for labour and its products). Moreover, it follows from the principle of equal exchange that all wages should be equal (which they demonstrably are not in modern society), since producers who exchange equivalent for equivalent should all be equally remunerated.[4]

The socialist alternative to the rule of property, therefore, is a society based on individual possession and free and equal trade – and this alternative is in fact the logical extension of the principles of political economy. Proudhon presents such a society as a 'synthesis' of original communism and the system of property. He envisages a society a small independent producers – peasants and artisans – who own the products of their personal labour, and then enter into a series of equal market exchanges. Such a society will, he insists, eliminate profit and property, and 'pauperism, luxury, oppression, vice, crime and hunger will disappear from our midst'.[5] Here again we encounter a clarion call for the realization of justice and equality through market exchange among petty producers.

What is Property? thus attempts to turn political economy's premises (labour as the basis of ownership, commerce as the exchange of equivalents) against its conclusions: defence of capitalist profit and property. It was this essentially critical side of the work which won Marx's praise. Nevertheless, Proudhon's argument did not subject those premises themselves to adequate criticism. As socialist thought developed, Proudhon's uncritical adoption of the presuppositions of bourgeois economics more and more became an obstacle to theoretical clarification of the tasks of the working-class movement. Rather than deepening and developing this analysis, Proudhon increasingly resorted to defences of liberal principles. There were six main features of his accommodation to liberal political economy.

First, Proudhon came increasingly to define justice in terms of the proportionality of prices to expenditures of labour. Indeed, the full meaning of the term justice seems for him to have been exhausted by the ideas of just prices and equal exchange. 'Equality', he argued, 'is produced by the rigorous and inflexible law of labor, the proportionality of values, the sincerity of exchanges.'[6] Equal market exchange among autonomous individuals was thus the foundation of justice and natural law:

> What is justice? the pact of liberty.

> Two men encounter each other, their interests opposed. The debate is joined; then they come to terms: the first conquest of *droit*, the first establishment of Justice. A third arrives, then another, and so on indefinitely: the pact which binds the first two is extended to the newcomers; so many contracting, so many occasions for Justice. Then there is progress, progress in Justice of course, and consequently progress in liberty.[7]

It follows from this, second, that commodity exchange becomes the model for the social contract. Indeed, Proudhon argues that an infinite series of voluntary contracts among individuals can replace the need for political institutions and a state.[8] We observe here a familiar pattern in which anarchist conclusions are reached from the premises of unfettered liberalism.

Third, Proudhon depicts exploitation as a product of monopoly and a violation of the true principles of commodity exchange. Under the prevailing system, he asserts, 'there is irregularity and dishonesty in exchange', a problem exemplified by monopoly and its perversion of 'all notions of commutative justice'.[9] The result of these market irregularities is that 'the *price* of things is not proportionate to their

VALUE: it is larger or smaller according to an influence which justice condemns, but the existing economic chaos excuses – Usury'.[10] This is a classic example of the 'adding on' theory of exploitation according to which illegitimate charges are added to the real value of some things (which simultaneously undervalues other goods). Exploitation becomes thereby a consequence of market disequilibria – the upward and downward deviations of price from value.

It should come as no surprise that, fourth, Proudhon looks to reform of credit and banking as the key to overcoming the inequities of the system of property. Indeed, the plan for a People's Bank became a fixture of Proudhonian social thought. During the short-lived republic created by the revolution of February 1848, Proudhon first set about organizing such a bank; a group of enthusiasts provided him with 20,000 francs, and a basic operational plan was drawn up. The repression which followed the defeat of the workers' revolution in June of that year led, however, to Proudhon's imprisonment and the collapse of the People's Bank, although its author was to revive the idea regularly throughout the 1850s.

Behind all Proudhon's banking schemes was the idea that the commodity basis of money should be abolished. This was to be accomplished by overturning 'the royalty of gold' and substituting for it a paper money based on labour time. All exchange would in this way be reduced to 'exchange of products for products', money would become nothing more than a symbolic representative of labour, and nobody would be able to profit from the possession of a scarce commodity – money like gold. The result would be a system of equitable exchange.[11] During the 1850s this scheme became known as 'mutualism' – a system aspiring to mutually satisfactory exchanges on the basis of a labour-money in ample supply. Implicit in this model is the notion that a common basis can be found for measuring and equating different acts of concrete individual labour. Proudhon sidestepped the real difficulties of this problem, however, by simply asserting the equality of each and every hour of labour performed within society.[12]

From this outlook it follows, fifth, that socialism equals the abolition of monopoly and the realization of free trade. Proudhon praises the virtues of market competition in establishing just prices and wages; he insists that all economic transactions should be governed by 'free contract and subject to competition'. In this light, he depicts mutualism as a synthesis of the principles of competition and association.[13] Finally, there is a political programme – or, more accurately, an *apolitical* program – which follows from this perspective. It was this orientation to the political struggle of the working class that Marx considered the most pernicious aspect of Proudhonism.

Proudhonian political strategy, if we can call it that, emerged first in *The System of Economical Contradictions* (1846) where its author claimed that 'if you are in a position to organize labour, if you have studied the laws of exchange, you have no need of the capital of the nation · or of public force'. Organize along lines of mutualism and equal exchange, he argued, and you 'shall envelop capital and the State and subjugate them'. It followed that there was no need for strikes – which were in any case self-defeating since they merely induced price rises – or political struggles for state power. Moreover, as Proudhon argued in *On the Capacity of the Working Classes* (1865), the legal right to trade union organization is 'contrary to the economic *right* of free competition'. Indeed, Proudhon claimed in that work that posterity would not condemn the soldiers who shot the striking miners of Rive-de-Gier since, while the former may have acted disgracefully, they sought only to maintain social order. In contrast to the destructive and destabilizing effects of strikes, mutualism would produce a gradual and inevitable victory.[14]

Proudhon thus rejected the idea of progress through class struggle. In his April 1848 electoral address, for example, he exhorted voters to embrace class harmony: 'Workers, hold out your hand to your employers and, employers, do not repudiate the advances of those who were your workmen', he exclaimed.[15] Indeed, Proudhon was never loath to proclaim his abhorrence of revolution. As he wrote about the revolutionary events of February 1848, 'the Revolution, the Republic, Socialism, were now approaching with giant strides … I fled before the democratic and social monster whose riddle I could not answer. An inexpressible terror froze my soul and paralyzed my mind.' And, he continued, 'I wept for the burgesses whom I saw ruined, driven into bankruptcy'. Moreover, he went on to explain that socialists were to blame for the hostility that now greeted them since they had threatened to apply their system 'by public authority and at the State's expense'.[16] Political action and revolution were thus condemned. The only acceptable route to a new society was one that posed no threat to the ruling class and the power of capital, one that disavowed political struggle and evolved slowly out of the interstices of mutualist exchange.

As the French workers' movement developed during and after 1848, a perspective which disavowed strikes, class struggle and revolution exercised an increasingly conservative influence. Proudhon was in fact quite explicit about the backward-looking tendency of his thought. 'You know me as a revolutionary who is profoundly conservative', he wrote an acquaintance in the summer of 1849. He later wrote to another ally declaring, 'my ambition is, after having been the most revolutionary thinker of my time, to become, without changing my opinions one iota, the *most conservative*'.[17] And stake out conservative positions he did. During the election campaign of December 1848, for example, he supported the presidential candidacy of Cavaignac, the general who had bloodily suppressed the workers' uprising in June of that year. Subsequently, he produced an apology for the dictatorship of Louis Bonaparte, arguing that the socialist Left should welcome his *coup d'état* as it would inevitably advance their cause.[18]

But nowhere is Proudhon's conservatism more conspicuous than in his attitude towards women. He opposed divorce, approved of those legal restrictions which denied women rights to deal with financial and business matters without paternal or spousal consent, and announced in *Pornocratie*, his diatribe against women's emancipation, that 'we men think a woman knows enough if she knows enough to mend our shirts and cook us a steak. I am one of those men.' His glorification of the patriarchal household was so extreme that he told his friend Karl Grun, 'far from applauding what is nowadays called the emancipation of women, I am inclined, rather, should it come to that extremity, to put them into reclusion!' Given the reactionary outlook of their leader, it comes as no surprise that the Proudhonists in the First International vigorously opposed proposals by Marx and his followers to support female labour subject to adequate health and safety legislation.[19]

What bothered Marx was not merely that Proudhon held such reactionary attitudes towards women's rights, unions, strikes and political action by the labour movement; he was equally dismayed by the wide influence of his ideas within the French working-class movement. Writing to his friend Kugelmann in October 1866, Marx explained that at the first congress of the International,

> the Parisian gentlemen had their heads full of the emptiest Proudhonist phrases. They babble about science and know nothing. They scorn all *revolutionary* action, that is action arising out of the class struggle itself, all concentrated social movements, and therefore also those which can be carried through by *political means* (for instance the *legal* shortening of the working day). Under the *pretext of freedom*, and of anti-governmentalism

or anti-authoritarian individualism, these gentlemen ... actually preach ordinary bourgeois economy, only Proudhonistically idealised! Proudhon did enormous mischief. His sham criticism ... attracted and corrupted first the '*jeunesse brillante*,' the students, and then the workmen, particularly those of Paris, who as workers in luxury trades are strongly attached, without knowing it, to the old rubbish.[20]

One sees evidence of Proudhon's influence on the French workers' movement in the 'Manifesto of the Sixty', published in 1864. After consultation with Proudhon, the Manifesto was produced by a group of workers whose leading figure was the engraver Henry Louis Tolain. Although the group chose – in decidedly non-anarchist terms – to field working-class candidates in the coming elections, their programme was essentially mutualist. Tolain and his supporters went on to form the core of the French section of the International Workingmen's Association (the First International), in which organization they often crossed swords with Marx and his adherents over questions such as strikes, unions, women's participation in production and state intervention in the economy.

Marx's view in the 1860s was that a revitalized and politicized trade union movement would serve as the point of departure for radical working-class politics. He thus took heart from the growing sympathy among European workers for a political cause – the national liberation of Poland – and from the fact that it served as the rallying point for launching the First International. Genuine socialist politics for Marx was rooted in militant trade unionism as the latter expressed the class struggle at its most basic level. To be sure, he hoped for a generalized trade unionism and often bemoaned the narrow sectionalism and lack of a 'spirit of generalization' which plagued the English labour movement.[21] But this did not prevent him from celebrating strikes and union struggles as the basis of all real working-class politics – an attitude which brought him into conflict with France's most famous socialist.

Proudhon's hostility to strikes and unions found an echo, albeit a somewhat muted one, among his working-class followers of the 1860s and 1870s. Tolain, for example, stressed the formation of economic associations by workers for the purpose of promoting free credit and free exchange as an alternative to union organization. And at the 1866 Congress of the International in Geneva, the Proudhonists condemned strikes as a 'war between masters ... to the detriment of all'. They extolled the necessary role of capital in production, claiming that relations between capitalists and workers were only perverted in the absence of reciprocal exchange. Moreover, true to their liberal impulses, they opposed the demand for legislation limiting the working day to eight hours on the ground that this interfered with freedom of contract.[22]

In the early years of the International, Marx's views were often in a minority, especially on economic issues. At the Lausanne Congress of 1867, for example, a resolution supporting a state bank based on the idea of free credit was carried with the backing of the Proudhonists from France and the English followers of Bronterre O'Brien.[23] Within England, the ideas of labour banks and equitable exchange were kept alive by the O'Brienite National Reform League, a number of whose members played an important role in the International. In fact, English branches of the International were often dominated by O'Brien's ideas and by lectures and debates on 'Land, Currency and Credit'.[24] While Marx admired the more revolutionary and less nationalist attitude of the O'Brienites relative to most English trade unionists, he had little patience for their 'currency quackery'.[25]

Marx's hostility to Proudhon's outlook was thus motivated by much more than personal antipathy. Believing that Proudhonist ideas were fatal to the struggle for the emancipation of the working class, and recognizing their wide influence within the French labour movement and, indirectly, among the O'Brienites in England, he considered the defeat of those ideas an urgent task of socialist theory and practice.

Marx and Proudhon: From First Encounter to *Poverty of Philosophy*

Marx's first mention of Proudhon appeared in an article in the *Rheinische Zeitung* late in 1842 where he states that communist doctrines such as 'those of Leroux, Considerant, and above all the sharp-witted work by Proudhon' should be subjected to 'long and profound study'. The comment occurs in the course of criticism of a German communism which is judged to be guilty of superficiality and phrase-mongering. To counter these traits Marx recommends a serious study of communist writings. With respect to the doctrines of Proudhon and others he appears non-committal; indeed, it is possible that Marx's knowledge of these writers was at this time derived largely from secondary sources.[26]

There is no real evidence that Marx had read Proudhon's *What is Property?* before 1844. He would have had a growing inclination to do so throughout 1843, however, as both his deepening interest in communism and his increasing concern with political economy pointed him towards Proudhon's first book. We know also that the young Engels had been strongly influenced by Proudhon's criticism of political economy, most obviously in the shaping of his *Outlines of a Critique of Political Economy*, which made an outstanding impression on Marx when he first saw it in November 1843. Indeed, in that same month Engels had published an article in the Owenite *New Moral World* in which he stated that *What is Property?* 'is the most philosophical work, on the part of the Communists, in the French language; and, if I wish to see any French book translated into the English language, it is this'.[27] Marx must therefore have turned to Proudhon's book with great interest; and there can be little doubt that *What is Property?* left a strong initial impression.

Yet, even at this early stage in his reading of political economy, Marx's admiration for Proudhon's work was tempered by criticism of its theoretical foundations. In his *Economic and Philosophic Manuscripts* of 1844, for example, Marx claims that Proudhon fails to transcend 'the level of political economy'. Proudhon, he claims, sees the antithesis of labour and private property and chooses to take the side of the first element in this antithetical relation. The author of *What is Property?* does not understand, first, that labour which produces private property for another is *alienated* labour and, second, that alienated labour and private property form two sides of a single relation. Rather than superseding this single relation (alienated labour/private property) – which would require revolutionizing society – Proudhon clings fast to one side of this relation. He argues that political economy should remain true to its starting point, labour as the source of wealth, while rejecting its conclusion – private property. Yet, argues Marx, this is to miss the essential nature of the dialectical relationship between these principles. Alienated labour is the source of capitalist private property; the latter would not be possible unless the products of wage-labour went into alien hands. Private property cannot be abolished without overturning the relations of alienated wage-labour. Proudhon fails to see this. By championing the cause of wage-labour he retains the very premiss of private property. As a result, he advocates 'equality of wages' as the solution to the poverty of labour. Rather than abolishing the wage-system and alienated labour, Proudhon makes everyone a wage-labourer. Yet this 'only transforms the relationship of the present day worker to his labour into the relationship of all men to labour. Society is then conceived as an abstract capitalist.'[28]

Unable to get to the root of capitalist private property, Proudhon merely fights its symptoms, as when he attacks interest on money. In so doing, he simply takes the side of productive capital against one of capital's unproductive forms. Marx concludes that criticism of political economy can advance beyond the inadequacies of Proudhon's analysis and arrive at a concrete understanding of the economic system 'only when *labour* is grasped as the essence of private property'.[29] This line of argument is recapitulated in Marx's collaborative effort with Engels of 1845, *The Holy Family*.

The Holy Family defends Proudhon against the sham criticism of the Left Hegelians. Marx and Engels praise the author of *What is Property?* for having made 'a critical investigation – the first resolute, ruthless, and at the same time scientific investigation – of the basis of political economy, *private property*'. Whereas political economy had hitherto proceeded from the side of wealth, 'Proudhon proceeds from the opposite side', that of poverty, and proves 'in detail *how* the movement of capital produces poverty'.[30] Nevertheless, they argue that criticism along Proudhonian lines merely sets the stage for a truly scientific criticism of political economy. Proudhon, they claim, 'has done all that criticism of political economy from the standpoint of political economy can do'. Because he uncritically adopts the liberal concept of individual 'possession' as the basis of the human being's relation to the objective world, Proudhon's standpoint cannot transcend that of political economy and the alienated human reality it describes.[31] That can be accomplished only from a standpoint which sees possessive individualism, to use the modern term, as itself a product of capitalism, not as the natural foundation of human life which is perverted by private property.

In 1844–5, then, Marx held that Proudhon had played an essentially positive role in advancing the critique of political economy while insisting that it was necessary to move beyond the limits of Proudhonian criticism. We know, however, that by 1847 Marx was moved to launch a much more vigorous denunciation of Proudhon with his book *The Poverty of Philosophy*. The increasingly polemical tone of Marx's discussion of Proudhon was occasioned, I believe, by two developments.

First, both Marx and Engels were engaged in sharp debate with the 'True Socialism' which dominated German communism at the time. The 'true socialists' advocated love of humanity, not class struggle, as the basis for transforming society. And this trend, led by Karl Grun in particular, was dominant within communist circles of German artisans in Paris. So concerned were Marx and Engels with combating this sentimental humanitarianism that Engels moved to Paris in August 1846 to confront directly Grun's influence among German communists. Grun, however, was closely associated with Proudhon; and France's leading socialist writer rejected Marx's request that he dissociate himself from the German true socialist. In order to criticize Grun effectively, it became necessary to confront head-on the doctrines of his French supporter.[32]

The second reason for the increasing sharpness of Marx's criticism of Proudhon is that the author of *What is Property?* showed no capacity to develop beyond the limits of his first book. At first, Marx had hoped to influence Proudhon and to win him over to a more consistently revolutionary position. But Proudhon's rejection of Marx's invitation to join a new Correspondence Committee of European socialists and his refusal to distance himself from the sentimental reformism of Grun led Marx to re-evaluate his initial enthusiasm for work with the French socialist. And this re-evaluation must have reached a point of no return with the appearance of Proudhon's *System of Economical Contradictions* (1846). This work demonstrated not merely that Proudhon's outlook was not developing but, worse from Marx's point of view, that it was regressing to a pure and simple petty bourgeois reformism. Rather than deepening his critique of political economy, Proudhon increasingly engaged in developing 'striking, ostentatious, now scandalous or now brilliant paradoxes'. Phrase-mongering had replaced serious analysis. And this was expressed in a tendency to depict surface modifications of bourgeois society, such as people's banks and free credit, as momentous revolutionary advances. Garbled theory produces muddled politics, Marx argued; indeed, 'charlatanism in science and accommodation in politics' followed hand in hand.[33]

By the end of 1846, then, Proudhon no longer appeared to Marx as a possible ally who could be won to a deeper and more revolutionary perspective. Moreover, in light of Grun's use of Proudhon to advance the cause of 'true socialism', the latter's ideas increasingly appeared as an obstacle to the revolutionary workers' movement – and one that would have to be confronted head-on. *The System of Economical Contradictions* provided just the opportunity he was looking for.

The Poverty of Philosophy: Petty Bourgeois
Socialism Under Attack

Whereas *What is Property?* had been a sharp-witted work of criticism, Proudhon's *System* was designed to be a more constructive and expository work. As Marx rightly saw, however, in theoretical terms the book offered little more than a vulgarized version of Ricardo and Hegel. Rather than departing from the highest achievements of these great bourgeois thinkers while overcoming their limits and contradictions by means of systematic criticism, Proudhon's *System* merely played with Ricardian and Hegelian ideas in order to arrive at the author's pre-established political conclusions. The result was not a piece of scientific criticism which deepened understanding of the contradictions of capitalism, but a blustering piece of eclecticism which could only do damage to the socialist workers' movement.

In his economic analysis, Proudhon sought to show the 'revolutionary' character of the doctrine that exchange value is determined by labour-time. From this Ricardian proposition Proudhon concluded that, since value theory posits the equality of the labour embodied in any two commodities that enter into exchange, it therefore follows that all acts of labour are equal (i.e. that any hour of concrete labour is equal to any other) and hence that all labourers should be paid equal wages. Yet as Marx points out, the Proudhonian conclusion does not follow from the Ricardian premiss. To say that commodities exchange on the basis of the labour-time needed for their production is not to say that each concrete hour of labour performed in society is equal to every other. The value of a commodity includes, after all, the indirect labour (embodied in the means of production) as well as the direct labour that enters into its production; it is not simply a question of the value created by direct labour and its remuneration (wages). More important, the equivalence of exchange-values does not imply the identity of each and every hour of labour performed. On the contrary, one of the functions of market competition is to determine precisely how much a given hour of labour is worth relative to other hours.

While Marx had not yet developed the crucial distinction between concrete labour and abstract labour which is at the heart of *Capital*, he had already grasped the idea that exchange on the basis of labour-time does not imply the identity of all specific, concrete acts of labour. He recognized that only on the market does the producer discover the (abstract) social value of a given hour of (concrete) labour performed. One hour of my labour may end up exchanging for only 45 minutes of someone else's labour (should the market deem my labour to be less productive than theirs). So, while it is true that Ricardo's theory of value presupposes the equal exchange of equal quantities of labour, this has nothing to do with the idea of an intrinsic equality of all individual acts of labour. The market does operate according to equal exchange; but this equality is established by over-riding the concrete particularity of each and every act of labour in order to transform them into quantifiable units of a common substance – human labour in the abstract. Thus, while average or 'socially necessary' labour is the *measure* of value (and hence of the social weight of individual acts of labour), this says nothing about the equality of each and every productive act *per se*. Proudhon's mistake, therefore, is to confuse 'measure by the labour time needed for the production of a commodity and measure by the value of the labour'.[34]

Proudhon fails to realize that the law of value (exchange on the basis of labour-time) operates only via the 'fluctuating movement' of the capitalist market and 'that there is no ready-made constituted "proportional relation"' which can provide an unchanging standard for just prices and equal exchanges. The 'anarchy of production' and market fluctuation are the actual mechanisms through which the law of value asserts itself.[35] Fluctuation, imbalance and over-production are thus inherent in any system of commodity exchange. Rather than violations of the the true principles of market exchange, these phenomena represent the actual economic life-processes necessary to any system of commodity production. Failure to grasp this leads to the hopeless confusion of seeking an egalitarian reform of society on the basis of the Ricardian theory of value – a false start which had been taken by a number of earlier socialist writers, among them John Francis Bray in his *Labour's Wrongs and Labour's Remedies*.

Marx offers two main challenges to Bray's theory of equal exchange (which he treats as an anticipation of Proudhon's position). First, he points out that if individual workers perform their concrete acts of production in isolation and without any collective co-ordination, there can be no guarantee that the requisite amounts of various goods will be produced. Too much labour time may have been expended on some commodities (e.g. chairs and shoes) and not enough on others (e.g. wheat and soap). Only if there is agreement among the producers *prior* to production about the amount of labour to be expended in various areas will there be a reasonable guarantee of equality of supply and demand (with the result that all hours of labour performed will in fact enter into exchange). 'But', Marx points out, 'such an agreement negates individual exchange.' And he goes on to argue that, since modern labour is based on co-operative acts of mass (not individual) production, planning the expenditure of social labour will require eliminating the struggle between capital and labour and allowing freely associated labour to direct economic decision-making. In such a co-operative arrangement based on socialized labour, 'there is no exchange of products – but there is exchange of labour which cooperated in production'.[36] It is worth emphasizing here that when Marx states that there is 'no exchange of products' under planned co-operative production he means no *commodity exchange* where the demand for and the value of a given product is established on the market *after* the act of production.

Bray's error, like that of Proudhon, was to treat one of the principles of modern bourgeois society as the basis for the recon-stitution of society on new principles. Exchange on the basis of equal labour times is in fact a consequence of private property and the rule of capital.

> Mr. Bray does not see that this equalitarian relation, this *corrective ideal* that he would like to apply to the world, is itself nothing but the reflection of the actual world; and that therefore it is totally impossible to reconstitute society on the basis of what is merely an embellished shadow of it.

And this problem emerges even more starkly in Proudhon, who seeks to reform the monetary system without ever asking why it is necessary within capitalism 'to individualize exchange value, so to speak, by the creation of a special agent of exchange'. Money, Marx goes on to point out, is not a mere thing, not simply an instrument of exchange, 'it is a social relation'. If money is necessary to exchange, this is indicative of a state of affairs in which human beings do not consciously regulate their economic relations, but in which 'a special agent' must intervene to regulate relations which escape human control.[37]

The Poverty of Philosophy thus continues the argument Marx ad-vanced in his writings of 1844–5 to the effect that Proudhon is unable to transcend the horizon of political economy and its presuppositions. As a result, Proudhon dehistoricizes the categories of political economy, treats them as expressions of eternal principles of social life, and attempts to purify those principles by liberating them from the encumbrances of monopoly rather than engaging in a critique designed to move entirely beyond the horizon of bourgeois economics. By accepting the premisses of political economy, Proudhon can merely engage in the tedious exercise of showing how political economy contradicts itself. He does not grasp that these theoretical contradictions are necessary results of the real contradictions of capitalist production. As a result, he hopes to resolve these contradictions through the purely intellectual exercise of separating the 'good' aspects of capitalism (individual production, competition, exchange of equivalents) from the 'bad' (private property, monopoly, exploitation). Rather than show the inevitable self-contradictions of modern society which need to be exploded, he regresses to the standpoint of an abstract moralizing – praising the 'good,' bemoaning the 'bad'. As Marx notes, with Proudhon 'there is no longer any dialectics but only, at most, absolute pure morality'.[38]

By dialectics Marx does not mean an abstract, transhistorical schema which runs through all stages of human development. What he has in mind here are the dialectics – the principles of self-contradiction and self-development – which grow out of the concrete activities of human beings within a given form of society. This involves abandoning attachment to 'eternal principles' of the sort invoked by Proudhon and turning instead to 'the real, profane history' of humanity. While this requires treating human beings as 'both the authors and actors of their own drama', it also involves delineating the structured contexts in which they act by situating human actions in terms of 'a definite development of men and their productive forces'. Such a mode of analysis leads one to the centrality of the class struggle between labour and capital, proletariat and bourgeoisie, as the driving contradiction of modern society. Socialist theory cannot be content, therefore, with the construction of abstract utopias or the creation of 'a regenerating science.' On the contrary, it must attempt to become the self-knowledge of a real historical process – the emergence of the revolutionary struggle of the proletariat out of the internal contradictions of capitalist society. Revolutionary socialist theory expresses, in other words, 'actual relations springing from an existing class struggle, from a historical movement going on under our very eyes'.[39]

Concrete, historical dialectics must be rooted, therefore, in the real self-activity and self-development of the working class. In terms of political theory, this involves the insistence that socialism can only be achieved through the *self-emancipation* of the working class. For this reason, Marx sharply attacks Proudhon's hostile attitude towards strikes and trade unions; while recognizing the limits of trade union struggle, Marx nevertheless treats unions as 'ramparts for workers in their struggles with the employers'. Moreover, these ramparts of working-class self-organization could provide the ground for an association 'which takes on a political character'. Marx dismissed Proudhonian opposition to working class political action. The class struggle discloses to workers that economics and politics are not truly separable; economic emancipation requires the conquest of political power. There is no way to shortcut the necessary 'moments' of the class struggle; rather than fearing them or attempting to transcend them, socialist revolutionaries try to raise them to their highest level – a working-class revolution which will lead to the abolition of classes and the state.[40]

The Poverty of Philosophy thus set out both the theoretical and practical orientations of Marxian socialism. At the level of theory this involved a rigorous critique of the phenomena through which capitalism most immediately confronts the individual – the commodity, money, market exchange – by showing them to be *necessary forms* taken by the alienated and antagonistic relations of capitalist production. And at the level of political practice it involves rejecting the idea that any of these necessary forms can be the means for a progressive regeneration of society, and asserting that a higher form of society can develop only out of the self-activity of the exploited class whose labour sustains the whole edifice of capitalism.

A Battle Continued: Marx's 'Economy' and the Critique of Proudhon

Much as Marx may have hoped to dispose of Proudhon in 1847, his adversary's influence was not to diminish in working-class and socialist circles. Indeed, throughout the 1850s Proudhon continued to be Europe's best-known socialist writer while Marx laboured in intellectual and political obscurity. Thus, although this decade was dedicated largely to work on his 'Economics', Marx regularly returned to the debate with his French opponent. In fact, criticism of Proudhon continued to provide a stimulus to his critique of political economy.

The appearance of Proudhon's *General Idea of the Revolution in the Nineteenth Century* provided the occasion for a development of key themes of *The Poverty of Philosophy*. In a letter to Engels in August of 1851, shortly after Proudhon's work appeared, Marx stated that he would like to write a short tract on *The General Idea* 'because of what it says about money'. Once more he attacked Proudhon's confusion with respect to the law of value and the role of money and banks. Two months later, Marx urged Engels to give him his 'views on Proudhon', noting that 'they are the more of interest now that I am in the middle of setting out the *Economy*'. Marx returned to the matter the following month, this time incensed by reading Proudhon's *Gratuité de crédit*, a work characterized by 'charlatanism, poltroonery, a lot of noise and weakness'. This time, in fact, Marx was moved to propose to his friend Joseph Wedermeyer a series of articles under the banner 'New Revelations on Socialism, or the Idée géneérale of P.J. Proudhon. A Critique by Karl Marx'.[41]

Although he did not produce this critique, Marx was prompted once again to undertake such a work in 1856–7. In January 1857 he wrote Engels that 'Proudhon is now publishing an "economic Bible" in Paris', and went on to note: 'I have a more recent work by one of Proudhon's pupils here: *De la Réforme des Banques, par Alfred Darimon*, 1865.'[42] This time Marx did write his critique – in the form of the opening section of the *Grundrisse*, the first draft of his 'Economics'. Although its significance has eluded most commentators, the first chapter of that work, 'The Chapter on Money', begins with a citation from Darimon's book, and the whole of the 124-page chapter (in the English translation) is framed by his confrontation with Proudhon's disciple.[43]

Beginning with the central flaw of Proudhonian theory, Marx points out that this doctrine 'proposes tricks of circulation' in place of a genuine transformation of society. At the heart of these 'tricks' is monetary reform via a people's bank. But no form of money 'is capable of overcoming the contradictions inherent in the money relation'. Abolish the monetary role of gold and silver and you must still address the persistence of this 'money relation'.[44] Much of the rest of the 'Chapter on Money' is devoted to delineating this relation, to demonstrating that the contradiction between money and commodities which the Proudhonians hope to suppress is a necessary aspect of any system of commodity production and exchange.

Marx's discussion departs from the point he had reached in *The Poverty of Philosophy*: that values of commodities can express themselves only through the constant fluctuations of the market. But he quickly links this issue to a more substantial problem not addressed in that earlier work: the necessity of money in any system of unplanned production governed by exchange acording to average labour-times.

The average (or socially necessary) labour-time required to produce a given commodity is something determined outside any one concrete production process. Only rarely will individual production times be identical with the average labour-time. 'This average appears as an external abstraction', but at the same time it is 'very real' – it is that average we glimpse through the 'constant oscillations' of commodity prices. Marx thus arrives at the conclusion that value can only manifest itself as price. But price and value only episodically coincide. The ever-changing relations of supply and demand, the introduction of new methods of production, and so on render prices inherently unstable. In a world of constantly changing market values, it is impossible to determine in advance the exact ratios at which commodities should exchange (as the proponents of labour money or 'time chits' would like). How, then, do we come to know the values of commodities and the ratios in which one should exchange with another? The 'time-chitters' conjure away the difficulties here with a pseudo-solution: treat every concrete act of labour as identical, they propose, and let each hour of labour exchange for any other hour. But individual acts of labour are not equal. Looked at concretely, they are radically different; they produce varying goods in quite different productive situations. As a result, two commodities produced independently can only be equated through the medium of a 'third party', which measures the average (or socially necessary) labour they represent. It is impossible for an individual commodity to provide this measure of itself since no specific act of labour can be assumed to represent the social average; put differently, no individual act of labour can be the measure of its own social value. The role of money, as we shall see in more detail below, is to act as a general representative of value (average social labour) and to provide the means of measuring the social value of specific commodities.[45]

Marx's discussion of the money relation in the *Grundrisse* operates at a very high level of abstraction and without the conceptual precision of his treatment of the problem in *Capital*. But its direction is clear: value is a social relation which can be expressed only by means of a specific commodity chosen from the world of commodities (money). Money is necessary in a system of commodity production since 'as a value, the commodity is general; as a real commodity it is particular'. And in order for a particular commodity produced in an unsocialized context to manifest its general or social nature (and thus to be exchangeable with another commodity), it requires something outside its own particular existence in which it can express its social being (its value). We have here a classic case of alienation: universal (value) and particular (commodity) are separated; their unification (in which the commodity attains a social value in the world of commodities) happens via a third party, a party external to the thing itself (commodity).

In capitalist society there is thus a complete separation between the general and the particular, the social and the individual. On the one hand, we have separate and isolated acts of production which are brought together through the medium of things (commodities) in the act of market exchange. On the other hand, we have a separate representative of the social being of these things and the labours which went into producing them. Under capitalism, the universality and social being of commodities can be expressed only 'as something alien to them, autonomous, as a thing'. Consequently, 'exchange value obtains a separate existence, in isolation from the product ... this is, *money*'. So long as the alienated relations of capitalism persist, it will not be possible to abolish the form in which that alienation manifests itself – money. It is not especially important whether gold or silver assumes the role of a universal 'third party' which measures the value of specific commodities; but something must assume this role or commodity exchange would not be possible. To abolish money, then, requires more than overcoming a worship of precious metals; it requires the abolition of commodity production (unsocialized production for market exchange). It follows, therefore, that it is 'impossible to abolish money itself as long as exchange value remains the social form of value'.[46]

There are a number of gaps in Marx's discussion of the commodity/money relation in the *Grundrisse*, due in part to what he described as 'the idealist manner of the presentation'.[47] Yet, as a critique of labour-money schemes, the essential argument is valid. Labour-money cannot transcend the contradictions of the money relation unless a balance of supply and demand is guaranteed, and unless individual and socially average labour-times are brought into harmony. But for this to happen, the Proudhonian national bank would have to be 'the general buyer and seller'. Moreover, this institution 'would have to determine the labour time in which commodities could be produced, with the average means of production available in a given industry, i.e. the time in which they would have to be produced'. To this end, 'social production in general would have to be stabilized and arranged so that the needs of the partners in exchange were always satisfied'. Most important, the purchase and sale of labour would have to be replaced – otherwise unemployment and/or changes in wage rates might upset price equilibrium – which presupposes 'common ownership of the means of production'. As Marx explains a bit further on in the *Grundrisse*, isolated and individualized labour can only become socialized through the intervention of an intermediary. Individual labour can avoid the intervention of an intermediary only if it is socialized from the outset: 'in order to be *general money* directly, it would have to be not a *particular*, but *general* labour from the outset; i.e. it would have to be *posited* from the outset as a link in *general production*.' It is clear that this presupposes socialized production: 'the communal character of production would make the product into a communal, general product from the outset'.[48] Changes of this magnitude require much more than the establishment of labour money; they presuppose the elimination of all the essential conditions of the capitalist mode of production. For, 'if the social character of production is presupposed', then consumption 'is not mediated by the exchange of mutually independent labours or products of labour'. Instead, consumption would be socially guaranteed. The only real alternative to capitalist production – and the exploitation attendant on it – is one which overcomes the separation of the producers from the means of production and which eliminates commodity exchange as the basis of subsistence. Short of this, any talk of abolishing money while retaining individualized production and exchange of commodities is a hopeless fantasy.[49]

By the time he had completed the *Grundrisse* 'Chapter on Money', Marx believed that he had demolished the theoretical underpinnings of Proudhonian socialism. His analysis of money, he wrote to Engels, aimed 'several opportune blows against the Proudhonists' and the 'absurdity' of their attempt to oppose the 'exchange of equivalents' to 'the inequalities etc. which this exchange produces and from which it results'. And his first attempt to present a systematic exposition of his economic theory, *A Contribution to the Critique of Political Economy*, would provide, he promised Wedermeyer, 'a scientific victory for our Party' since 'the basis of Proudhonist socialism ... will be run into the ground.' One of the achievements of the book, he reminded Engels, was that 'Proudhonism has been extracted by its roots'.[50]

The *Contribution* concisely restates the basic theory of money developed in the *Grundrisse*. Marx criticizes petty bourgeois socialism for its failure to understand the necessity of a money-commodity to any system of independent production and exchange. The target this time is John Gray:

> Commodities are the direct products of isolated independent individual kinds of labour, and through their alienation in the course of exchange they must prove that they are social labour, in other words, on the basis of commodity production, labour becomes social labour only as a result of the universal alienation of individual kinds of labour. But as Gray presupposes that the labour-time contained in commodities is *immediately social* labour-time, he presupposes that it is communal labour-time or labour-time of directly asociated individuals. In that case it would be impossible for a specific commodity, such as gold or silver, to confront other commodities as the incarnation of universal labour.[51]

While Marx criticizes Gray's theoretical confusion in trying to abolish the exchange of commodities (by centralizing exchange in the hands of the bank) while preserving commodity production by isolated producers, the bulk of his scorn is reserved for Proudhon. For Gray at least was 'compelled by the intrinsic logic of the subject matter to repudiate one condition of bourgeois production after another' with his calls for nationalization of the land, public ownership of the principal means of production, and a national bank which would direct and regulate production. Gray's inability to theorize the commodity/money relation leaves his argument suspended in mid-air, repudiating many of the conditions of bourgeois production but not bourgeois production *per se*. Yet Proudhon does not advance even this far. He simply wants to rid society of a monetary commodity (like gold or silver) – and thereby abolish usury and monopoly – in order to enable the pristine relations of commodity production to realize themselves in a true society of justice. Proudhon's standpoint is thus a significant regression from that of a socialist writer like Gray (not to mention Thompson and Bray whose works achieved an even higher level of clarity):

> it was left to M. *Proudhon* and his schools to declare seriously that the degradation of *money* and the exaltation of *commodities* was the essence of socialism and thereby reduce socialism to an elementary misunderstanding of the inevitable correlation existing between commodities and money.[52]

Capital: 'The Real Battle Begins'

Important as it was to the critique of Proudhonism, the *Contribution* had broken off, Marx believed, right where the crucial battle should begin. As he explained in a letter to Ferdinand Lassalle, the *Contribution* covered the ground only of the chapters on the Commodity and on Money from the original outline for the 'Economy'. The crucial third chapter, on Capital, he had held back from the *Contribution*. And he had done so 'for *political* reasons, for the real battle begins in chapter 3, and I thought it advisable not to frighten anyone off from the very beginning'.[53] In fact, chapter 3 in Marx's original outline grew into the entirety of the first volume of *Capital* after 'Part One: Commodities and Money'. It was there, he believed, in the theory of capital, that petty bourgeois socialism would find its definitive repudiation. Yet even the opening chapters of *Capital* advance Marx's critique of petty bourgeois socialism by developing his clearest exposition of the relation between commodities and money, and of the contradictions inherent in schemes for 'market socialism'.

Whereas the *Grundrisse* commenced with an analysis of money, *Capital* starts with the commodity. Commodities, Marx explains, have a *dual character*, they are both use-values (useful objects capable of satisfying some human need) and exchange-values (products that can be exchanged for other goods). Commodity exchange, however, is governed not by usefulness but by exchange-value. The latter is regulated by labour-time. But just as commodities have a twofold character – being both use-values and exchange-values – so does the labour that goes into their production. On the one hand, there is the concrete (useful) labour directly expended in the production process; and, on the other hand, there is the abstract (socially necessary) labour this represents. The whole mystery of commodities and money is embodied in these two pairs: use-value/exchange-value, and concrete labour/abstract labour. It is of the nature of the commodity that each element of these pairs is separated from the other: the use-value of a commodity is realized only if it can transform itself into an exchange-value, just as the concrete labour that went into producing it is validated only when it is translated into abstract social labour through exchange on the market. The mysterious nature of the commodity has to do with the internal divisions it embodies, which can be transcended only through complex external relations.

The secret of the mystery of commodities can be arrived at, Marx claims, by means of a comprehensive analysis of any exchange equation such as 20 yards of linen = 1 coat. When we say that the value of the linen is expressed in the coat, we indicate that the coat is the material expression of the value of the linen. Since the value of the linen cannot be expressed in its own use-value (since it does not exchange with itself), it finds its expression in the use-value of the coat. As we have already noted, the translation of concrete individual labour into abstract social labour requires an external relation, something outside the commodity whose exchange-value we wish to know. Because commodities are 'products of mututally independent acts of labour, performed in isolation', individual labour is separated from social labour. Produced in isolation, without social co-ordination, the linen requires another commodity (in this case the coat) to function as the medium for expressing its social being.

But linen and coats are concretely different objects which satisfy different human needs. For one to serve as a means of expressing something inherent in the other, they both must share a common characteristic separate from their concrete utility. This common characteristic is general (abstract) human labour. The equation 20 yards of linen = 1 coat refers not to a material relation between these goods, but rather to a social relation between the labour embodied in them. The social character of the coat – the fact that it represents an expenditure of average social labour as well as of concrete, useful labour and can thus be exchanged with other commodities – can only be 'activated' by bringing the coat into a relationship with linen (or some other commodity).

So long as we restrict ourselves to this simple or accidental relation between two commodities selected at random, we can say no more than that the use-value of the coat expresses the exchange-value of the linen, since to know the exchange-value of the coat we would have to bring it into an active relation with another commodity and thus extend our exchange sequence to at least a third good, e.g. 20 yards of linen = 1 coat = 10 pounds of tea. At the simple level of a two commodity relation, the abstract labour represented by the linen is expressed in the concrete labour embodied in the coat (whose social value could be discovered only by bringing it into an exchange relationship with tea or some other commodity). As Marx puts it, 'this concrete labour therefore becomes the expression of abstract labour'. This, moreover, is just another way of saying that within every commodity there is an 'internal opposition between use-value and value' which is 'represented on the surface by an external opposition, i.e. by a relation between two commodities'.[54]

The relationship between money and commodities is merely an expanded (and in principle infinitely expandable) form of the equation 20 yards of linen = 1 coat. With money, one particular commodity, let us say gold, is selected to play the role of *general equivalent* to the world of commodities. Every commodity thus enters into a relationship with gold in the same way as the linen did with respect to the coat, i.e. as a commodity which finds an external object (gold) in which to express the value inherent in itself. The money relation is thus inherent in a system of commodity production (production for exchange). This is a crucial point, which eludes market socialists who wish to retain unregulated, individualized production for a market while abolishing the 'tyranny' of a money-commodity. Yet that very tyranny – the fact that a single commodity can require that every other commodity take it as the universally accepted means of expressing their values (that they achieve social being as worth *so much gold*) – derives directly from the fetishism inherent in the commodity form.

Marx's theory of commodity fetishism refers to the fact that within capitalism the social relations between people as producers take the form of material relations between things – commodities. It is impossible for the products of unsocialized production relations to express themselves in a directly social fashion. Yet commodity production is ultimately social in nature; it is production not for private use but for exchange with others. However, the social relations inherent in commodity production 'do not appear as direct social relations between people in their work, but rather as material relations between persons and social relations between things'.[55] Commodity fetishism – in which the social relations between people can only manifest themselves as relations among things – derives directly from the separation (alienation) among commodity producers. And it expresses itself in the fact that a thing – money – is necessary to endow the private labour of the individual with social being. Without its metamorphosis into money, a commodity would remain a private thing lacking any social reality. As Marx puts it in the *Grundrisse*, 'the individual carries his social power, as well as his bond with society, in his pocket'. And this is a direct result of the alienation peculiar to capitalism since 'money can have a social property only because individuals have alienated their own social relationship from themselves so that it takes the form of a thing'.[56]

For Proudhon to hope that 'all commodities can simultaneously be imprinted with the stamp of direct exchangeability' is therefore an illusion of the same order as desiring 'that all Catholics can be popes'. To make all Catholics popes would be to abolish *the* pope, which would be to abolish Catholicism. Similarly, to make all goods directly exchangeable without the mediation of money would be to socialize their production, to make them products of communally organized production, i.e. to abolish their status as commodities. Yet Proudhon is unwilling to take these steps; he remains mired in a 'philistine utopia' in which he views 'the production of commodities as the absolute summit of human freedom and individual independence' while aspiring to remove 'the inconveniences resulting from the impossibility of exchanging commodities directly, which are inherent in this form' of economic life.[57]

Proudhon's confusion involves opposing the forms in which commodity relations necessarily express themselves while accepting the relations which create them. Petty bourgeois socialists become hopelessly entangled in self-contradiction since they focus on one side of the commodity/money relation without grasping that both sides are *internally* related, that one cannot have commodity relations without a money commodity. In addition, the market socialists' failure to grasp the necessity of money in a system of commodity production also results in an inability to understand the connection between value and price.

As we have seen, at the heart of Smithian socialism is the attempt to reconcile price with value, to create a regime of 'natural prices' free from unfair monopolistic additions to commodity prices. Yet Marx's theory of the commodity/money relation demonstrates that divergence between price and value will tend to be the rule. After all, the value immanent in the commodity can only manifest itself as a monetary price. Indeed, unless it can realize itself as a price by exchanging with money, value does not achieve concrete existence. Prices, however, are the products not simply of general economic laws – such as the determination of value by socially necessary labour-time – but also of innumerable fluctuations in supply and demand, changes in the costs of inputs, and so on. Given the incessant fluctuations of such factors, only rarely will market price coincide with immanent value. Rather than undermining the laws of market exchange, then, the expression of value in a monetary price separate from immanent value is necessary to a law of value which can manifest itself only in the form of fluctuating prices which regularly diverge from underlying values. The discrepancy between price and value is thus not a flaw, as the Smithian socialists believed; it is an essential feature of any system of commodity production. Divergence between price and value, as Marx put it, 'is inherent in the price-form itself. This is not a defect, but, on the contrary, it makes this form the adequate one for a mode of production whose laws can only assert themselves as blindly operating averages between constant irregularities.'[58]

The efforts of the petty bourgeois socialists to suppress the power of a money commodity and to establish an immediate identity between value and price demonstrates a thoroughgoing confusion as to the nature of market regulation and production for exchange. Proudhon and his English predecessors may perceive the alienated relations between commodities and money, value and price; but they are unable to see the *necessity* of such relations in a system of production governed by exchange. It is worth quoting Marx at some length on this point:

> Commodities first enter into a process of exchange ungilded and unsweetened, retaining their original home-grown shape. Exchange, however, produces a differentiation of the commodity into two elements, commodity and money, an external opposition which expresses the opposition between use-value and value which is inherent in it. In this opposition, commodities as use-values confront money as exchange-value. On the other hand, both sides of this opposition are commodities, hence themselves unities of use-value and value. But this unity of differences is expressed at two opposite poles: the commodity is in reality a use-value; its existence as value appears only ideally, in its price, through which it is related to the real embodiment of its value, the gold which confronts it as its opposite ... These antagonistic forms of the commodities are the real forms of motion of the process of exchange.[59]

Because commodities cannot express their values directly they require an external relation to money. And this external relation creates the formal possibility of economic crises, which the market socialists had hoped to eliminate by abolishing the commodity character of money. By demonstrating that it is impossible to abolish the binary relation commodity/money within the confines of commodity production, Marx also shows that crises are inherent in this relation. Although Marx's full theory of capitalist crisis was only developed at the much more concrete level of analysis found in the third volume of *Capital*, he insisted that crisis was rooted in the commodity/money relation. Put simply, a crisis occurs when some commodities cannot complete their metamorphosis, when they are unable to realize themselves as values because they fail to exchange with money. Because the social being (value) of a commodity is not immediately given, and because it can only be realized through exchange with a separate commodity (money), it is always possible that this process of self-realization and self-transformation of the commodity will not transpire, that it will remain in its immediate form (use value/concrete labour) and not realize itself in exchange. A crisis is precisely such a moment in which commodities fail to enter fully into their external relations with money; then the separation between commodities and money reaches a breaking point. 'In a crisis, the antithesis between commodities and their value-form, money, is raised to the level of an absolute contradiction.'[60] Contrary to the market socialists, then, crises are not a contingent fact deriving from a distortion of the market economy by money; they are inherent in the commodity relation *per se*.

Part One of *Capital* (Volume One) thus demonstrates the inability of petty bourgeois socialism to grasp the commodity/money and value/price relations and the possibility of crises these entail. Marx turns in parts Two to Six to a discussion of capital, the labour process and the production of surplus value. The burden of much of these parts is to demonstrate how it is that capital systematically appropriates a share of the unpaid labour (surplus value) created by wage-labourers. At the centre of Marx's argument is the claim that it is the availability of labour-power on the market (offered by those who have no alternative means of subsistence) which enables capital to appropriate a surplus-value from the direct producers. It is not unequal exchange that accounts for exploitation of labour; rather, it is the appearance of labourers on the market as sellers of their working power as a result of their dispossession from means of production. This labour-power can then be consumed by capital in the process of production for a duration and at an intensity which results in the creation of a value greater than that which was originally paid for it as wages. Building on this analysis, Marx returns in Part Seven (Volume One) to the problem of petty bourgeois socialism once more – this time in an effort to illustrate the confusion behind Proudhonian opposition to *capitalist* appropriation in the name of *individual* apropriation. In this case as well, Marx attempts to show the necessary relationship involved: individual appropriation and capitalist appropriation are two sides of a single relation *within the framework of capitalist production*.

Marx confronts this issue directly in chapter 24 of *Capital*, 'The Transformation of Surplus-Value into Capital'. The first subsection of this chapter bears the heading: 'Capitalist Production on a Progressively Increasing Scale. The Inversion which Converts the Property Laws of Commodity Production into Laws of Capitalist

Appropriation'. This subsection, which Marx expanded significantly in the French edition of 1872, challenges the very axis of Proudhonian economic theory – the critique of capitalist appropriation of a share of the products of labour, according to the principle of individual appropriation (the right of all labourers to ownership of the products of their labour). Central to Marx's argument is the claim that commodity production and capitalist appropriation are entirely compatible, even if the former is 'inverted' in its development into the latter. Marx claims that this 'inversion' grows out of the nature of individual production, exchange and appropriation. By thus insisting that capitalist appropriation grows out of individual appropriation – that the seizing of a share of the labourer's output by capital does not contradict, but is in fact consistent with, the principle of free and equal exchange among individual proprietors – Marx is attempting to drive the final nail into the coffin of Proudhonian theory.

Too often, Marx's treatment of this issue has been misunderstood as implying that simple commodity production automatically gives rise to fully capitalist production.[61] Marx's claim is different: it is that the property right established according to the principle of individual appropriation and equal exchange, which Proudhon saw as in conflict with capitalist exploitation, can and does become the legitimating principle of such exploitation. As soon as a full-scale labour market is created (by the dispossession of masses of producers), then, Marx argues, exploitation can occur under conditions of equal exchange. If the employer pays the prevailing market rate for labour-power, then there is an exchange of equivalents – labour for wages. But in paying the value of labour (wages), the capitalist receives its use-value (labour-power). This enables exploitation to occur *after* this free and equal exchange has taken place, when, by productively consuming labour-power in the production process, the capitalist receives commodities whose value exceeds what was paid out in wages (and other initial costs of production). It is crucial to realize, however, that this exploitation does not contradict the equal exchange which preceded the process of production.

The fact that capitalists own means of production upon which they can set wage-labourers to work is an inequality established *prior* to any specific transaction in the labour market. Within that market, every transaction can in principle be entirely equitable – i.e. capitalists pay the full value of labour as established on the market – yet the equivalents exchanged will not be personal labour for personal labour. From the moment one party has the means to exchange capital for labour, then labour market transactions become the exchange of living labour for portions of unpaid past labour. Henceforth, 'each individual transaction continues to conform to the laws of commodity exchange, with the capitalist always buying labour-power and the worker always selling it at what we will assume is its real value'. But now this ongoing process of equal exchange is also an incessant process of capitalist appropriation – since a surplus value can be extracted in the sphere of production – without any violation of the principles of free market exchange. In this way, 'the laws of appropriation or of private property, laws based on the production and circulation of commodities, become changed into their direct opposite through their own internal and inexorable dialectic'. While we continue to observe an exchange of equivalents – labour for the wages determined in the market – the equivalence is merely formal; in substance there is a fundamental inequality at work, but one which originates outside the sphere of exchange (however much it is reproduced by it):

> The relation between capitalist and worker becomes a mere semblance belonging only to the process of circulation, it becomes a mere form which is alien to the content of the transaction itself, and merely mystifies it. The constant sale and purchase of labour-power is the form; the content is the constant appropriation by the capitalist, without equivalent, of a portion of the labour of others.[62]

Given these class arrangements, equal exchange sustains the separation of workers from their products, of labour from property. This is the 'inversion' Marx has in mind: whereas private appropriation and exchange were initially justified in terms of the right of individuals to exchange the products of their labour, from the moment that some are propertyless and have only their labouring ability to sell, then the same principle justifies the buyer of their labour-power in 'fairly' claiming the commodities they produce. Yet legal ownership of the means of production enables the capitalist, while paying the value of labour as determined by the market, to appropriate more value than was advanced as wages. What these buyers acquire is a unique commodity, labour-power, which has the special property of being able to generate more value than that which is necessary to its own production/reproduction (represented by wages). But this 'surplus-value' is not appropriated as a result of fraud; it takes place 'in the most exact accordance with the economic laws of commodity production and with the rights of property derived from them'.[63]

The key to the entire process, of course, is the proletarianization of a substantial proportion of the working population. Without that precondition, simple commodity production cannot develop into fully capitalist production. But that precondition is the very defining characteristic of a genuine system of commodity production:

> This result becomes inevitable from the moment there is a free sale, by the worker himself, of labour-power as a commodity. But it is also only from them onwards that commodity production is generalized and becomes the typical form of production; it is only from then onwards that every product is produced for sale from the outset and all wealth goes through the sphere of circulation. Only where wage-labour is its basis does commodity production impose itself upon society as a whole.[64]

The process that Marx is describing at this level of theoretical abstraction corresponds to the historical processes I have discussed in chapter 1: petty commodity production becomes a breeding ground for capitalist exploitation once a significant number of producers have been forced onto the market as sellers of labour-power. Indeed, given adequate supplies of labour-power on the market, petty commodity production will undergo a systematic process of class differentiation; the capital/wage-labour relation will grow out of the soil of petty production. Given that condition, which is the very key to the development of capitalism, exploitation can take place through pure economic transaction untainted by the use of monopoly power. It should come as no surprise, then, that towards the end of this section of chapter 24 of *Capital*, Marx takes another jibe at 'the cleverness of Proudhon, who would abolish capitalist property – by enforcing the eternal laws of property which are themselves based on commodity production!'[65]

The cumulative effect of the argument set forth in the first volume of *Capital* is thus devastating for petty bourgeois socialism. Whereas the latter had attempted to counterpose the law of value to capitalist exploitation and inequality, Marx demonstrates that the value form – in which products of labour interact according to the laws of market exchange – implies all the results rejected by petty bourgeois socialism: the 'tyranny' of a money-commodity, divergence of price from value, economic crises and class polarization. As Engels was to put it in *Anti-Dühring*, his critique of a similar sort of German 'socialist' economic theorizing:

The value form of products therefore already contains in embryo the whole capitalist form of production, the antagonism between capitalists and wage-earners, the industrial reserve army, crises. To seek to abolish the capitalist form of production by establishing 'true value' is therefore tantamount to attempting to abolish catholicism by establishing the 'true' Pope.[66]

This, then, is the central flaw in all notions of market socialism: by accepting market relations (commodities, prices and wage-labour), market socialists must logically accept the inevitable consequences of these relations – exploitation, class inequality and economic crises. But market socialists fail to see this because they do not understand that without the market in human labour-power there is no generalized commodity exchange. If labour-power is not bought and sold, it will not have a market-determined value. And if this crucial input into every production process is not marketized, then commodity exchange will not be general, and goods will not have true market values (since the labour embodied in them will not have been priced by the market). The only true market economy is thus a capitalist economy with a generalized labour market – a point pursued in more detail in the next chapter. Market socialism thus means 'socialism' with wage-labour and exploitation – i.e. a non-socialism. All talk of market socialism is for this reason illogical and incoherent. This is why Marx insists that socialism requires the abolition of wage-labour – which can only mean the de-commodification of labour-power. The elimination of exploitation and class inequality is impossible without the abolition of the labour market. And this can only mean the *demarketization* of economic life. A consistent socialism can only be unrelentingly hostile to the market as regulator of economic relations.

6

Beyond the Market

> There can be nothing more erroneous and absurd than to postulate the control by the united individuals of their total production, on the basis of *exchange value*, of *money*.[1]

Central to the Marxian conception of socialism is the idea that it is possible to 'defetishize' economic life, to free human beings from subjection to impersonal economic laws, to organize the production of goods and services according to a conscious plan rather than through the blind working of the market. At the heart of Marxian socialism, then, is the vision of a society beyond commodity exchange, the law of value and money. It has been common in recent years for many on the Left to dismiss this view as the stuff of 'wild-eyed dogmatists' clinging to a 'fundamentalist-millenarian' outlook not worthy of discussion by responsible individuals.[2] Yet the current enthusiasm for 'market socialism' as an alternative to Marx's position too often fails to recognize that there is a serious case to be answered. It has become acceptable to talk about the persistence of commodities, prices, money and profit in a future socialist society without the slightest recognition that one ought at least to acknowledge the powerful case put by Marx against the first market socialists – Thomas Hodgskin, John Gray, John Francis Bray and Pierre-Joseph Proudhon in particular. Indeed, most of this discussion proceeds in virtual ignorance of Marx's critique of those socialist currents which looked to labour exchanges and labour money schemes as means of transforming the market in an egalitarian direction.[3]

Thus, without even the slightest attempt to clarify the stakes of the argument, Alec Nove tells us that 'the idea that "value" will not exist under socialism makes no sense'. And Alan Carling, whose species of 'rational choice Marxism' often provides a theoretical underpinning to contemporary market socialism, writes that 'the marketplace really is a free space' – as if there were not a critique of the market that merits discussion. Similarly, Robin Blackburn commends Proudhon's 'greater sensitivity than Marx to the significance of petty production and exchange' without so much as a nod to the thoroughgoing critique of Proudhon's muddle concerning commodities, exchange, value and money to be found in *The Poverty of Philosophy*, the *Grundrisse*, *A Contribution to the Critique of Political Economy* and volume 1 of *Capital*. And he proceeds to put at the centre of his account of the crisis of socialism the 'acuteness of the theoretical critique developed by Mises and Hayek' of any form of socialist economic planning. Moreover, he fails to note that, in Marxian terms, the Austrian critique represents an extreme case of 'vulgar economics' – a perspective which treats human labour as a mere technical factor of production, and the market as the only mechanism for rational allocation of goods and means of production among competing ends – and that this has profound implications for the very way 'economy' is conceptualized.[4]

Most market socialists will argue that they do not underestimate the deficiencies of the market system, that they accept much of the Marxian critique of untrammelled market competition. It is precisely to offset the inequalities inherent in market economy that they support public ownership of the principal means of production, a guaranteed annual income, provision of free social services, and the like. At the same time, they will insist, socialism confronts a crisis of *economic rationality* rooted in its failure to delineate and construct efficient non-market means of regulating the production and allocation of goods and services. Relying on the horrific example of the Soviet Union and Eastern Europe, they will argue that non-market allocation of goods and services has proved grossly wasteful and inefficient. If the basic objectives of socialism are to be salvaged, they conclude, this will require utilizing the rationality inherent in market regulation of the economic process.

It is in this spirit that Alec Nove looks to the market in outlining the features of his 'feasible socialism'. Nove proposes a competitive market which will generate 'prices that balance supply and demand, that reflect cost and use-value'. He accepts the necessity of profit, interest and rent, and of a labour market that will determine wage scales. And he argues that 'value' will still govern the basic interrelations of the economy.[5]

Yet this perspective entails much more than a continuing role for some market mechanisms within a socialist economy – if that were all there was to it, there would be little cause for debate. But the issue is much larger than that: it concerns the implications of an economy regulated by a competitive price mechanism, one in which all inputs into the production process – including labour-power – are priced by the market, since this is the only way in which 'rational market prices' can be formed and goods and services allocated on the basis of price signals to producers and consumers. The issue of contention, therefore, is not the use of market mechanisms within the framework of socialist planning; it is more fundamental than that – it concerns the compatibility of socialism with market *regulation*.

Much of this chapter is devoted to pursuing this question. Without underestimating the complexities of democratic socialist planning on a national – let alone international – level, I believe that socialists must be clear on the basic issues at stake in such a discussion – and that such clarity has been conspicuously absent in much recent discussion. There is no point jumping into an argument over the technical instrumentalities of socialist economy if issues of fundamental principle are misconstrued. And one of the noteworthy things about the recent 'turn to the market' within much of the Left is that the market has been adopted as a purely technical means of allocating goods and services without consideration of its deeper social and economic implications. Yet before we can make any progress in discussing socialist economy, we must come to terms with first principles.

Let us begin, then, with the basic assumption shared by all market socialists: that the market is the most efficient means of allocating goods and services because of the automatic process through which it sends price signals to producers and consumers about changes in the supply of and demand for goods. Given the enormous number of goods and services produced in a modern economy, and the complexity of gauging their demand and determining the inputs (raw materials, technologies, skills, etc.) required to produce them, efficiency dictates that the market govern their allocation. Thus far, the argument appears innocent enough. But what is usually ignored in such discussions is that an economy governed by price signals is one in which market principles determine the value of all inputs and outputs within the economic process. It follows, as Nove recognizes, that all goods and services, including human labour-power, should be priced through their exchange against a universal equivalent (money). Yet this has consequences that deserve to be explored. And given that the ultra-liberals whose arguments have loomed large in recent discussions of socialism and the market are clear about at least some of the terms of the debate, their argument provides a useful point of departure for our discussion. Let us take Mises's classic anti-socialist statement, 'Economic Calculation in the Socialist Commonwealth', as a case in point.

At the heart of Mises's argument are a number of crucial claims about economic rationality. First, he asserts that 'without economic calculation there can be no economy'. Second, in the absence of such calculation it is 'impossible to speak of rational production'. Third, calculation and rational production are impossible without 'a pricing mechanism'. Fourth, for the pricing mechanism to operate there must exist a free and competitive market. Fifth, a competitive market economy – the only genuine, i.e. rational, economy – requires 'private ownership of the means of production' since production goods will not have rational market prices unless they are sold by private producers and purchased by private firms whose only criterion is profit maximization by means of price competition.[6] It follows from all of the above that the market cannot regulate an economy in the absence of private ownership of the means of production, competition, market-determined monetary prices and profit maximization.

Spelled out in these terms, it is difficult to see how there could be any accommodation between socialism and the neo-liberal position. Blackburn makes no effort to confront this issue head-on, seemingly unaware of the full terms of debate. But Brus and Laski clearly recognize what is at stake. In *From Marx to the Market* they observe that, in proposing to remove parts of the economy from market regulation, even market socialism 'is still exposed to criticism from the extreme liberal position' of Mises and Hayek. Inherent in that position is the notion that *all* economic transactions and relations should be regulated by the market; the persistence of a sector regulated by criteria other than those of the market will subvert the whole edifice of economic rationality. Grasping the force of this argument Brus and Laski note that 'if marketization is the right direction of change, it must be pursued consistently'. This would involve accepting the need for a capital market in which profit-maximizing firms compete for credit, as well as the inevitability of unemployment and economic fluctuations. Not surprisingly, Brus and Laski conclude with the observation that if marketization is the only viable strategy, then 'not only the original Marxist promise has to be cast aside as anachronistic, but also the very concept of transition from capitalism to socialism'.[7]

These are indeed the true stakes of the argument. If the market is the only mechanism of rational economy, then it should govern all aspects of economic life. And, as I argue in detail below, it is no good saying that market socialism proposes to combine socialist objectives with market-governed allocation. For that is to dodge the crucial issue: whether it is possible to have an economy regulated by market prices which obeys, at least in part, a non-market logic. It is not the persistence of market transactions and mechanisms that is at issue here; it is the question of the economic logic inherent in market *regulation* of the economy – i.e. whether the allocation of goods, services, labour and investment funds will be determined by the opportunities for profit indicated by the price signals given in competitive markets. The latter, I argue, spells the death of any meaningful notion of socialism, as Brus and Laski concede. The choice, therefore, is socialism *or* market regulation. And it is better to be clear on this than to pretend, as Frederic Jameson puts it, 'that socialism really has nothing to do with socialism itself any longer'.[8]

For what market socialists propose, unwittingly in most cases, is a 'socialism' based on a labour market and wage-labour – i.e. a system in which labour-power is commodified. Market regulation, as I outline below, is not possible unless labour-power is bought and sold on the market. Genuine commodity prices can be formed only if the value of the labour input to the production process is itself determined (priced) through the market. And this requires that workers receive market-determined wages, that their labour take the form of *wage-labour*. Again, Mises could not be clearer on the matter. In the market economy, he writes, 'man deals with other people's labor in the same way he deals with all scarce material factors of production'. And, he continues, 'as far as there are wages, labor is dealt with like any material factor of production and bought and sold on the market'.[9]

Yet these statements take us onto Marx's terrain. For it was he who demonstrated that the innermost secret of capitalism is the commodification of labour-power and that the latter underpins exploitation and capitalist accumulation. The key to the capitalist economy, therefore, is the market in human labour-power. And this insight, systematically pursued, explodes the entire fetishistic universe of classical political economy and renders nonsensical all notions of 'market socialism'.

Wage-Labour, Accumulation and Market Regulation

The essential character of capitalist society is determined by the fact that the *market in labour* comes to structure and dominate the overwhelming bulk of economic activities. What distinguishes capitalism is not the existence of a market *per se*, but rather the fact that the basic social relation between producing and exploiting classes is structured in market terms – around the sale and purchase of human labour-power. This has the consequence that the capitalist economy is governed by the law of value (expressed through the market) which reduces human labour-power to a thing, and establishes the domination of living labour (human productive activity in the here and now) by past products of labour (dead labour, capital). Moreover, the market cannot be the regulator of economic reproduction until labour-power is commodified; it follows, therefore, that a market-regulated economy is an economy based on wage-labour. Most defences of market socialism make no effort even to address, never mind confront, these arguments concerning labour-power, the law of value and market regulation. Given their vital importance to any thorough understanding of market economy, it is worth clarifying a few of these key points at this stage in our discussion.

The existence of commodity production, of production for exchange, is not unique to capitalism. Elements of commodity production have existed within diverse modes of social production. But the laws of commodity exchange do not come to govern the regulation and reproduction of the economy without the commodification of labour-power: 'only where wage-labour is its basis does commodity production impose itself upon society as a whole'.[10] For without the transformation of labour-power into a commodity, the fundamental law of commodity production and exchange (the law of value) – which dictates that commodity exchange take place according to socially necessary labour times established competitively on the market – will not regulate the economy.

This can be seen if we consider commodity production by peasant proprietors whose subsistence is not dependent on access to the market. To the degree to which a share of the output of the household is produced for the market, we have production oriented to exchange; the peasants discover the exchange-value of their commodities once they are brought to the market. But, because the peasant household is not separated from the means of production and subsistence (the peasants possess land and can thus produce a wide range of goods for consumption), these commodities will not as a rule exchange at their values (according to the socially necessary abstract labour they contain). On the contrary, since the economic survival of peasant proprietors such as these does not depend on exchange – they produce much of what they consume directly on the land they possess and could in principle withdraw entirely from the market and revert to producing only for direct consumption – the labour they devote to commodity production is not priced by the market. Much of their labour is concrete, private labour producing use-values for direct consumption. As a result, it is entirely rational for them to engage in commodity production (in order to procure certain use-values available through market exchange) even when the price provided by the market in no way corresponds to their costs of subsistence during the time they devote to producing for the market. Given their non-market access to means of subsistence, this need not be disastrous for members of the peasant household. Their economic reproduction is not governed by market exchange. Consequently, they could continue to subsist on their own direct production and enter into market exchanges which do not conform to market rationality. They are under no economic compulsion to conform to the (abstract) standards of the market since their survival is not *market-dependent*, i.e. they have non-market means of reproducing themselves.

Although they are entering into exchange, in other words, they are producing for the market not as a result of economic compulsion, but because of choices with respect to use-values. They are deciding whether it is worth it to them to work x hours in order to produce commodity y for the market which can be sold so that they might purchase so much of commodity z (which they do not produce for themselves). This is not production governed by exchange (and hence by value and abstract labour). The labour-time of peasant proprietors such as these remains concrete. Their economic reproduction is not dependent on the pricing of their labour by the market; they do not run the risk of starving should they be unable to transform their concrete useful labour into abstract social labour, or should the terms of that transformation (the market price of their commodity) be inadequate to recompense their costs of production. Their labour thus remains private and need not conform to social norms.

But things are radically different in an economy where the direct producers have been separated from the means of production – or even where independent producers are market-dependent, i.e. their costs of production are determined by the market and their survival depends upon market prices for their commodities which meet or exceed their market-determined costs. Now the products of concrete labour must exchange with money at a price sufficient to enable the direct producers to reproduce themselves. Moreover, this exchange must be on terms that meet or exceed their original costs of production. Only now do we have production *governed* by exchange, a situation in which economic reproduction depends on producers organizing their concrete labour processes according to the standards of the market (human labour in the abstract). All inputs into the production process now pass through the market and are monetized (receive a money price). And only now can it be said that the market regulates the allocation of labour and all goods and services:

> the product wholly assumes the form of a commodity only – as a result of the fact that the entire product has to be transformed into exchange-value and that also all the ingredients necessary for its production enter it as commodities.[11]

Short of the domination of direct producers by the market – which determines the money costs of their means of production and subsistence and forces them to produce for the market and at average levels of productivity – the value of labour-time will not be determined by the market. Historically, the separation of workers from the means of production and subsistence and the creation of a system of wage-labour were the crucial historical preconditions of generalizing commodity/market relations. This was so for two reasons: millions of producers were made market-dependent through dispossession of non-market means of subsistence (land, common rights, etc.); and the subsequent commodification of their labour-power created a genuine labour market in which 'labour' became yet another market-determined cost of production. In these circumstances, there is a constant drive to have the concrete labour processes involved in commodity production conform to the average levels of social productivity, i.e. to transform concrete into abstract labour. Short of this, the market cannot produce 'rational market prices', i.e. prices based on market determination of the values of commodities. The commodification of labour-power has historically been the key to 'rational' market prices. Before proceeding further, let us take a moment to clarify a few essential terms.

Concrete labour refers to the unique production process undertaken by an individual, while abstract labour describes the *social value* of that labour as it is expressed through the exchange of commodities on the market (a value which is determined by the labour time 'socially necessary' to produce a commodity). Thus, 10 hours of concrete labour expended in producing a commodity may be worth only 8 hours of average social labour when it comes to exchanging with other products on the market. The market, in other words, translates concrete (individual) labour into abstract (social) labour, and it does so via the medium of money.

In a system of unsocialized production for exchange, the social value of a commodity appears only on the market. It is the market which confers social being and social value on the commodity by telling the producer the price at which it will exchange. The specific commodity must therefore express its social value in something outside itself. It is impossible, after all, for any specific commodity to present the labour which went into producing it as directly social labour. Since there is a gap between individual (concrete) and social (abstract) labour, the commodity can express its social value only indirectly, through the medium of something else. And this is the role of money – to function as a 'general equivalent', a representative of human labour in the abstract, which mediates every exchange transaction and quantifies the social value of each and every act of concrete labour.

This takes us to the danger that haunts producers who are governed by exchange (as opposed to those whose reproduction is not governed by the market). For it is in the nature of the commodity form that the translation of use-value into exchange-value, of concrete into abstract labour may not occur, that specific acts of concrete labour may fail to achieve universality as exchange values. It is an ever-present possibility that some producers will fail the test of the market, that they will be unable to find a buyer for the use-values they have produced. Nearly as dangerous is the possibility that the terms of the translation of concrete into abstract labour, the ratio between market price and original costs of production, will not be adequate to reproduce the commodity-producing unit.

For it is not enough simply that a use-value realize itself as an exchange-value (by exchanging for money), that its concrete labour be translated into socially necessary abstract labour. Even should that translation occur, the bigger the gap between the two terms, the less concrete labour approximates to the average level of productivity reflected in socially necessary labour-time, the greater the risk that the translation will take place on terms which prevent the producing unit from reproducing itself (i.e. that market revenues fall short of costs of production). For this reason, commodity producers experience the law of value – exchange governed by socially necessary labour time – as an external pressure. Should they fail to produce efficiently enough, the prices which rule the market will be insufficient to redeem their actual costs of production. The result will be a failure of self-reproduction of the producing unit (bankruptcy).

Because exchange is not guaranteed, there is a competitive scramble to meet or exceed average levels of productivity (socially necessary labour-times). The divisions inherent in the commodity form thus reproduce themselves as relations of competition between the producing units. And this means that producing units whose interactions are regulated by the market relate to one another as *capitals*. Capital, as Marx never tired of repeating, is a social relation, a key aspect of which is the compulsion of individual units of production (by the threat of bankruptcy) to try to better the productivity of other units. The necessity of translating concrete into abstract labour, of exchanging commodity for money, makes competition an essential feature of the relations between the individual producing units – indeed, this is a fundamental part of what makes such market-regulated entities *capitals*.

It is this which Marx has in mind when he writes that 'the reciprocal repulsion between capitals is already contained in capital as realized exchange-value'; and it is why capital can only exist in the form of *many capitals*. Because individual (concrete) and social (abstract) labour are separated under a system of commodity production, they can only be reunited by means of a competitive struggle among individual producers to realize the social value of their products. The divisions at the heart of the commodity and capital thus manifest themselves in competition between capitals: 'Conceptually, *competition* is nothing other that the inner *nature of capital*, its essential character, appearing in and realized as the reciprocal interaction of many capitals with one another, the inner tendency as external necessity.'[12]

And what is this 'inner nature of capital', its 'inner tendency'? Put simply, it is the drive to accumulate by means of exploitation. For it is of the nature of the commodity/market economy that the producers feel the external pressure of the law of value (production according to socially necessary levels of productivity) as a pressure to develop the forces of production. The surest means of surviving the competition of the market is continually to raise the productivity

of labour, to produce a given good in less time. 'Capital therefore
has an immanent drive, and a constant tendency, towards increasing
the productivity of labour, in order to cheapen commodities and
by cheapening commodities, to cheapen the worker himself.'[13]

And this can only mean systematic exploitation. For the key to
increasing the productivity of labour is the utilization of the most
advanced means of production; and this requires the expenditure
of enormous sums which must be generated through the profits
(surplus value) of the producing unit itself. It follows that successful
accumulation will rest on a constant drive to maximize surplus-value
– unpaid labour which takes the form of capital as means of production. The drive to accumulate is thus a drive to maximize surplus-
value which can be transformed into new and more efficient means
of production: 'Accumulate, accumulate! That is Moses and the
prophets! ... Therefore save, save, i.e. reconvert the greatest possible
portion of surplus-value or surplus product into capital.'[14]

One of the greatest misconceptions about capitalism is the notion
that these tendencies flow from the motivations of a class of private
owners of the means of production. Yet the reality is quite different:
the drive to accumulate by means of exploitation is inherent in the
generalization of the commodity form. An economy based on that
form, in which economic reproduction occurs by means of exchange
according to market criteria (socially necessary labour-time), will
inevitably produce all of its basic relations, irrespective of the precise
form of ownership. For what is crucial to capitalism is not a specific
form of ownership of the means of production, but rather the *capital
relation*, that relation in which the direct producers are dominated
by the means of production and the incessant drive to develop and
expand them. 'The rule of the capitalist over the worker', insists
Marx, 'is nothing but the rule of the independent *conditions of labour*
over the *worker*.' It is not the capitalist who creates these conditions;
these conditions create the capitalist: 'The capitalist functions only
as *personified* capital, capital as a person ...' This is what it means
when Marx writes elsewhere that 'capital is essentially *capitalist*',
capitalism refers to that specific set of social relations in which
workers are subjected to the pressures of exploitative accumulation
in order that the producing unit can survive in the world of commodity exchange.[15]

Indeed, these relations can exist even where there is no apparent
capitalist. It makes little difference if workers 'sell' their labour-power
to collectives under their own control. So long as these enterprises

are engaged in commodity production, so long as their revenues are governed by market prices, then wage-labour will prevail since the fund for wages will be determined by the market prices for their commodities. And so long as they are forced to accumulate in order to meet socially necessary labour-times, which are determined on the market, then the provision of these wages themselves will depend on the success of strategies of 'self-exploitation', i.e. the accumulation of a surplus from their own labour which enables the workers to utilize a quality and quantity of means of production which ensure the market viability of the firm. This is why even workers' co-operatives producing commodities for the market will tend inevitably to 'become their own capitalist' – they will be driven by market competition to accumulate a growing surplus from their own labour in order to invest in new means of production which give them a fighting chance to meet the survival conditions established on the market.[16]

Workers acting as 'their own capitalist' may sound odd to those who have accepted the image of capital as identifiable private owners and employers. But once we grasp capital as a social relation inherent in the generalization of the commodity form – especially with respect to labour-power – then it becomes clear that the precise form in which capital is personified is an entirely secondary question. The key issue is the compulsion to competitive accumulation which entails the domination of living labour by dead labour – something which can occur even within a worker-managed firm producing for ex-change. The struggle for socialism is thus not just, or even principally, about the struggle against a certain group of capitalists, however crucial that may be as a point of departure. More important, it is about overturning capital – the system of wage-labour and its basic dynamic, competitive accumulation:

> the idea held by some socialists that we need capital but not the capitalists is altogether wrong. It is posited within the concept of capital that the objective conditions of labour – and these are its own product – take on a *personality* towards it, or, what is the same thing, that they are posited as the property of a personality alien to the worker.[17]

Capitalist relations and imperatives are thus built into an economy regulated by commodity production and exchange, an economy in which each producing unit is under a constant pressure to accumulate at the expense of labour in order to raise levels of productivity. This is why it is not enough for workers to establish control of their places of work. As important as workers' self-management within the enterprise may be, it cannot break free of the logic of the market unless the working class can establish democratic, planned control of the economy. Reuniting workers with the means of production is thus about more than workers' control at the level of the firm; it also requires democratic control of the economic reproduction of society – otherwise the means of production will continue to be subject to the market-driven imperative to accumulate at the expense of living labour. And the latter is a form of the separation of workers from the means of production. Overcoming that separation involves reuniting the 'collective worker' – the whole working class – with society's means of production. That means overcoming the separation between producing units which characterizes the market system. Workers' control is not possible, in other words, in a situation in which groups of workers continue to relate their labour and its products to those of other workers by means of the market. So long as acts of concrete labour are connected only through the market, society's means of production will obey the competitive imperative to accumulation as an end in itself and will thus continue to evade the control of the direct producers – which is to say that they will remain a form of capital.

One can see some of these effects in the case of the Yugoslav economy of the 1960s, 1970s and 1980s. Yugoslavia was that Stalinist state which most seriously tried to co-ordinate elements of workers' participation in the firm with market regulation. And the results were entirely consistent with the analysis we have presented: inherent tendencies towards unemployment (partially relieved for a time through emigration), inflation, *increasing* social inequality, and concentration and centralization of capital.[18] The Yugoslav case demonstrates that market regulation imposes its own imperatives on the firm irrespective of its structure of ownership or the degree of workers' self-management (which in the Yugoslav case was often exaggerated by commentators). As one socialist critic rightly notes, 'Yugoslav history suggests that self-management can be destroyed by economic conditions external to the firm, even when supported by a full panoply of intra-firm self-management laws and institutions'.[19]

All the basic tendencies of classical capitalism are thus inherent in an economy regulated by the market. If the market is to price the bulk of goods and services in order to provide signals guiding production and consumption, then labour-power will have to be commodified, i.e. its price (wages) will have to be determined competitively through the market. And the wages which the market determines will have to be held to a level adequate to the drive to accumulate as an end in itself (in order to maintain the market viability of the firm). There can be no market regulation, in short, without a labour market, the wages system, and the unplanned drive to accumulate for the sake of further accumulation. For market socialists to argue that they intend something else, that they intend to guarantee the reproduction of human beings independently of the market, or that their objective is to regulate and direct accumulation according to social objectives, is to accept the subordination of market processes to non-market criteria – and thus to abandon any reasonable notion of market socialism. Yet not to do so, to insist on the rationality of market regulation, is to accept wage-labour and the law of value – and the relations of exploitation these entail.

Failure to grasp this point produces enormous confusion among market socialists. One writes, for example, that 'exploitation is not the consequence of the market *per se*'. He then proceeds to argue that the market could be put to good use 'in a society where the means of production were publicly owned and where workers controlled the polity and the enterprise'.[20] However, this is to evade the crucial issue. For while non-exploitative relations could indeed exist in the context of various market mechanisms subordinated to socialist planning (a point to which I shall return), this is not the argument made by modern market socialists. Their claim is for the superiority of the market as a *regulator* of economic life. Yet market regulation in a context in which 'workers controlled the polity and the enterprise' presupposes that, having established social ownership and workers' control of production and the state, workers would accept that wages, conditions, hours and the structure and intensity of the work process should all be dictated by production for the market on the basis of the law of value. If so, then capitalist social relations would congeal once again whether they expressed themselves in terms of capitalist competition between workers' co-operatives, state capitalism (control of publicly owned means of production by a bureaucratic group which 'personifies' capital), or through the crystallization of a new class of capitalist managers within the enterprise itself.

If instead workers resist the logic of market regulation, if they insist upon the priority of non-market criteria (and thus on their right to determine the structure of social production on the basis of some attempt to ascertain social need), then they have committed themselves to transcending the market, to regulating their labour and the allocation of goods and services according to criteria other than those of prices and profits. This would mean moving the economy in the direction of demarketization, however much market mechanisms might be utilized in a context of planned regulation.

The debate between classical Marxism and market socialism is thus not over different means of achieving a shared goal. What is at issue is the very possibility of defetishizing economic life, of uniting 'freely associated producers' in a democratic process in which they regulate and plan the expenditure of human labour and the utilization of means of production in order to satisfy freely expressed needs. To reject this possibility is to embrace the inevitability of alienated labour, exploitation and the unplanned and anarchic drive towards competitive accumulation – and it is to renounce the achievement of anything that might recognizably pass as socialism.

The Political Economy of the Working Class

Compelling as this analysis of commodities, money and the market may be, it invites an obvious question: can this critique realize itself, can it pass from theoretical investigation to practical politics? Is it possible, in other words, to develop a meaningful political practice oriented to the transcendence of commodities and the market? And can it delineate principles which would guide the economic regulation of a non-market socialism? These questions are crucial given Marx's well-known aversion to abstract speculation and utopian prognostication about the future order of society.[21] For Marx, criticism is meaningful only if it is based on a real social movement. It follows that any serious discussion of the economics of socialism must take as its point of departure the actual political economy of the working-class struggle against capitalism.

Commentators have generally ignored the extent to which Marx attempted to do precisely that. His *Inaugural Address of the Working Men's International Association* (September 1864) describes two victories for 'the political economy of the working class': the Ten Hours Bill, which imposed some limits on the length of the working day; and the creation of co-operative factories run by workers.[22] The nature of these 'victories' is a key to deciphering the political economy of the working class.

The essence of the political economy of capital is the exploitation of labour, the maximization of surplus-value for capital. But whereas capital defines wealth in terms of the maximization of surplus labour, for workers 'wealth is disposable time and nothing more'. The Ten Hours Bill, like more than a century of subsequent working-class struggle internationally, demonstrates that workers strive to limit the time in which they are subject to the dictates of capital, to win time for their own free self-development. For workers, 'free time, disposable time, is wealth itself, partly for the enjoyment of the product, partly for the free activity which – unlike labour – is not dominated by the pressure of an extraneous purpose'.[23]

From this principle flows the basic dynamic of a socialist economy, its tendency to develop the forces of production not in order to produce surplus value, but in order to reduce the amount of necessary social labour performed by its members. A society of freely associated producers would thus organize production with the following principle to the fore:

> The free development of individualities, and hence not the reduction of necessary labour time so as to posit surplus labour, but rather the general reduction of the necessary labour of society to a minimum, which then corresponds to the artistic, scientific, etc. development of the individuals in the time set free, and with the means created for all of them.[24]

This principle, embodied in workers' struggles to shorten the working day, had for Marx already found its corresponding form of production: the co-operative factory. The co-operatives, he suggested, 'have shown that production on a large scale, and in accord with the behests of modern science, may be carried on without the existence of a class of masters'. Not that Marx was starry-eyed about co-operative production within capitalism. On the contrary, he recognized that, because they operated in the atomized framework of commodity exchange, they would inevitably reproduce the 'defects of the existing system' by forcing workers to become 'their own capitalist' and to subject themselves to competitive pressures to exploit their own labour.[25] However, notwithstanding this severe deficiency, co-operative production prefigured a society based upon 'associated labour'; indeed, the very deficiencies of co-operative workplaces within capitalism underlined the need for workers to overthrow the rule of capital. The limits imposed by capitalism on workers' co-operatives highlight the fact that 'to convert social production into one large and harmonious system of free and co-operative labour, *general social changes* are wanted,' changes which can be realized only 'by the transfer of the organized forces of society, viz. the state power, from capitalists and landlords to the producers themselves'.[26] And, as I have noted above, reuniting workers with the means of production involves much more than instituting workers' control at the level of the firm; it also requires establishing democratic control of the whole process of economic regulation of society. The battle for the political economy of the working class is thus a struggle for the reconstruction of the economic system on radically new principles.

On their own, reductions in the working day and co-operative factories are not incompatible with the rule of capital. But they represent principles – the maximization of free, disposable time and co-operative production – which are antithetical to the imperatives of capitalism. Further, struggles based on these principles underline the incompatibility of the rule of capital with the political economy of labour. Whereas the political economy of capital requires 'the blind rule of supply and demand', the struggle for an alternative political economy of the working class points towards 'social production controlled by social foresight'. Moreover, the constant efforts of capital to dilute, undermine and roll back workers' gains within capitalism highlight the need for workers to conquer political power. Without this, the political economy of the working class cannot become the basis of a new society.[27]

But what does Marx mean by a society based on 'social production controlled by social foresight'? Part of the answer is that he intends a society in which production is carried on 'by freely associated men ... under their conscious and planned control' – a society of 'freely associated producers'. There is a crucial political notion involved in the concept of 'free association' – the idea that a socialist society will be self-regulating, a form of society in which there is no need for an external agency (the state) which stands over and against individuals. Indeed, Marx's hostility to the capitalist market is internally related to his hostility to the state: both express modes of social alienation in which human beings are unable to regulate and govern their economic and political affairs democratically, and in which institutions and mechanisms outside their control dominate and direct their life activities. It is worth underlining this point, since part of Marx's argument is that *a society governed by the market requires a state*. The state, Marx tells us in his critique of Hegel's *Philosophy of Right*, is an expression of alienated life activity. And the burden of his early writings was to show that where human beings do not control their labour, their most fundamental activity as a species, they will be unable to control their social and political interactions. Where an alienated mechanism – the market – is required to govern economic life, so a separate and alien institution (or set of institutions) will be necessary to impose order on the political community. Contrary to some market socialists, then, the market is not an alternative to the state; the one presupposes the other.[28] For this reason, only a revolutionary democratization of economic life which transcends the market can lead to the dissolution of alienated political power. The struggle against the state is integrally connected to the struggle against the market.

Social production thus necessitates democratic control. We have seen that it also requires 'social foresight'; and this can only mean economic planning. Marx speaks, for example, of 'a society where the producers govern their production by a plan drawn up in advance'; and he maintains that the most fundamental part of such a process would be the 'apportionment' of labour-time 'in accordance with a definite social plan'.[29] The conscious organization of human labour and its products is the index of a qualitatively higher form of social organization. Marx's concern is not for some grandiose administrative plan for the social direction of all economic phenomena; rather, it is for the liberation of that essential human life activity – labour – from the dictates of an alienated and not yet fully human mode of existence.

Social planning of production means first and foremost the involvement of the producers in determining how their labour will contribute to the satisfaction of freely determined social needs. This is not a problem settled unconsciously through interactions among things; rather, it is to be resolved through conscious interaction among the producers themselves. This is what it means to speak of 'social foresight' governing social production. It follows that 'the labour of the individual is posited from the outset as social labour ... He therefore has no particular product to exchange. His product is *not an exchange value*.' For this reason, in 'a co-operative society based on common ownership of the means of production', the labour expended in creating products does not 'appear here *as the value* of these products, as a material thing possessed by them, since now, in contrast to capitalist society, individual labour no longer exists in an indirect fashion but directly as a component part of the total labour'.[30]

This takes us to the threshold of the problem of economic calculation, the indices which would be used to guide socialist economic planning. But before proceeding to this, it is important to address five main objections that the Marxist perspective typically encounters. In responding to these, we will be in a better position to discuss the real challenges that confront socialist planning of economic life.[31]

Five Objections: Individuals, Needs, Abundance, Plan and Transition

The first objection to the Marxian conception of socialism we shall consider is the flimsiest of the lot: the claim that Marx's socialism envisages the suppression of any private sphere, the absorption of individuality by society. Acccording to Jean Cohen, Marx's famous 'social individual' is divested even of that 'moment of particularity' which comes from belonging to one social class among others. 'Since Marx never discussed the "private" or the "particular" except as that which has to be abolished with the abolition of capitalism', she writes, 'one can only presume that in the fully transparent socialized communist society envisioned in *Capital* it would no longer exist.'[32] This is a staggering claim. That Cohen's 'presumption' is belied by even the most cursory examination of the texts seems not to matter. Note, for example, that Marx does not simply refer to 'social individuals', but to '*free* social individuals' and that he treats 'the *free* development of individualities', or, alternatively, 'the full development of individuality' as the hallmark of a socialist society. Moreover, Marx's overwhelming insistence on time as 'the room of human development' is a nonsense without some recognition that it is unique individuals who will be using the time freed from social production to pursue their own self-development.[33] But this central goal of socialism – the free development of the individual – has an essential precondition: the subjection of economic life to collective and democratic control. The emergence of the 'free social individual' must be 'based on the universal development of individuals and on their subordination of their communal, social productivity as their social wealth'.[34]

This brings us, second, to a more serious argument: the assertion that Marx's whole discussion of production for needs involves a fundamental incoherence. This claim has been advanced most convincingly by Kate Soper in *On Human Needs*. Soper recognizes the great strength of Marx's insistence that needs are not fixed and predetermined, but open-ended and historical. Yet this very position, she insists, undermines his critique of capitalism in terms of its failure to satisfy the 'true needs' of the majority. After all, a critique from the standpoint of 'true needs' presupposes some standard of fixed, demonstrable needs whose lack of satisfaction constitutes the ground for condemnation of capitalism. There is thus an irresolvable tension between the 'cognitive and normative discourses' one finds in Marx, between his historical and open-ended conceptualization of needs and his normative critique of capitalism from the standpoint of 'true needs'. As a result of this tension, Marx allegedly lapses into a naturalization of politics by reverting to the idea that there are identifiable natural needs whose satisfaction would be the central goal of socialist society.[35]

The whole of this argument pivots on a failure to grasp the theoretical foundation of Marx's critical theory. For the entire thrust of Marx's position, the very reason that he eschewed the abstract moralizing of the Left Hegelians and utopian socialists, has to do with his commitment to the idea of *immanent critique*. Put simply, Marx transformed Hegel's claim that philosophy 'is its own time apprehended in thought' into the view that a profound and comprehensive critique of society must disavow abstract speculation and flights of fancy by grounding itself in the actual social and historical forces pressing towards a societal transformation.[36] The forces of socialist transformation must develop within capitalist society; otherwise socialism is a purely abstract (hence unreal) utopia. And in terms of the human beings who constitute those forces – the working class – this can only mean they develop needs whose satisfaction requires the overthrow of the existing mode of production. Marx does not require an abstract and ahistorical theory of natural needs to underpin his critique of capitalism; that critique stands or falls on the evidence of workers pushing for the satisfaction of historically created needs which conflict with the imperatives of the present system (accumulation of capital).[37]

It seems clear that, however important a whole range of needs may be, the most significant of these for Marx is the need for individual self-development. Broadly categorizing society in terms of the development of human freedom, Marx sees three great phases in the evolution of economic life: first, forms of society characterized by ties of personal dependence, in which members are bound to the community (often in hierarchical and exploitative relations); second, a form of society based on the 'emancipation' of individuals from such ties to the community, and the development of personal 'independence' by way of alienation through exchange relations involving commodities, prices and money; and, finally, developing within the latter he finds the potential for a form of concrete universality in which communal arrangements provide the framework for an association 'in which the free development of each is the precondition for the free development of all'.[38]

Capitalism constitutes the second of these three phases. It is here, Marx writes, that 'a system of general social metabolism, of universal relations, of all-round needs and capacities is formed for the first time'. Marx insists that without the development of these 'universal relations', albeit relations which are merely abstractly universal, and of 'all-round needs and capacities' (which cannot be fully realized), there could be no basis for concrete socialist criticism: 'if we did not find concealed in society as it is the material conditions of production and the corresponding relations of exchange prerequisite for a classless society, then all attempts to explode it would be quixotic.'[39]

Marx's position does not require a naturalistic theory of needs. It requires merely a theorization which demonstrates: (1) that capitalism generates needs (especially for individual self-development), which it systematically fails to satisfy; (2) that this failure of need-satisfaction induces class struggle which, on the side of the working class, creates an impetus toward societal transformation; and (3) that the productive forces and system of universal exchange developed within capitalism are capable of being mastered collectively and democratically (a capacity that is prefigured in workers' co-operatives).

We now arrive at the third objection: the notion that Marx's account of universal and all-round development of individuals presupposes conditions of unlimited availability of goods and services. This objection is formulated, especially by Alec Nove, in a manner which suggests its complete absorption in bourgeois economics. Mainstream economics characteristically conceives of the individual as a consumer, not as a producer. The shopping mall, not the workplace, is the basis of its models. Consistent with this premiss, Nove imagines that Marx's discussion of a society of abundance can only mean an unlimited (and potentially infinite) supply of consumer goods (and the producer goods necessary to their production). And this, he objects, is to conjure away the central category of economics – scarcity. Marx, he claims, thus 'solves' the problems of economics by a sleight of hand.[40] But it should now be obvious that abundance for Marx has a radically different meaning. Starting from the view that human beings are productive creatures, Marx recognized that the supply of goods and services presupposed the expenditure of human labour. Further, he held that, however much conditions of work can be transformed for the better, labour will always remain a 'realm of necessity'. Indeed, 'the realm of freedom really begins', Marx writes, 'only where labour determined by expediency and external necessity ends; it lies by its very nature beyond the sphere of material production proper'. It follows that for Marx abundance means not simply a decent and secure level of provision of material goods and services; it also entails time away from labour, time for 'the free intellectual and social activity of the individual'.[41]

Abundance thus means raising the productivity of labour through the application of the powers of science and co-operation. It means shortening the working day (or week) to create a greater amount of time outside the sphere of necessary labour, and it ought as well to mean radically reducing socially necessary reproductive labour performed privately (childrearing, cooking, cleaning) by socializing significant amounts of such necessary labour. Marx's concept of abundance is thus integrally connected to his view of human freedom. It requires a recognition of the finitude of the life and time of individuals so that a balance can be achieved between needs for material and cultural goods, and needs for 'free intellectual and social activity'. As in all economy, therefore, time is the crucial issue. Clearly, then, any post-capitalist economy will have to negotiate two different imperatives: on the one hand, the necessity to provide a decent and secure standard of living for all; and, on the other, the need of working people for more time for 'free intellectual and social activity'. To be sure, there is a real tension here. The hallmark of a workers' state will be the participation of citizens – through workers' councils and neighbourhood committees – in processes of mass democracy which attempt to reconcile these different needs. But if they are to be conducted in a manner consistent with the aspiration towards free individual self-development, these decision-making processes require a framework in which

the associated producers govern the human metabolism with nature in a rational way ... accomplishing it with the least expenditure of energy and in conditions most worthy and appropriate for their human nature. But this always remains a realm of necessity. The true realm of freedom, the development of human powers as an end in itself, begins beyond it, though it can only flourish with this realm of necessity as its basis. The reduction of the working day is the basic prerequisite.[42]

This is the 'value problem', which persists in a post-capitalist society: democratic and communal regulation of individual labour-time in accordance with the need for self-development. When Marx writes that 'economy of time, to this all economy ultimately reduces itself', it is this human criterion he has in mind. As biological beings, humans must produce their means of subsistence, and the means of production which make this possible. This is the foundational principle of the materialist conception of history. But in a society which has developed the forces of social production to a point where it is possible to banish that scarcity which threatens biological existence and, indeed, to sustain a significant level of cultural expression and interaction, and in which the exploitation of labour has been elimi-nated, 'economy of time, along with the planned distribution of labour time among the various branches of production, remains the first economic law'. Rather than the asocial arrangement in which human beings first labour, and, then, through the media of money and the market, discover the match between their productive activity and social need, socialist economy rests on a democratic process for creating the framework for such a match through conscious human regulation.

In such a situation, 'the labour of the individual is posited from the outset as social labour'. The individual 'has no particular product to exchange. His product is *not an exchange value*.' Nevertheless, this does not abolish all problems of economy: 'On the basis of communal production the determination of time remains, of course, essential.'[43] What it does, however, is remove this problem from the reified world of commodities and money, and subject it to the democratic delib-eration of social individuals.

This brings us to the fourth objection, the claim that the Marxist conception of planning implies some sort of omniscience on the part of the direct producers – a thesis which is central to Nove's argument and is echoed by Blackburn. Yet, Marx's position was that a degree of error was inevitable, as were accidental and unanticipated changes in material and socio-economic circumstances. As a result, he sug-gested that the dominant tendency within a socialist economy should be 'a perpetual relative overproduction'. Only in this way could the prospect of shortages be guarded against. And for this reason, he spoke of planned creation of a 'surplus product' in the form of 'an insurance and reserve fund' to offset the possibility of underproduc-tion and shortage. Indeed, planned overproduction is for Marx 'equivalent to control by society over the objective means of its own reproduction,' for it signifies that human beings have deliberately produced to avoid that condition which is most deleterious to human life – underproduction and scarcity.[44]

There is no great difficulty in principle with planned over-production. The bulk of producer and consumer goods are not perishables; a planned overproduction of, let us say, 5 per cent poses no insurmountable technical or logistical problems. The real issue in dispute here is not omniscience, but democracy. What the critics of socialist planning need to demonstrate is why elected delegates of workers and neighbourhood committees could not be involved in establishing a framework plan for the economy which started from a democratically established scale of social priorities with respect, for example, to food, housing, health, education and childcare facilities, clothing, libraries, transportation, electricity and cultural and recreational goods. To be sure, this would require detailed information on technical coefficients of production, investment of resources in producer goods industries, the scales of socially necessary labour-time appropriate to various plans, differential environmental effects of various alternatives, the trade-offs between levels of output of different goods, and so on. And all of this undoubtedly requires an important amount of 'expert' information, which will not readily be available to each and every individual. But why could not the agencies responsible for accumulating and providing such information be subjected to democratic regulation? And why could not computerized inventory control and just-in-time delivery systems be adapted to democratic planning? Are the problems here so insurmountable that we would do better to stick with commodities and money, exploitation and crisis?

Nove has a simple answer: the only alternative to markets, commodity prices and money is a dominating, Stalinist-type bureaucracy. But this is an assertion which ultimately falls back on claims that individuals are naturally lazy and self-interested (in the narrow, asocial sense of the term characteristic of bourgeois economics). Thus, since democratic planning is not possible, the best we can hope for is the 'democracy' of consumer sovereignty established through personal choice in competitive markets.[45] As with most versions of market socialism, we end up with the market *and* with a state that looks remarkably like the bureaucratic machinery of capitalist society. We are thus left with a perspective in which 'commodity production and markets' are depicted as the only alternative to bureaucratic state tyranny – with the claim, in other words, that there is no attainable form of society more conducive to freedom than one regulated by the market. Small wonder that at the end of his study Nove feels compelled to ask of his model: 'is it socialism?' It is a question which begs to be asked – and answered in the negative.

This takes us finally to the most subtle objection to Marx's position: the claim that his sketch of an alternative economic order conjures away the real problems of an actually existing society making the transition from a recognizable capitalism towards a feasible socialism. Marx, we are told, had little, if anything, to offer with respect to the burning problem of socialist economy – the road to be taken by a society embarking upon a transition to socialism. Even if Marx's socialist ideal is defensible – which for Nove it is not – it is said to be irrelevant to the issue at hand.

It is true that Marx rejected the elitist game of fashioning blueprints for a future society; but he was not averse to sketching out broad principles derived from a study of the developmental tendencies of capitalism and workers' struggles within the system.[46] Thus, in his *Critique of the Gotha Programme*, he explicitly addressed the problem of

> a communist society, not as it has *developed* on its own foundations, but, on the contrary, as it emerges from capitalist society; which is thus in every respect, economically, morally, and intellectually, still stamped with the birthmarks of the old society from whose womb it emerges.

Here, he points out, it would not yet be possible to organize economic life according to the principle of 'to each according to their need'. That principle presupposes a level of economic and cultural development which would not yet have been achieved. In the first instance, then, distribution would be governed by the principle of 'to each according to their ability', i.e. that each would draw from the stock of social wealth in proportion to their individual contribution. This, Marx suggests, would be done on the basis of 'a certificate' entitling each individual to withdraw 'from the social stock of means of consumption' to the degree to which they have contributed. This involves, of course, the same principle 'which regulates the exchange of commodities' in capitalist society – exchange on the basis of labour-time. But, Marx insists, here 'content and form are changed, because under the altered circumstances no one can give anything except his labour, and because, on the other hand, nothing can pass into the ownership of individuals except individual means of consumption'. We have then, transitional arrangements which are 'still stigmatized by a bourgeois limitation': since individuals are unequal

in various ways (age, strength, training, etc.), distribution acccording
to labour is 'a right of inequality'. What prevents it from becoming
the basis of structural inequalities and exploitation, however, is the
political form of the state, mass workers' democracy and social
ownership of the means of production. The latter cannot be subject
to criteria of market competition, individual ownership or profitability, otherwise bourgeois right would give rise to bourgeois relations
of production.[47]

What, then, of Marx's discussion of labour 'certificates'? Isn't this
merely an admission that money will still be the regulator of such
a transitional society? Here we encounter an area of fundamental
confusion in much of the recent debate over market socialism.
Certificates which simply represent a sum of hours of labour performed are not 'money' in any recognizably capitalist sense. Money,
as we have spelled out above, is the mechanism which defines and
measures the value of alienated labour performed in an asocial
context; indeed money is that 'thing' which transforms concrete
labour into abstract labour. Where labour is communal, and its
allocation determined in advance, a certificate or voucher is not
money; it is not the mechanism which validates the social character
of individual labour, nor does it transform the latter into the former.
While such certificates represent a means of exchange, they do not
perform the function of informing the producers of the social value
of their private labour. Labour certificates would merely establish
a basis on which a given expenditure of labour could be exchanged
for a share of the general stock of the products of social labour. But
this is not *commodity exchange* since the 'value' of labour, its entitlement
to share of social wealth, is established prior to production. As a result,
'the communal character of production would make the product into
a communal, general product from the outset'. Elaborating on such
a system of production, Marx contrasts it with commodity production
in the following way:

> On the basis of exchange values, labour is *posited* as general only through
> *exchange*. But on this foundation [communal economy] it would be *posited*
> as such before exchange; i.e. the exchange of products would in no way
> be the medium by which the participation of the individual in general
> production is mediated.[48]

The role of labour certificates is to allow mediation of individual
and social labour to take place. But this is not a mediation which
establishes the social value of individual labour, since this has been

established from the start; it is merely a means of mediating the exchange of labour for labour. Thus, what Marx says about Owen's 'labour money' applies with equal force to his own labour certificate: it 'is no more "money" than a theatre ticket is.'[49] Nevertheless, social allocation by means of labour certificates is merely a transitional form, one 'still stigmatized by a bourgeois limitation'. How, then, does this form of social allocation wither away?

The heart of the issue here is the continued growth of the socialized consumption sector of the transitional economy, that sector governed by need not ability. To the degree to which housing, basic diet, clothing, health care, education, childcare, electricity, water, sanitation, transportation and access to cultural and recreational activities are guaranteed as social rights, the realm of 'bourgeois right' contracts. Within advanced capitalism, tendencies towards the socialization of services such as health and education have existed for a long time, as a result of working-class pressure and capital's need for the physical and cultural reproduction of labour-power – albeit tendencies distorted by and subordinated to capital accumulation. In an economy freed from the dynamics of exploitation, and disengaging from the pressures of accumulation, this realm of guaranteed social consumption could increasingly encroach on that governed by exchange. Material and cultural subsistence would decreasingly depend on transactions involving labour certificates or any such pseudo-money.

The expansion of the guaranteed consumption sector would thus be one side of the *decommodification* of labour-power. Subsistence, enjoyment and cultural self-development would decreasingly depend on individual purchases governed by the value of individual labour performed (although the requirement of social labour for healthy adults would always remain). Indeed, with the development of productive forces and cultural levels, socially guaranteed consumption would regularly expand. Increasingly, the allocation of social wealth would be governed by rights based on individual needs. Thus, the sphere of individual consumption through the market – in which many prices might be regulated as I discuss below – would contract in relative, although perhaps not absolute, terms. While they would play a subsidiary role for the satisfaction of unique, personal needs best realized outside the socialized consumption sector, such markets would occupy a marginal, if nevertheless significant, role as the expansion of the socialized sector pursued the logic of demarketization, decommodification and demonetization of economic life.

The model I am discussing need not dictate individual consumption patterns. There is no reason, for example, why a socially guaranteed consumption package could not be constructed to cater to individual preferences by allowing a variety of 'menus' with a range of possible 'substitutions' – e.g. a trade-off of better than average housing for reduced claims elsewhere, or of transportation vouchers (some combination of air, rail and automotive transport coupons) for increased claims for clothing or musical instruments, or by allowing individuals to engage in more social labour (and thus forgo time for personal self-development) so that they might make more purchases from the regulated market. Moreover, flexibility would also be provided through face-to-face exchanges by individuals of various goods, vouchers or coupons (e.g. transport coupons for tickets to cultural events). Such transactions are not, of course, commodity exchange (they are merely the exchange of use-values) and even when they are governed by regulated market prices, they do not involve universal regulation of the reproduction of individuals by a representative of abstract labour.

The Question of Calculation

At this point my argument is likely to be attacked on the grounds that I betray a 'fundamentalist' unwillingness to come to terms with the calculation problem which would exist in a socialist economy (or in a society transitional towards socialism). Robin Blackburn in particular believes that Marxists have failed to produce an adequate reply to the arguments of Ludwig von Mises and Friedrich von Hayek, according to whom rational economic decision-making is not possible without the price signals provided by genuinely competitive markets based on private ownership of the means of production and investment on the basis of profit-maximization. Not that Blackburn supports the anti-socialist case put by Mises and Hayek; but he clearly believes that these critics correctly identified the Achilles' heel of socialist economic thought.[50]

Most remarkable about this line of argument is that those who pursue it most vigorously fail to grasp its full implications. The Mises–Hayek critique of socialism according to the criterion of calculation is inseparable from an underlying theory of economic life – one that rests on the most thoroughgoing methodological individualism – and lacks coherence outside the framework of that theory. Grant the conclusion — that rational economic calculation is not possible without competitive market prices – and one must logically accept large chunks of the underlying theory *and* the view that socialism is an inherently irrational project.

To reject the Mises–Hayek perspective on calculation is not, therefore, a simple manoeuvre designed to evade difficulties. Rather, it is to proclaim one's opposition to an entirely fetishistic vision of economic life. For, as Joseph Schumpeter pointed out, the Austrian anti-socialists proceed from 'the model of a Crusoe economy' in which atomistic, self-seeking individuals choose to exchange the products of their isolated labours. More than this, they then push the subjectivism and individualism of this model to the most absurd extremes. All of economic life, they insist, is driven by consumer needs, thereby conveniently ignoring the role of labour in economic life. Having reified both the individual and his or her status as a consumer, they then simply conflate all of economic life with market exchange. To live is to exchange. It follows, in the words of a modern follower of Mises and Hayek, that 'the core of economic theory is the theory of markets'.[51]

Having reduced economic relations to subjectively driven market exchanges between atomized, self-seeking individuals, the neo-Austrians are free to treat pure profit as a subjective phenomenon, as a function of discovery by entrepreneurs. And since we are all potential discoverers, it follows that 'we are all entrepreneurs'. Moreover, the entrepreneurial opportunities offered to us all provide the moral justification of capitalist private property: discoverers, we are told, should be free to enjoy the fruits of their discovery. The ethical justification of capitalism thus comes down to the principle of 'finders, keepers'.[52] That the neo-Austrian position culminates in such a pathetic banality is not accidental. Every step of the way, the argument is crudity piled on crudity. Rampant subjectivism, extreme methodological individualism and capitalist apologetics combine to produce what must be judged among the poorest performances in the history of economic thought.[53]

It is not the purpose of this study to offer yet another critique of neo-Austrian economics. I develop these points only to illustrate a key blindspot in recent arguments which take the ultra-liberal position on economic calculation as the point of departure for claims that the market is the only mechanism that can regulate a socialist economy. With respect to this argument, two crucial points need to be made about the nature of markets.

First, the best that markets can do is to provide information to people about a range of private economic choices available to them as isolated individuals. Markets are incapable of providing any meaningful information about the *social effects* of private economic transactions. Yet as an important body of literature in welfare economics has shown, virtually all allegedly private economic acts have such public effects, or 'externalities' to use the jargon of modern economics. Even Robinson Crusoe could not act in isolation. And in real-world situations, as E.K. Hunt points out,

> most of the millions of acts of production and consumption in which we daily engage involve externalities ... Since the vast majority of productive and consumptive acts are social, i.e., to some degree they involve more than one person, it follows that they will involve externalities.[34]

Thus, whatever may be said about the ability of markets to provide information relevant to individual decision-making – and this has been vastly overrated – they are not equipped to calculate trans-individual effects and are thus biased against social decision-making. Calculation of public effects of economic action requires information that markets do not and cannot provide. Not only do markets presuppose atomized individuals; by depriving people of information about social effects, and by rewarding only acts judged according to private, asocial criteria, they perpetuate atomism. Moreover, because they produce unregulated social effects, markets create enormous social inefficiencies. It is no overstatement, therefore, when the authors of *Quiet Revolution in Welfare Economics* write that

> markets bias and obstruct the flow of essential information, promote antisocial incentives over equally powerful motivations that need not be socially destructive, and generate increasingly inefficient allocations of resources. In sum ... markets promote snowballing individualism that is demonstrably non-optimal regardless of whether they are combined with private or public enterprise.[36]

It is also worth noting in this regard that an important line of argument has demonstrated convincingly that market-based hierarchies within the firm also create inefficiencies within the individual unit of production.[56]

This brings us to the second general point that needs to be made about markets: market information is equally incapable of providing rational criteria for investment. Austrian and neo-Austrian economics have been unable to construct a meaningful theory of capital and investment – a failing which is thinly disguised by rhetoric about 'uncertainty', 'entrepreneurship' and 'discovery'.[57] Markets provide no rational criteria which could guide the building of roads, sewers, steel mills, communication networks, schools, parks, clothing factories, childcare centres, hospitals, bakeries or hydroelectric stations. 'No individual entrepreneur', writes one economist,

> can estimate on the basis of market data alone, the productivity of investment until the investment plans of other entrepreneurs are determined. How can they say what the productivity of investment in a particular town will be until one knows whether or not that new railway line is to be laid down? We have here something analogous to external effects in production.[58]

Such investment decisions require long-run estimates of collective needs. Yet the whole point about prices is that they reflect present data. Investment inevitably changes these data over time by creating new incomes, changing technical conditions of production, altering consumer preferences (by providing new goods), and so on. The longer the time-horizon, the more glaring this problem becomes. How is the market to regulate decisions with respect to public goods which will, at least in large measure, be consumed by the next generation?

Once we move outside the fictionalized world of Crusoe economics, it becomes clear that markets are entirely incapable of guiding economic decisions that affect the well-being of large numbers of people, whether these involve a long time-horizon or choices concerning public goods like hospitals and parks. For this reason, one economist rightly notes that market theory offers 'no satisfactory "competitive solution" to the problems of the horizon and terminal capital equipment or of investment generally'.[59] Indeed, the neo-Austrians implicitly recognize this fact when they reject the fictional world of general equilibrium theory. Precisely because investment decisions are a step into the unknown in a world governed by price signals, they create enormous instability. In an unregulated system, many investments will fail, some will be precarious, others will be too successful (hence inflationary). It follows that investment in a market-regulated system will produce *disequilibrium*, not the self-adjusting equilibrium of neo-classical economics.[60]

The ultra-liberal theory of calculation rests, therefore, on the flimsiest of assumptions: that rational economic decision-making can reasonably be conceptualized according to a model of consumption choices by isolated individuals. Recognize the inherently social nature of economic action and the problem of the time-horizon associated with investment, however, and market calculation stands exposed as little more than an ideological construct with almost no explanatory power. That socialist writers could so blithely treat the market as a central mechanism of socialist economy is testimony to the current sway of fetishistic thinking on the Left.

But if the market cannot provide the sort of information needed to regulate a socialist economy – and, indeed, is structurally biased against the provision of such information – by what mechanisms and processes might a socialist economy regulate itself? A number of general points can be made in response to this question.

First, the key variables in establishing the framework of the economy are the structure of social consumption and the rate and direction of investment. The structure of consumption determines the order of priority given to a whole range of needs, and thus the allocation of productive resources to the provision of food, clothing, means of transportation and communication, housing, healthcare, education, and so on. The structure of investment similarly prioritizes such things over time. The rate of investment, on the other hand, 'determines what can be called the intertemporal distribution of welfare': how much of today's output will be devoted to meeting needs in the here-and-now and how much will be devoted to future needs.[61] The division of the social product between consumption and investment thus reflects social choices with respect to present and future needs.

Capitalism 'resolves' these issues according to the criterion of profitability. The structure of consumption is determined by capitalist decisions as to the production of those goods which, given the existing distribution of income, are expected to provide the highest rate of return. Similarly, the structure and rate of investment are determined by capital's assessment of the potential profit of various investment projects. In both cases, democratic public discussion of these issues is irrelevant. These are 'private' decisions which pertain to capital by virtue of its property rights, however much the welfare of the majority may be affected by them.

Central to the political economy of socialism is the attempt to establish democratic control over macroeconomic decisions which determine the fundamental structure of consumption and the rate and structure of investment. This involves asserting the inherently social nature of such processes, and the basic priority of macroeconomic decision-making in economic life. And it involves challenging the methodological individualism of market economics and its mystified view of such decisions as mere aggregates of private microeconomic decisions.

By treating macroeconomics as a sum of individual micro-decisions, market theory maintains that 'if the environment is being destroyed, if housing and health are inadequate while deodorants and hair sprays are abundant, or if products are unsafe, it is because people "want" it this way'.[62] One of the central achievements of Marx's critique of market economics was to expose the inversion of subject and object, means and ends which characterizes this outlook. Contrary to the view that commodity-market mechanisms are purely technical in nature and can be accommodated to any range of choices, Marx demonstrated that market regulation (expressed through the law of value) treats as natural what are in fact thoroughly social relations and processes: the commodification of labour-power, the subordination of use-value to exchange-value, of need to profit, and of consumption to accumulation.

By demonstrating that subordination of human needs to reified automatic laws is the very essence of market regulation, Marxism proposes the socialization and demarketization of economic life. Indeed these are simply two sides of the same coin. To socialize macroeconomic decisions – by subjecting them to genuine democratic and public control – is to push back the frontiers of the market, to affirm the right of the majority to regulate processes which have hitherto governed their lives.

Related to this first principle, the socialization of macroeconomic decision-making, is a second: demarketization of subsistence. The ideology of the market holds that the market is a mechanism for the expression of needs (which are reflected in prices) and that the level of demand for a given commodity is a reflection of the 'need' for it relative to other goods given existing supplies. The absurdity of this view has been pointed out by countless critics: if a shortage of some good drives up prices and reduces demand and consumption, then it follows that the 'need' for that good has diminished. Since 'human needs only exist in markets', notes one such critic, market ideology implies that 'raising prices thereby reduces human needs' (since these can only be measured by market demand).[63] A simple example – that of 'famine' – illustrates the obscenity of this argument. It is commonplace in a market-regulated economy for people to starve while food is being exported from the famine region.

This is a completely 'rational' outcome in terms of market principles. Indeed, since domestic demand for food (measured by ability to pay) is low, market economics suggests that there is no domestic 'need' for the exported food. Here a basic truth is revealed: the market does not and cannot acknowledge needs which do not obey its dictate – the provision of means of exchange (a representative of abstract human labour). For it is not needs which are the issue; it is 'entitlement', the ability to pay in terms of the universal equivalent of the market. Thus, in the words of Amartya Sen, 'food being *exported* from famine-stricken areas may be a "natural" characteristic of the market, which respects entitlements rather than needs'.[64]

Against this inverted logic, socialism asserts the priority of directly ascertaining needs. It rejects the notion that these exist only to the degree to which they are mediated by market relations and money. Socialism thus aspires to detach access to subsistence from market exchange – which entails, as I have argued above, the growth of the 'social wage' provided through the socialized consumption sector. The struggle to liberate distribution of wealth from market regulation is a drive to supersede the principle of fee for service. What applies to socialized healthcare and education (at least to some degree in most advanced capitalist nations) can equally apply to housing, basic diet, transportation, communication, energy, recreation, and so on.

It is obvious that a whole range of material, cultural and historical factors would determine the rate at which progress towards this goal could be achieved. But that such a goal is possible and feasible is demonstrated by the partial socialization of a limited range of services within capitalist society. Market socialists have offered no compelling argument as to why socialization, freed from the rule of capital, could not be radically extended. And those who accept that it is feasible seem unable to recognize that the expansion of free social services necessarily involves the contraction of the market and undermines market regulation of the economy.

At this point the impatient critic is likely to throw down two more challenges. First, can one reasonably imagine that social planning could provide appropriate supplies of the multiplicity of goods and services to which most people in advanced capitalist society have become accustomed? And second, do I mean to suggest that socialist economy will be indifferent to efficiencies of production and distribution? To both questions my answer is no. But this involves much less of a concession to the market than my critic is likely to believe.

Let me start by granting that it is not reasonable to expect society to plan precise output levels for hundreds of thousands of goods. I see no reason, however, to be especially troubled by this fact. To begin with, the bulk of human subsistence consists of a fairly limited range of basic goods. Even in the case of the advanced capitalist countries, Ernest Mandel points out, 'private consumers may purchase a few thousand different goods in the course of their whole life-cycle (even that would be an exaggerated estimate for many of them)'. Production schedules for such goods could easily be devised without price signals since, even in capitalist societies, 'the bulk of current production corresponds to established consumption patterns and predetermined production techniques that are largely if not completely independent of the market'.[65] As for fluctuations in demand, again, for most of these goods, lack of price information poses little problem. There is little lost by way of efficiency, after all, in choosing to overproduce a wide range of goods with a reasonable shelf-life, e.g. soaps and shampoos, canned and many packaged foods, household appliances, clothing goods, pencils, pens, notepaper, and so on. The same applies to many industrial goods, from ball bearings to aluminium and electrical generators. Furthermore, inventory control systems are far more effective than price signals for tracking changes in the demand for goods – which is precisely why capitalists devote so much effort and investment to perfecting them. As Pat Devine notes, price changes are not

> necessary to provide the information that changes in capacity are needed. A change in demand first becomes apparent as a change in the quantity being sold at the existing price and is therefore reflected in changes in stocks or orders. Such changes are perfectly good indicators or signals that an imbalance between demand and current output has developed. … Price changes in response to changes in demand are therefore not necessary for purpose of providing information about the need to adjust capacity.[66]

It is worth noting that this argument does not apply only to supplies of consumer goods. The development of computer-regulated just-in-time delivery systems for parts and components in manufacturing processes demonstrates that price signals are not required to assure the availability of all the elements necessary to manufacture a final product. Modern corporations engage in much more planning than mainstream economics likes to acknowledge. There is no reason why a socialist economy could not refine and develop such systems of planning within the firm.

Still, there are good reasons for not including all goods and services in a social planning process. Goods of lower overall priority to the community, those whose scarcities are a significant factor, and those which cater to highly specialized needs could best be left to individual market exchange. Which goods would enter this sphere depends in the first instance on the make-up of the socialized sector. But let us assume that a range of 'luxury' goods would be allocated according to market exchange: fine wines, exotic teas and coffees, speciality clothing and home furnishing, some electrical goods, and the like. Let us also assume that this sector allocates goods whose consumption society prefers to discourage, such as cigarettes. Further, let us assume that a range of personal services are available in this sphere, e.g. hairdressing and cosmetic surgery.

The existence of a sector such as this would provide for a large number of individual preferences to be accommodated according to supply and demand. But this need not involve much of a concession to market principles for reasons which should now be clear. First, the scope of this sector would be limited. So long as the bulk of subsistence goods are not procured through the market, then the latter will not regulate the social and material reproduction of human beings. Second, even in such a sphere, there is no reason that the market should reign supreme. Many market prices could be regulated by public policy. Cigarettes provide an obvious case in point. If society wishes to discourage consumption of such goods, or to force consumers to pay for obvious external effects, it can easily 'tax' them (as do modern capitalist societies) by setting prices well above costs of production and making them unresponsive to a decrease in demand. The 'taxes' accrued in this way could be appropriated by public authorities to subsidize the socialized consumption sector, to create special funds (e.g. for environmental clean-up), or to lower the prices of certain goods still allocated through the market (hardcover books perhaps). The crucial point here is that even this limited market sector could be regulated according to social criteria and need not, therefore, involve any move towards market regulation.[67] In the words of Wlodzimierz Brus,

A society which consciously constructs a mechanism for the functioning of its economy chooses between different combinations of direct and market forms of allocation, and subordinates commodity relations to autonomously defined goals and criteria of rationality. In this way society can overcome commodity fetishism.[68]

This comment takes us to our critic's second challenge – the problem of efficiency. Note that Brus refers to 'criteria of rationality' which are 'autonomously defined'. The emphasis here is on the plural form: criteria. For one of the characteristics of an economy moving beyond the market is its liberation from domination by the law of value, the relentless drive to reduce socially necessary labour-time in order to maximize surplus-value and the rate of accumulation. As I have argued above, this does not mean that the economy of time disappears in socialist society. It does mean, however, that the problem of time is situated within the political economy of the working class.

The cardinal principle of that political economy is 'the free development of individualities', the 'development of human powers as an end in itself'.[69] Human labour ceases to be a means to an end – the self-expansion of capital. Increasingly, the development of the many-sided creative energies and capacities of individuals becomes the ultimate goal of society. Of course, our biological and social constitution make necessary social labour inevitable. But socialist society strives to reduce such labour in order to maximize time for individual self-development. For 'wealth', as Marx puts it, 'is disposable time and nothing more'.[70]

It follows that socialist economy does possess an inbuilt drive to increase the efficiency of production: the impetus to maximize free, disposable time. And this drive can be developed as a structural incentive within the worker-controlled firm. Once output targets are set for the individual workplace – on the basis of planning according to social demand, available resources and technology and the allocation of labour – workers should be free to introduce innovations which enable them to meet those targets in fewer hours *subject to quality control criteria*.[71] So long as workers meet their output target in less time than anticipated with no diminution in quality, they ought to be free to dispose of their increased time away from social labour as they please. Their options should include taking on more social labour elsewhere in order to meet an unanticipated increase in demand for some good (provided they have the requisite skills) so that they might supplement their 'money wages' for increased purchases from the market.

But if socialism is based on the maximization of time for self-development, what does it mean to insist on a plurality of criteria of economic rationality in socialist society? Part of the answer to this question is implied in our reference above to quality control. While wealth consists to an important extent of disposable time, it is also more than this for the political economy of the working class. The key thing is not just the quantity of time at workers' disposable; it is also the *quality* of time – within and beyond necessary social labour. For wealth is also for Marx measured by the multiplicity and richness of needs that are satisfied (which involves a combination of goods, services and time for self-development).

Indeed, one of the progressive features of capitalism according to Marx is that it develops new needs in people, it awakens and cultivates their senses and expands the range of their enjoyments: in the course of capitalist development of the productive forces, 'the producers change, too, in that they bring out new qualities in themselves, develop themselves in production, transform themselves, develop new powers and ideas, new modes of intercourse, new needs and new language'.[72] This takes place, however, in a contradictory and one-sided way. While developing new aspirations for self-development among the producers, capitalism also restricts their opportunities to realize them. Socialism takes over and develops capital's tendency to cultivate the human being 'in a form as rich as possible in needs, because rich in qualities and relations'. But it does so in a way which liberates this positive side of capital's self-expansion from the alienation and exploitation associated with it.[73]

Three things follow from this. First, the reduction of necessary social labour cannot be at the expense of the range of human satisfactions. On the contrary, the productivity gains brought about by the development of the forces of production would in all probability be distributed in two ways, not one: by increasing the social output to raise consumption levels (and perhaps to move some goods from the sphere of market exchange into the socialized consumption sector) and, after that, by reducing necessary social labour. The second thing which follows from our qualitative criteria is that reduction in necessary labour-time could not be at the expense of the conditions of work itself. It is contrary to the political economy of the working class to increase the drudgery, monotony or hazards of work. This is why, in the very passage in which he advances the criterion of 'the development of human powers as an end in itself' as the goal of socialism, Marx also insists that this objective has as its precondition that the producers work in 'conditions most worthy and appropriate to their human nature'.[74]

Finally, reduction in necessary labour cannot be at the expense of the natural and social environment outside the workplace. Central to Marx's outlook is the view that 'man is a part of nature'; that nature is the human being's 'inorganic body'.[75] The health and well-being of this 'body' is a genuine human need. It would be unacceptable, therefore, to have one group of workers introduce an innovation which improved productivity within the workplace while adding dangerous pollutants to the land, water or atmosphere. Moreover, environmentally hazardous increases in productivity within the workplace would be socially inefficient since they would require increased labour inputs for new pollution control systems, environmental clean-up projects, and the like. It is characteristic of capitalism that, as Engels puts it, 'in relation to nature, as to society, [it] is predominantly concerned about only the immediate, the most tangible result'. Capitalism thus treats nature as a mere means to an end, the self-expansion of capital. But this leads to terrible devastation. Moreover, 'nature takes its revenge on us' for violating its inherent characteristics – as part of nature, human beings suffer from its despoilation. Using the example of capitalist agriculture, Marx argued that this mode of production only increases output 'by simultaneously undermining the original sources of all wealth – the soil and the worker'.[76]

Socialism would obey a different logic. The short-run efficiencies which dominate a mode of production governed by the maximization of surplus-value result in degradation of the worker and despoilation of the environment. For the political economy of the working class, the health of the environment – clean air and water, protection of the ozone layer, restoration of rain forests and so on – is just as much a need as is the disalienation of the labour process.

The needs of socialist citizens could not be reduced, therefore, simply to the desire to minimize necessary social labour, however important that would be. Their needs would be rich and varied. And as there is no single measure of the multiplicity of human needs, it follows that a number of separate but interrelated criteria would have to guide the planning process. In general terms, we can summarize the most fundamental objectives that would guide socialist planning as follows: (1) increasing the quantity and quality of per capita consumption (and especially its guaranteed component); (2) decreasing necessary social labour in order to maximize disposable time; (3) improving the conditions of work in order to eliminate hazards and reduce monotony and drudgery; (4) reducing private labour performed in the household (e.g. cooking, cleaning, laundry) through the creation of communal kitchens, dining areas and laundries (whose use would be entirely voluntary) and through the provision of household appliances; (5) protection of the well-being of the natural and social environment; (6) planned relative overproduction. Of course, these objectives will often point in different directions. And the choices involved cannot be translated into a single measure or means of calculation – a point which was neglected by socialist writers who intervened in the calculation debate, thus weakening their critique of the neo-Austrian position.

One of the advances represented by socialist planning is precisely that the rich and varied needs which are central to modern human existence would not be subordinated automatically to a monolithic economic law. The essence of socialist planning is that people democratically participate in the deliberations by which these criteria (and others) are balanced. Indeed, this is what it means to move from the realm of blind necessity to the realm of freedom. There is nothing metaphysical in the idea. It simply refers to the fact that democracy and conscious human deliberation would direct the basic pattern of economic reproduction of society. In such a context, the criterion of efficiency would become a means to human ends, not an end in itself to which all needs are subordinated.

But what of calculating efficiencies where these are consistent with the criteria which would guide socialist planning? Aren't indices of relative costs crucial here? And is not the great advantage of prices that they provide precisely such indices? How does one calculate the greater or lesser efficiency of various methods of production without a means of measuring all the inputs involved according to some common standard?

The very way in which these questions are posed indicates much of what is wrong with current thinking about the market. For it betrays an inability to conceive of calculation without market prices. Yet, as Oskar Lange pointed out in his principal contribution to the calculation debate, such a position confuses 'prices in the narrower sense, i.e., the exchange ratios of commodities on a market, with prices in the wider sense of "terms on which alternatives are offered"'.[77] And, notwithstanding Mises, Hayek and their accolytes, there is in principle no reason why such relative indices – or `planning prices' – could not be devised without resorting to market regulation. Indeed, one enormous advantage of devising them outside the market is that the cost of 'externalities' could enter directly into 'price' calculation. Planning prices could thus be freed from the information constraints inherent in market calculation. In addition, unlike the static data provided by the market, planning prices could be adjusted (through an equational system) to take account of the changing economic parameters brought about by investment. Posed in these terms it is clear that Schumpeter was right when he concluded that 'there is nothing wrong with the pure logic of socialism' and, indeed, that at the level of logical analysis, 'the socialist blueprint is drawn at a higher level of rationality than the pure theory of capitalism'.[78]

A common objection to this argument is that, logic aside, the sheer scale of the calculations involved would render any planning process impracticable. Let us note that this objection involves a wild exaggeration of the number of price solutions with which planning would have to cope.[79] Equally important, there is little doubt that Lange was right too when he pointed to the superiority of computers over markets for solving a system of simultaneous equations – a superiority which has to do principally with calculating economic dynamics. Computer programs can incorporate the effects of changes brought about by growth, investment and public policy decisions in a way that completely eludes the price system of the market. The computer is not just a substitute for the market, therefore; it has calculative capacities different from those of the market:

> After setting up an objective function (for instance maximising the increase of national income over a certain period) and certain constraints, future shadow prices can be calculated. These shadow prices serve as an instrument of economic accounting in long-term development plans. Actual market equilibrium prices do not suffice here, knowledge of the programmed future shadow prices is needed.
>
> Mathematical programming turns out to be an essential instrument of *optimal* long-term economic planning. ... Here, the electronic computer does not replace the market. It fulfills a function the market was never able to perform.[80]

Non-market 'prices' thus have a number of real advantages over market prices with respect to economic calculation: they can incorporate social costs ('externalities'), they can respond to changing parameters brought about by decisions outside the scope of a single firm, and they can be adjusted to take account of the anticipated effects of long-term development plans. Let me emphasize again that I am discussing 'planning prices' here, i.e. a measure of relative costs that would guide economic decisions where this is the operative criterion. This has nothing to do with market regulation of the economic reproduction of society. As far as the technical question of devising planning prices is concerned, however, my own view is that Maurice Dobb's elaboration of a model of measuring past, present and future labour inputs could serve quite effectively as a means of calculation for these purposes.

I have largely ignored Dobb's contribution to the literature on economic planning since his approach is undermined by a reliance on the Russian experience as his point of departure and, not surprisingly, on the labour market to determine wages, and by his failure even to acknowledge workers' democracy as a key to socialist planning. For these reasons, much of Dobb's work is of little or no value to the development of a political economy of socialism. But with respect to this technical problem, devising a measure of average labour inputs for purposes of socialist economic calculation, Dobb's discussion is instructive. This is especially so because, as he points out, a dated-labour system of calculation could provide a measure not merely 'of labour-expenditures actually incurred, but of potential labour-expenditures that would be imposed elsewhere if the input in question were to be put to a sub-marginal use'.[81]

Let me hasten to add, once again, that any such quantitative method of calculation would have to be subordinate to qualitative criteria (a point that is absent in Dobb). Efficiency calculations are relevant only where all other considerations are equal, or nearly so. Precisely because a range of qualitative concerns would operate autonomously, socialist society could choose methods of production which would be less cost-efficient in the short or medium term because of the less satisfactory conditions of work or the long-run depletion of natural resources associated with alternative methods. And this possibility, I repeat, is one of the features which distinguishes a planned economy from one regulated by the market.

My discussion of the calculation debate may be summarized, then, as follows. I argued, first, that the challenge thrown down by Mises and Hayek is not merely a technical one. To accept the terms of debate as they pose them is to accept that all aspects of economic life must be reduced to a single measure. All concrete labour must be reduced to a single abstract form; all human needs must be expressed via a common medium which quantifies them; human labour and the natural environment must be treated as simple commodity inputs into a production process and thus regulated according to short-run cost-efficiencies; and social needs must be treated as mere aggregates of individual market decisions.

Second, I attempted to show that socialism would set its basic economic parameters by establishing communal ownership of the means of production and social control of the structure of consumption and the rate and direction of investment. Remove these macroeconomic issues from the market and a framework plan for the economy would be in place. Connected to this, third, is the idea that the economic reproduction of human beings would be demarketized. The bulk of means of subsistence would increasingly be provided through a socialized sector based on provision of free goods and services not governed by market prices. I pointed out, fourth, that provision of a whole range of consumer goods could be regulated by inventory control systems more efficiently than by price signals (a fact that is recognized by modern capitalist firms). And I suggested in this regard that the methods of just-in-time delivery of parts and components could provide much of the information necessary to the supply of these items within manufacturing systems.

Fifth, I argued that, given the sorts of parameters involved in democratically establishing a framework plan for the economy, there need be no insoluble problem involved with calculating 'planning prices' which would allow efficient choices to be made with respect to the implementation of an economic plan. None of this need involve notions of omniscience. It involves the claim that there is an alternative to market regulation, the shortcomings of which have been obscured by the fetishistic notions prevalent among market socialists. At the same time I claimed, sixth, that there are valid reasons for leaving the allocation of a wide range of goods to individual market exchange. But even here, I pointed out, many prices could be regulated (through 'taxes' and subsidies) according to public policy.

I then took up, seventh, the efficiency argument. I maintained that the governing efficiency criterion of socialism would be the maximization of disposable time and that this provides an impetus to the development of the forces of production. But I insisted that the richness of human needs – itself a key measure of wealth – would require that this efficiency criterion be balanced by a number of qualitative concerns with respect to the quality of products, of the work process, and of the natural and social environments. While there is a single logic guiding the political economy of socialism – the satisfaction of human needs – these cannot be reduced to a single measure. Democratic debate and decision-making will be the very heart and soul of a (far from infallible) process by which people will weigh their needs and come to a set of 'tradeoffs' incorporated in an economic plan.

Finally, I argued that where a measure of efficiency is relevant, a number of comparative measures of 'costs' could be devised. I am inclined to think that Dobb's method of measuring past, present and future labour inputs could be especially useful here. Whether I am right on this technical question is not decisive. But it seems clear that Schumpeter was correct to acknowledge the economic rationality of socialism. And given the possibilities of using computers for linear programming, there is in principle no reason why accountable agencies could not devise 'planning prices' much more comprehensive and dynamic than those which regulate the market. A socialism that does not capitulate to the market is both feasible and viable. It is, ironically, market regulation, not socialist planning, which should be on trial.

Socialized Markets or Market Reformism?

At first glance my position may seem close to Diane Elson's theory of 'socialized markets'. Elson advocates an economic arrangement in which 'the process of production and reproduction of labour power is the independent variable to which the accumulation process accommodates'. She suggests, in other words, that the social and material reproduction of people should be guaranteed outside of exchange. To this end, she argues for 'public provision of health, education, water and sanitation services free of charge', the guarantee of 'a minimum money income to cover the purchase of sufficient food, clothing, shelter and household goods for a very basic living standard', and, finally, for 'free provision of access to information networks: print, telephone, photocopiers, fax machines, computers, etc'.[82]

This approach clearly has the merit of implying that labour-power be decommodified and that society move in the direction of demarketizing economic life. Yet Elson recoils from the full implications of her own analysis. She criticizes 'anti-price Marxists' for failing to appreciate 'the progressive aspects of market coordination', and for not understanding 'that a decentralized socialist economy needs a decentralized price mechanism'. Indeed, she reverts at times to an entirely mainstream view of economy, as when she claims that 'the crucial point about money and prices is that they enable us to consider alternatives'.[83] Now, as I have shown, this is not at all the case. The crucial thing about money and prices is that they embody a profound social contradiction, the alienation of individual from society, of use-value from exchange-value, of concrete from abstract labour, which requires an alien third party, a 'thing' beyond labourers and their products, to reconcile these separated elements. And this thing then comes to dominate the economic lives of the producers:

> The existence of money presupposes the objectification of the social bond ... money ... can have a social property only because individuals have alienated their own social relationship from themselves so that it takes the form of a thing.[84]

Elson appears to see none of this. It comes as no surprise then that her discussion of Marx's concept of commodity fetishism is woefully inadequate. Rather than seeing it as a theory of the value-form specific to capitalism – where the sociality of human labour takes the abstract, externalized form of a thing – she reduces it to merely 'a dramatic metaphor for the isolation problem' in which a given individual or firm does not have access to all the information necessary to make fully informed market decisions. As a result, Elson dulls the razor-sharp edge of Marx's critique of capitalism. Where Marx had intended his notion of commodity fetishism to underline the inherently alienating nature of economic life governed by commodity–money relations, Elson treats it as little more than a critique of restricted access to market information. In the end, she discusses 'socialization' of economic life not principally as a question of decommodification, but rather as a problem of fair and equal access to market information.[85]

Given this confusion, Elson ends up trying to reconcile the irreconcilable. Her useful insights as to how the production and reproduction of labour-power could be guaranteed outside the market are vitiated by her efforts to cling to market-determined money prices as the regulators of a wide array of economic transactions. For, in so far as she grants real autonomy to a 'decentralized price mechanism' to allocate labour, goods and services, she gives an asocial mechanism the power to govern the economic metabolism of society – and thus undermines socialization. If enterprises are to be governed by the laws of the market, after all, they will be compelled to accumulate in order to achieve (or better) socially necessary labour-times. The organization, intensity, hours and rhythms of work will have to be determined ultimately by the forces of market competition. Moreover, there will be a constant tension between the principles of socialization and market regulation. Either the system will allow the bankrupting of relatively inefficient enterprises (and the layoffs and unemployment that entails), or more efficient firms will have to be taxed at a higher level in order to keep those firms afloat and to continue to sustain the provision of free social services and a guaranteed minimum income – thereby undermining the market reward for successful accumulation and diluting market rationality. The clash between the logics of market-regulation on the one hand and socialization on the other will inevitably generate social discontent – either among those who are driven out of work or whose wages are driven down by market competition, or on the part of those whose market efficiency is 'penalized' by higher taxes which inhibit their ability to accumulate as rapidly as possible in the face of present or future competitive threats.

Whichever route the system chooses, the benefits of socialization will continually be undermined by the reality of market imperatives. The same conflict which is at work in the advanced capitalist countries at the moment will sooner or later come into play: either society will choose to break with market regulation in order to preserve the benefits of socialization, or it will be forced to erode the socialized sphere in order to allow market forces freer play. In the end, Elson's 'socialized markets' embody a fundamental contradiction: the coexistence of market and non-market logics of economic regulation. One or the other must ultimately assert its dominance. If Elson claims that she always intended the market to be subordinate to the logic of socialization, she will have to accept that her model will not have a genuine 'decentralized price mechanism', nor will it strictly speaking provide for the choice between economic alternatives on the basis of money prices.

This is not to deny that different mechanisms can be incorporated within a single economic system. It is to insist, rather, that the combination of utterly different economic logics is not viable. My argument has been that socialism represents the increasing subordination of market transactions to non-market regulation by the direct producers and their fellow citizens. Recognizing that autonomous markets are inherently asocial, I have argued that socialism must strive to limit, restrict and subordinate them within a framework governed by a commitment to decommodifying economic life. Elson fails to come to terms with what is at stake here: a choice between principles of economic regulation. Her position ends up entangled in a welter of contradictions which she tries to resolve with a thoroughly unconvincing appeal to the liberal notion that the key economic task is to challenge 'capital's prerogatives over information'.

We observe here a phenomenon which runs through the history of market socialism since the 1820s: a rapid descent from the lofty heights of 'socialization' to the depths of market reformism. Lack of clarity about commodities, money and market regulation continually results in attempts to revamp the market without transcending it. In Elson's case, market reformism fixes itself not on a call for co-operative stores and workshops or currency reform, but on an appeal for a 'campaign around open access to information'.[86]

This, regrettably, is the inevitable fruit of adaptation to the ideology of the market. The effort to distance onself from the barbaric legacy of Stalinism by means of compromise with the market can only lead to retreat from genuine socialism. Indeed, the trajectory of much of the Left in the aftermath of the collapse of Stalinism has been precisely that – towards accommodation with liberalism, as if trying to fit in with the dominant ideological discourse is the best way to preserve critical thought. The result has been a series of efforts to depict socialism as little more than spruced up liberalism, or as entirely compatible with the market principles of liberal economics. Considered in these terms, modern market socialism is just one facet of a general intellectual and political retreat.[87] Moreover, this retreat threatens the very integrity of the revolutionary socialist project. 'There is a real danger', notes one critic, 'that the chilling experience of Stalinism and the sobering experience of social democracy is producing a lowering of sights, a loss of focus on the priorities and values that make the socialist/communist project revolutionary and worthwhile.'[88]

Yet it is precisely now, as the laudable efforts of working people in Eastern Europe to put an end to the tyranny of Stalinism are being channelled into the dead-end of marketization, that revolutionary socialism cannot afford confusion on the question of the market. For what is happening to the economies of Eastern Europe at the moment is merely a local example of a global process of restructuring according to the dictates of the market – price competition, cost minimization, profit maximization. Now, as the world economy experiences its third major recession since the mid 1970s, is hardly the time for socialists to retreat from the fundamental idea that there is an alternative to the twin tyrannies of the market and the state: the democratic system of workers' self-government and conscious planning of social production that Marx termed a 'free association of the producers'.

The history of the working-class movement is a history of resistance to the tyranny of the market and its laws. From anti-enclosure riots to Luddite rebellions, from the campaign against the New Poor Law to struggles against factory closures and wage-cuts today in Brazil, Poland, South Africa or the United States, the working class has continually fought against domination by the market in human labour power.

It was the great achievement of Karl Marx to have theorized that struggle, to have shown the inherently alienating, competitive and exploitative nature of an economy based on the commodification of labour-power, and to have constructed a socialist perspective which demonstrated that proletarian struggles could triumph only by breaking the rule of capital – and that this meant overturning commodity and market relations. The trend of many on the Left today to embrace the market, to denounce 'anti-price Marxists', to turn to Mises and Hayek for the challenge necessary to renew socialism leads towards a renunciation of that entire legacy, and of its vision of socialism as a society in which human beings are no longer dominated by the products of their own labour.

Following that path is not the service we owe the working class movement as it confronts the immense misery and destruction of the late twentieth century. Socialist advance today requires a recovery of all that was best in Marx's critique of the capitalist market and the vision of self-emancipation which flowed from it. There, not in the ideology of the market, will we find resources for socialist renewal.

Conclusion

We have covered a lot of ground. Now let us draw some conclusions.

It has been the central argument of this book that the market economy, in which market exchange is the mechanism through which society reproduces itself economically, is necessarily a capitalist economy. Market regulation presupposes the commodification of human labour-power, without which the market cannot impose its 'rationality' on the economic process. As I have demonstrated in the first three chapters, this was grasped, however crudely, by the earliest ideologists of the market.

The ideology of the market was constructed as part of a multi-faceted attack on the working class. Its proponents set themselves on a crusade to destroy the moral economy of the poor, to undermine their claim to a right of subsistence. From Edmund Burke's objection to the old poor law that 'labor is a commodity', to Malthus's insistence that the individual has 'no claim of *right* on society for the smallest portion of food, beyond that which his labor would purchase', the ideology of the market has been concerned centrally with the creation and maintenance of a market in human labour-power.[1] To that end, all fetters on that market – from common lands, to perquisites, to the old poor law – were defined as violations of economic liberty which would have to be destroyed. And destroyed in large measure they were.

Belying its pompous declarations about the sanctity of property, the market glorified in this ideology has always rested on the propertylessness of the direct producers. Until the working poor were divested of any significant means of production of their own, there could be no truly 'free' market in labour. The original market ideologists – from early advocates of enclosure to hard-nosed opponents of poor relief – understood this. And they insisted that, since the poor would 'not seek for labour [i.e. wage-labour] until they are compelled to do it', economic compulsion would have to be the order of the day.[2] Through enclosure, extinction of common rights, elimination of perquisites, erosion of apprenticeship regulations and more, labourers were rendered increasingly dependent on the market for their economic survival. And the destruction of the old poor law sealed the process. With the New Poor Law of 1834, pre-capitalist forms of economy were essentially destroyed; as a result of the abolition of a supposed 'right to live', 'the market system proper was released'.[3]

Released from the restraints of customary and communal rights, a market system can be made to appear the most natural of things; and an ideology of the market can grow up in which the propertylessness of the poor, their utter dependence on the market for their subsistence, appears as something which has existed from time immemorial. By identifying the market in labour as an essential feature of humanity's march to liberty – that condition which best conforms to its nature – Adam Smith contributed to precisely such a naturalistic doctrine. Uncritical acceptance of the labour market defeated his social ethics, just as it did the efforts of Smithian socialists to construct a market-based alternative to exploitation.

Smith's great blindspot was his thoroughly unhistorical attitude towards wage-labour. The actual history of enclosure and expropriation, a legacy of force and violence, makes no appearance in the *Wealth of Nations*. In this one crucial respect, Smith was surpassed by his contemporary, Sir James Steuart. For Steuart posed the creation of a class of wage-labourers as a problem in need of explanation. As a result, commented Marx,

> he gives a great deal of attention to this *genesis* of capital ... He examines the process particularly in agriculture; and he rightly considers that manufacturing industry proper only came into being through this process of separation in agriculture. In Adam Smith's writings this process of separation is assumed to be already completed.[4]

From Smith onward, uncritical acceptance of this separation (the secret of the primitive accumulation of capital) became a cornerstone of the ideology of the market. While earlier writers had acknowledged the compulsion necessary to create a labour market, the *Wealth of Nations* contributed decisively to the tendency to treat the dispossession of the poor as a fact of nature. But debate over the matter was not closed. It raged again during the upsurge of British radicalism associated with the French Revolution. And this time the principal point of contention was not enclosure – it was the poor law.

It was Malthus's achievement in this context to have completed political economy's 'naturalization' of the labour market (which involved vulgarizing Smith) by making relief of poverty incompatible with the laws of nature. The ideology of the market thus culminated in a harsh fatalism with respect to the plight of the poor. Poverty and hunger were no longer issues of social and political policy; they were inevitable products of nature's laws. Capitalist social relations were thus made to appear as unchanging as the law of gravitation. 'We have every reason to believe', wrote Malthus, that society 'will always consist of a class of proprietors and a class of labourers.'[5] Wage-labour had become part of the natural order of things.

This naturalization of wage-labour corresponded to an underlying reality: once workers are separated from the means of production and subsistence, a market-regulated economy tends to perpetuate this state of affairs. The surplus product of wage-labourers continuously sustains and augments capital, and thus reproduces its monopoly of the means of production. Even if real wages rise, workers will as a rule remain dependent on the market for their means of subsistence. The market in labour thus tends to perpetuate capital and that essential condition on which it rests, the separation of labour from property.[6] This gives rise to that fetishism unique to the capitalist economy. Since the interaction of things on the market tends to reproduce wage-labour and capital, these appear to be material (not social) phenomena. Moreover, since the original compulsion on which capitalism rests (the separation of producers from means of production) is now reproduced automatically through the market, extra-economic force can pull back from centre-stage. The perception of capitalist social relations as natural is thus reinforced. For the ideologists of the market, nothing is easier, therefore, than to believe that these relations 'are themselves natural laws independent of the influence of time. They are eternal laws which must always govern society.'[7]

Precisely such fetishism plagued the efforts of the first popular critics of political economy. While seeking to eliminate exploitation, these radicals sought to do so within the framework of commodity/market relations. They undertook to purify these relations, not transcend them, by pouring new content into capitalist forms. This involved them in the fruitless exercise of trying to retain commodities and prices without a money commodity, profits without exploitation, capital without capitalists. To be sure, these popular political econo-mists often sensed the magnitude of the problems that confronted them and were thus driven 'to repudiate one condition of bourgeois production after another'.[8] When they did so, they pointed beyond the horizon of generalized commodity production and the market. But they could do little actually to move beyond that horizon, handicapped as they were by a desire to retain specifically capitalist forms of economic life.

The great achievement of Marx's critique of political economy was to show the inseparability of production for the market, money, wage-labour, competitive accumulation and exploitation. Marx's theory is simultaneously a critique of market regulation *and* a critique of all efforts at market socialism. By defetishizing the world of commodities, Marx showed that the reified laws of the market are the necessary forms in which the alienated and exploitative relations of capitalist production manifest themselves. One cannot transcend capitalism, therefore, on the basis of market regulation; the one presupposes the other.

Marx was not the first to recognize the alienated and fetishistic nature of the capitalist market system. Before him, the young Hegel, in his Lectures of 1803–4, had described the system of bourgeois economy as 'a self-propelling life of the dead, which moves hither and thither, blind and elemental', as 'a wild animal' which 'stands in constant need of being tamed and kept under control'.[9] It was clear to Hegel that the sphere of capitalist market relations did not conform to any reasonable notion of human freedom since the prerequisite of the latter is that human powers be expressed in an objective realm of self-actualization and self-determination. Because, in Hegel's words, market relations are based on the 'blind depend-ence' of individuals on one another, they constitute a system of alienation in which things of human creation take on a life and laws of their own.[10] Yet Hegel tried to work out arrangements for taming and controlling the market economy without superseding bourgeois relations. Unlike those socialists who hoped to humanize the market, however, Hegel looked to an agency outside the market – the state – to impose a universality foreign to the 'blind and elemental' particularity which characterizes market economy.

Marx saw the blatant flaw in such a solution – the market and the state are two sides of the same system of alienation, the one cannot cure the other – but he never abandoned the Hegelian insight that the capitalist market formed a 'self-propelling life of the dead', which evaded the control of its participants. Rather than calling in the state (a particularistic force in a capitalist society) to act as a universalizing force, Marx sought a genuinely dialectical solution by identifying as the key contradiction of capitalism the barrier the market represents to satisfying the needs of those who are forced to sell their labour-power as a commodity. The antagonisms at the heart of the commodity status of human labour-power drive its bearers – the working class – to break with the market and the commodity form. Rather than look for a solution outside the sphere of market economy, Marx found within that sphere the contradiction which can explode the system from within.[11]

Market socialists, however, have abandoned the critical-revolutionary import of this Marxian insight. Indeed, by adopting the view that the market is a necessary means to the satisfaction of human needs, market socialists often revert not only to a pre-Marxian position, but even to a pre-Hegelian one. Whereas Hegel recognized the thoroughly reified nature of market relations, albeit while posing a pseudo-solution, market socialists tend not to grasp even the insights he provided, let alone their powerful development by Marx into a systematic critique of market regulation and the reification of economic life. Mesmerized by the credit-based 'boom' of western capitalism throughout the 1980s, and traumatized by the disintegration of Stalinist regimes, which they depicted, incorrectly, as species of socialism or workers' states, many on the Left have turned to the market as their last hope for preserving the possibility of a better society. Yet they have done so at a time when the enormous *irrationality* of the market is re-emerging with a shocking brutality. As I write this Conclusion, the world economy is mired in its third slump since 1974. Estimates suggest that as many as 43 million people are living in hunger in the richest nation on the planet. Meanwhile, General Motors, the world's largest corporation, has announced plans to lay off 74,000 North American employees; and IBM, the world's biggest producer of computer goods reports that it will have to cut 20,000 jobs more than the 40,000 it predicted only a few months ago.

These are just local examples of the 'laws of the market' imposing their imperatives during a period of crisis in the world economy. And, short-lived 'recoveries' notwithstanding, the worst is yet to come. Already, half of Africa's 645 million people are living, according to a United Nations report, in 'absolute poverty' – and their conditions are worsening with each year. Meanwhile, that policeman of the world market, the International Monetary Fund, sucks $580 million per year out of Africa as a result of 'fair' market transactions with respect to debt repayment. In the poorest part of Africa, forty sub-Saharan countries are paying out $1 billion every month to finance their crushing debt load. And on top of all this, more than $30 billion in capital has fled the continent since 1986, all in conformity with the market's imperative to maximize profits. As for the claim that Africa's crisis derives from its insufficient absorption into the world market, one need merely examine the brief record of marketizaion in Eastern Europe: unemployment is soaring in Poland and the former East Germany; gross national product in Bulgaria has plummeted by one half; and Yugoslavia, that Stalinist state which most fully sought the therapy of the market, has disintegrated into rival nationalisms and civil war in the context of a debilitating market-driven economic crisis.[12]

It is impossible to predict the outcome of this situation, in part because it will be determined by political responses as much as by economic dynamics. The indications are, however, that we are living through a period of continuing crisis whose devastating impact imperils the well-being of millions. Indeed, the system's crisis tendencies mean that it will continue to do so with a regularity and brutality which endangers the very survival of our species.[13] It is no use saying that these phenomena are not inherent in the market, that the market could be 'tamed' and used for human purposes within different institutional arrangements. For the issue in dispute, as I have shown, is not the survival of various market mechanisms in a society moving away from capitalism, but whether the market can be the prime regulator of a socialist economy, whether human beings are capable of regulating their economic relations other than through the blind and elemental tyranny of things. The choice is either the socialization of economic life (and the subordination of markets to social regulation), or market regulation and its systematically asocial effects.

It is for these reasons that the trend to embrace market socialism represents such a profound retreat. For it involves a renunciation of the heart and soul of the socialist project: the struggle for a society beyond alienated labour, exploitation, competition and crisis, a society in which human beings begin to direct their economic relations according to conscious plan. What Rosa Luxemburg wrote of Eduard Bernstein more than ninety years ago applies with equal force in this case: the market socialist 'does not really choose a more tranquil, surer and slower road to the *same* goal. He chooses a *different* goal.

Instead of taking a stand for a new social order, he takes a stand for the surface modifications of the old order.'[14]

Now, as humanity experiences the crises of the late twentieth century, is hardly the time for lowering socialist sights, for settling for 'surface modifications of the old order' by attempting a reconciliation with the market. It is precisely now that we need a vigorous reassertion of the socialist critique of the tyranny of the market, and a spirited defence of the view that working people can emancipate themselves from that tyranny, abolish their alienation from the means of production, and establish collective and democratic control of economic life. That goal, in various forms, has been the inspiration for millions who have braved repression, jail, torture and death in their fight for a world based on the emancipation of labour. And so it will continue to be for those who are today resisting the devastation wrought by the market, be they in Asia, Africa, North or South America, Eastern or Western Europe. However much the ideology of the market may have come to dominate political discourse, even in socialist circles, the *reality* of the market will produce opposition and revolt. A perspective which abandons the critique of alienation, exploitation and the market developed by Marx, and which seeks a reconciliation with the market, can be no guide for those who wage such struggles. And it does not deserve the mantle of socialism.

Notes

Introduction

1. The dominant text in the turn to market socialism is Alec Nove, the *Economics of Feasible Socialism* (London: George Allen and Unwin, 1983). For a representative sample of recent writing which attempts to reconcile socialism with the market, see Geoff Hodgson, *The Democratic Economy* (Harmondsworth: Penguin, 1984); Wlodzimierz Brus and Kazimierz Laski, *From Marx to the Market: Socialism in Search of an Economic System* (Oxford: Clarendon, 1989); Diane Elson, 'Market Socialism or Socialization of the Market?' *New Left Review* 172 (November–December 1988); Robin Blackburn, 'Fin de Siècle: Socialism After the Crash' *New Left Review* 185 (January–February 1991). While there are significant and important differences between these authors – indeed Elton would disavow the label 'market socialism' – they are all concerned with the use of the market as a key mechanism of socialist economy. I critically discuss their views in chapter 6 of this study. Extravagant claims for the end of history and the uncontested reign of liberal capitalism were the stuff of Francis Fukayama's 'The End of History', picked up by a number of periodicals and serialized in twelve parts in the Toronto *Globe and Mail*, 'Canada's National Newspaper', December 1–18 1989.

2. Ludwig von Mises, 'Economic Calculation in the Socialist Commonwealth', in *Collectivist Economic Planning*, ed. Friedrich von Hayek (London: George Routledge and Sons, 1935), p. 105.

3. Blackburn, p. 41; Hodgson, p. 171; Nove, p.77

4. Brus and Laski, Preface, n.p., p. 151. I should note that these authors equivocate as to the desirability of full-scale marketization; but their argument represents an increasing capitulation to the cult of the market.

5. My own view on the nature of Stalinist Russia derive from the 'state caapitalist' analysis developed within the Trotskyist tradition. The classic work is Tony Cliff, *State Capitalism in Russia*, 2nd edn (London: Pluto, 1974). The roots of this perspective in the post-World War 2 Trotskyist movement are sketched in Alex Callinicos, *Trotskyism* (Minneapolis: University of Minnesota Press, 1990), especially ch. 5.

1. Origins of Capitalism and the Market

1. Ludwig von Mises, *Human Action: a Treatise on Economics* (New Haven: Yale University Press, 1949). For the term 'fetish-worshipper', see Karl Marx, *Theories of Surplus Value*, Part 3 (Moscow: Progress, 1971), p. 130. The most developed version of the theory of commodity fetishism is to be found in Karl Marx, *Capital*, vol. 1, trans.

Ben Fowkes (Harmondsworth: Penguin, 1976), pp. 163–77.

2. Mises, *Human Action*, pp. 615, 616.

3. Marx, *Capital*, vol. 1, p. 874.

4. Ibid., p. 876.

5. For a brief overview of these developments, see David McNally, *Political Economy and the Rise of Capitalism* (Berkeley: University of California Press, 1988), pp. 2–8.

6. On average peasant holdings, see M.M. Postan, *The Medieval Economy and Society* (Harmondsworth: Penguin Books, 1975), p. 144; and C.G.A. Clay, *Economic Expansion and Social Change: England 1500–1700*, vol. 1 (Cambridge: Cambridge University Press, 1984), p. 61. On the development of large peasant farms, see Rodney Hilton, *The Economic Development of Some Leicestershire Estates in the Fourteenth and Fifteenth Centuries* (Oxford: Oxford University Press, 1940), pp. 94–100; and his *The English Peasantry in the Later Middle Ages* (Oxford: Oxford University Press, 1975), pp. 46–8, 164–6; R.H. Tawney, *The Agrarian Problem in the Sixteenth Century* (1912; rpt New York: Harper and Row, 1967), pp. 70–81; and W.G. Hoskins, *The Midland Peasant: The Economic and Social History of a Leicestershire Village* (London: Macmillan, 1957), pp. 72, 87, 141–2; Mildred Campbell, *The English Yeoman under Elizabeth and the Early Stuarts* (New Haven: Yale University Press, 1942), p. 102.

7. Hilton, *English Peasantry*, p. 168. See also Tawney, p. 139; John E. Martin, *Feudalism to Capitalism: Peasant and Landlord in English Agrarian Development* (London: Macmillan, 1983), pp. 118, 129; and Clay, 1: p. 78.

8. Tawney, p. 74. Sources for the data in Table 1.1 are described in Richard Lachmann, *From Manor to Market: Structural Change in England, 1536–1640* (Madison: University of Wisconsin Press, 1987), p. 129. See also J.C.K. Cornwall, *Wealth and Society in Early Sixteenth Century England* (London: Routledge and Kegan Paul, 1988), pp. 16–17, 200–10.

9. See, for example, F.M.L. Thompson, 'The Social Distribution of Landed Property in England Since the Sixteenth Century', *Economic History Review*, 2nd series, 19 (1966), pp. 505–17; and Gordon E. Mingay, *Enclosure and the Small Farmer in the Age of the Industrial Revolution* (London: Macmillan, 1968).

10. See, for example, the purely technical definition of agricultural history offered by J.D. Chambers and G.E. Mingay, *The Agricultural Revolution 1750–1880* (London: B.T. Batsford, 1966), p. 1.

11. H.J. Habakkuk, 'English Landownership, 1680–1740', *Economic History Review* 9 (1940), p. 16.

12. Robert Brenner, 'Agrarian Class Structure and Economic Development in Pre-Industrial Europe', in *The Brenner Debate*, eds T.H. Ashton and C.H.E. Philpin (Cambridge: Cambridge University Press, 1985), pp. 48, 61. See also Philip Jenkins, *The Making of a Ruling Class: The Glamorgan Gentry 1640–1790* (Cambridge: Cambridge University Press, 1983), p. 51.

13. F.M.L. Thompson, 'Landownership and Economic Growth in England in the Eighteenth Century ', in *Agrarian Change and Economic Development*, eds E.L. Jones and S.J. Woolf (London: Methuen, 1969), p. 45.

14. Charles Wilson, *England's Apprenticeship, 1603–1763* (London: Longman, 1965), p. 33; Clay, 1, p. 118; Gordon Mingay, 'The Size of Farms in the Eighteenth Century', *Economic History Review*, 2nd series, 14 (1961–2), pp. 473–9.

15. Chambers and Mingay, p. 84; Clay, 1, p. 118. On the cost of enclosure, see Barry Holderness, 'Capital Formation in Agriculture', in *Aspects of Capital Investment in Great Britain, 1750–1850*, eds J.P.P. Higgins and Sidney Pollard (London: Methuen, 1971), pp. 159–83. The expression with respect to this crucial century comes from E.P. Thompson, 'The Peculiarities of the English', in his *The Poverty of Theory and Other Essays*

(London: Merlin, 1978), p. 42.

16. J.D. Chambers, 'Enclosure and the Labour Supply', *Economic History Review*, 2nd series, 5 (1953), pp. 319–43.

17. Chambers and Mingay provide the classic account of this position.

18. Tawney, p. 217. For background on common fields, see Joan Thirsk, 'The Common Fields' and 'Origin of the Common Fields', in her *Rural Economy of England* (London: Hambledon Press, 1984).

19. J.R. Wordie, 'The Chronology of English Enclosure, 1500–1914', *Economic History Review*, 2nd series (1983), pp. 492–4.

20. Joan Thirsk, *Tudor Enclosures* (London: Routledge and Kegan Paul, 1959), pp. 20–21; Martin, pp. 134–8. See also John T. Swain, *Industry Before the Industrial Revolution: North-East Lancashire c. 1500–1640* (Manchester: Manchester University Press, 1986).

21. Wordie, pp. 486, 495.

22. Barrington Moore Jr., *Social Origins of Dictatorship and Democracy* (Boston: Beacon Press, 1966), p. 29.

23. Marx, *Capital*, 1, pp. 878, 895.

24. N.F.R. Crafts, 'Enclosure and Labor Supply Revisited', *Explorations in Economic History* 15 (1978), pp. 176–7, 180. K.D.M. Snell, *Annals of the Labouring Poor: Social Change and Agrarian England 1660–1990* (Cambridge: Cambridge University Press, 1985), pp. 197–206. See also Hoskins, pp. 269–73.

25. Mingay, *Enclosure*, p. 31.

26. Ibid., pp. 27–32.

27. Mingay, 'Size of Farms', pp. 472–3.

28. R.A. Butlin, 'The Enclosure of Open Fields and Extinction of Common Rights in England, *circa* 1600–1750: a review' in *Change in the Countryside: Essays on Rural England 1500–1900*, eds H.S.A. Fox and R.A. Butlin (London: Institute of British Geographers, 1779), p. 75.

29. J.R. Wordie, 'Social Change on the Levenson-Gower Estates, 1714–1832', *Economic History Review*, 2nd series, 27 (1974), pp. 596–601. See also Clay, 1, p. 97; and Peter Kriedte, *Peasants, Landlords and Merchant Capitalists: Europe and the World Economy, 1500–1800*, (Leamington Spa: Berg, 1983), p. 55.

30. J.H. Clapham, 'The Growth of an Agrarian Proletariat 1688–1832: A Statistical Note', *Cambridge Historical Journal* 1 (1923), pp. 92–5. These figures are reproduced by Chambers and Mingay, p. 103, and, ironically, by Maurice Dobb, *Studies in the Development of Capitalism*, rev. edn (New York: International, 1963), p. 230.

31. John Saville, 'Primitive Accumulation and Early Industrialization in Britain', *Socialist Register 1969*, pp. 256–7.

32. Ibid., p. 258.

33. Hoskins, p. 269.

34. Lachmann, p. 17.

35. Alan Everitt, 'Farm Labourers' in *The Agrarian History of England and Wales. Volume 4: 1500–1650*, ed. H.P.R. Finberg (Cambridge: Cambridge University Press, 1967), p. 398. See also David Hey, *an English Rural Community: Myddle under the Tudors and the Stuarts* (Bristol: Leicester University Press, 1974), p. 178. See also Cornwall, pp. 200–10. I will explore below the slightly ambiguous status of 'servants' in husbandry and the proletarianization they experienced.

36. Eric Hobsbawm and George Rudé, *Captain Swing: A Social History of the Great English Agricultural Rising of 1830* (New York: W.W. Norton, 1975), p. 36. See also J.M. Neeson, 'The Opponents of Enclosure in Eighteenth-Century Northamptonshire, *Past and Present* 105 (1984), p. 138.

37. Joan Thirsk, 'Seventeenth Century Agriculture', in her *Rural Economy*, p. 211.

38. Donald Woodward, 'Wage Rates and Living Standards in Pre-Industrial England', *Past and Present* 91 (1981), pp. 39, 41; Everitt, pp. 425, 427.

39. Marx, *Capital*, 1, p. 871.

40. On the timing of this development, see Kriedte, p. 142. As will become clear below, while believing that Kriedte's observation here is useful, I reject his general theoretical framework.

41. Everitt, pp. 429, 403. See also Hey, p. 165.

42. As cited by Snell, p. 177.

43. Everitt, pp. 405, 406.

44. As cited by J.L. Hammond and Barbara Hammond, *The Village Labourer* (London: Longman, 1978), p. 9.

45. As cited in ibid., p. 196.

46. As cited by Snell, pp. 171, 172.

47. Cited in ibid., p. 172.

48. I am indebted to Colin Barker for pointing out the importance of this shift in the moral rhetoric of poverty in ruling circles. I would also like to register my debt to his insightful, but regrettably unpublished manuscript, 'State-building and Poverty: the *Poor Law Report* of 1834'.

49. E.L. Jones, 'Agricultural Origins of Industry', *Past and Present* 40 (1968), p. 71.

50. As cited by Hammond and Hammond, p. 50.

51. E.L. Jones, 'Editor's Introduction' in *Agriculture and Economic Growth in England 1650–1815*, ed. E.L. Jones (London: Methuen, 1967), p. 23.

52. Snell, pp. 28, 28, n14, 195–206.

53. Chambers and Mingay, p. 101.

54. Ann Kussmaul, *Servants in Husbandry in Early Modern England* (Cambridge: Cambridge University Press, 1981), pp. 3, 4, 11.

55. Ibid., pp. 100–101; Hobsbawm and Rudé, pp. 44–6.

56. Kussmaul, pp. 81–2, 116, 128–9; Snell, p. 74.

57. Snell, p. 81–2. See also Hobsbawm and Rudé, p. 44.

58. Everitt, pp. 437–8.

59. Hobsbawm and Rudé, p. 44.

60. Anthony Brundage, *The Making of the New Poor Law: The politics of inquiry, enactment and implementation, 1832–39* (London: Hutchinson, 1978), ch. 1; J.R. Poynter, *Society and Pauperism: English Ideas on Poor Relief, 1795–1834* (London: Routledge and Kegan Paul, 1969), ch. 1.

61. Adam Smith, *The Wealth of Nations*, 2 vols, eds R.H. Campbell and A.S. Skinner (Oxford: Oxford University Press, 1976), 1, p. 157.

62. R.A. Soloway, *Prelates and People: Ecclesiastical Social Thought in England 1783–1852* (London, 1969), pp. 81, 126.

63. Snell, p. 105.

64. The classic discussion of 'moral economy' is E.P. Thompson, 'The Moral Economy of the English Crowd in the Eighteenth Century', *Past and Present* 50 (1971). Snell, pp. 72, 99, extends Thompson's concept in several important respects.

65. This view has been advanced perhaps most strongly by Joan Thirsk, 'The Farming Regions of England', in *The Agrarian History of England and Wales*, vol. 4, ed. H.P.R. Finberg (Cambridge: Cambridge University Press, 1967). For arguments designed to qualify this picture, see Rab Houston and K.D.M. Snell, 'Proto-Industrialization? Cottage Industry, Social Change, and Industrial Revolution', *Historical Journal* 27 (1984), p. 477; and Maxine Berg, Pat Hudson and Michael Sonenscher, 'Manufacture in Town and Country before the Factory', in *Manufacture in Town and Country Before the Factory*, eds Maxine Berg, Pat Hudson and Michael

Sonenscher (Cambridge: Cambridge University Press, 1983), pp. 20–23.

66. Jones, 'Agricultural Origins', p. 61. See also John T. Swain, p. 205; and David Hey, *The Rural Metalworkers of the Sheffield Region* (Hertfordshire: Leicester University Press, 1872), p. 21.

67. David Underdown, *Revel, Riot and Rebellion: Popular Politics and Culture in England 1603–1660* (Oxford: Oxford University Press, 1987), p. 18.

68. Charles Wilson, *England's Apprenticeship 1603–1763*, 2nd edn (London, 1984), p. 36.

69. Joan Thirsk, 'Seventeenth-Century Agriculture and Social Change', in her *The Rural Economy of England* (London: Hambledon Press, 1984); Hey, *Rural Metalworkers*, p. 12.

70. On Sheffield see Hey, *Rural Metalworkers*, pp. 10–13; for north-east Lancashire, consult Swain, pp. 110–12, 120–21, 192. The Yorkshire and Lancashire clothing industries are discussed by Alfred P. Wadsworth and Julia De Lacy Mann, *The Cotton Trade and Industrial Lancashire* (New York: Augustus M. Kelley, 1968), pp. 4, 25, 55–6; Herbert Heaton, *The Yorkshire Woollen and Worsted Industries*, 2nd edn (Oxford: Clarendon Press, 1965), pp. 89, 92–3, 97; S.D. Chapman, 'James Longsdon (1745–1821), Farmer and Fustian Manufacture', *Textile History* 1 (1970), pp. 266–70; idem, 'Industrial Capital Before the Industrial Revolution', in *Textile History and Economic History*, ed. K.G. Ponting (Manchester: Manchester University Press, 1973), pp. 114, 128–9; idem, 'The Textile Factory Before Arkwright', *Business History Review* 48 (1974), p. 455.

71. W.B. Crump and Gertrude Ghorbal, *History of the Huddersfield Woollen Industry* (Huddersfield: Alfred Jubb and Son, 1935), p. 31; Heaton, p. 92.

72. Donald Woodward, 'Wage Rates and Living Standards in Pre-Industrial England', *Past and Present* 91 (1981), p. 39. See also Alan Everitt, 'Farm Labourers', in *The Agrarian History of England and Wales, Vol. 4: 1500–1650*, ed. H.P.R. Finberg (Cambridge: Cambridge University Press, 1967), pp. 425–9; and W.H.B. Court, *The Rise of Midland Industries 1600–1838* (1938; London: Oxford University Press, 1953), p. 42.

73. Court, p. 22.

74. The notion of 'more fully capitalist forms of production pivots on Marx's important distinction between the formal subsumption and the real subsumption of labour-power to capital – a point to which I shall return. See Karl Marx, 'Results of the Immediate Process of Production', in *Capital*, 1, pp. 1019–38.

75. Hey, p. 49. On this general point, see also François Crouzet, *The First Industrialists* (Cambridge: Cambridge University Press, 1985), pp. 132, 137.

76. Hey, p. 52.

77. Court, pp. 112–13; Wilson, pp. 300–301.

78. Crump and Ghorbal, pp. 43–6.

79. On Hill, see Frank Atkinson, *Some Aspects of the Eighteenth Century Woollen and Worsted Trade in Halifax* (Halifax: Halifax Museums, 1956); and R.G. Wilson, *Gentlemen Merchants: The Merchant Community in Leeds 1700–1830* (Manchester: Manchester University Press, 1971), pp. 58–60.

80. Pat Hudson, 'Proto-industrialisation: the case of the West Riding Wool Textile Industry in the 18th and early 19th centuries', *History Workshop* 12 (1981), p. 48; idem, 'From Manor to Mill: the West Riding in Transition', in *Manufacturing in Town and Country*, p. 140.

81. John Goodchild, 'Pildacre Mill: an Early West Riding Factory', *Textile History* 1 (1970).

82. Marx, *Capital*, vol. 3, trans. David Fernbach (Harmondsworth: Penguin, 1981), p. 452.

83. See Peter Kriedte, Hans Medick and Jurgen Schlumbohm, *Industrialization Before Industrialization*, trans. Beate Schemp (Cambridge: Cambridge University Press, 1981), pp. 2–3, 21, 34; and Peter Kriedte, *Peasants, Landlords and Merchant Capitalists* (Leamington Spa: Berg, 1983), pp. 1, 10, 40, 42, 59, 78, 80, 90, 131. For critiques of this thesis, see Hudson, p. 34–60; and Rab Houston and K.D.M. Snell, 'Proto-Industrialization? Cottage Industry, Social Change, and Industrial Revolution', *Historical Journal* 27 (1984), pp. 437–92.

84. One of the shortcomings of Marx's discussion in chapter 20 of *Capital*, vol. 3 is that he does not consider this question of the origins of merchants. Thus, to illustrate 'Way 2', he refers to 'the English clothier of the seventeenth century, who brought weavers who were formerly dependent under his control' (p. 452). As I have tried to demonstrate, this was not always an example of a merchant becoming an industrial capitalist, but could just as well illustrate the path by which a small producer became both a merchant and/or putter-out.

85. Crump and Ghobal, pp. 90, 94.

86. S.D. Chapman, *The Early Factory Masters* (Newton Abbot: David and Charles, 1967), pp. 19–25, 34, 79–80, 94; idem, 'The Transition to the Factory System in the Midlands Cotton-Spinning Industry', *Economic History Review*, 2nd series, 18 (1965), p. 537. For an interesting discussion of similar patterns in London, see R.G. Lang, 'Social Origins and Social Aspirations of Jacobean London Merchants', *Economic History Review*, 2nd series, 27 (1974).

87. J.D. Chambers, *The Workshop of the World: British Economic History from 1820 to 1880*, 2nd edn (London: Oxford University Press, 1968), p. 14. See also Crump and Ghorbal, pp. 66, 92; Crouzet, p. 123; Chapman, *Early Victorian Factory Masters*, pp. 53–4, 79; idem, 'James Longsdon', pp. 273, 283–4; Heaton, p. 298.

88. See Chapman, *Early Victorian Factory Masters*, pp. 19–25, 78–82.

89. Ibid., p. 277. See also Julia de Lacy Mann, 'Clothiers and Weavers in Wiltshire during the Eighteenth Century', in *Studies in the Industrial Revolution*, ed. L.S. Pressnell (London: Athlone Press, 1960), p. 83.

90. Crouzet, p. 123.

91. Marx, *Capital*, 2, pp. 927–31.

92. Ibid., p. 274.

93. Ibid., pp. 590–91, 600, 602, 604.

94. Ivy Pinchbeck, *Women Workers and the Industrial Revolution 1750–1850* (1930, rpt London: Virago, 1981), p. 121.

95. Ibid., pp. 121–2. See also Snell, p. 307.

96. Snell, p. 311; Mary Lynn McDougall, 'Working Class Women During the Industrial Revolution, 1780–1914', in *Becoming Visible: Women in European History*, eds Renate Bridenthal and Claudia Koonz (Boston: Houghton Mifflin, 1977), p. 275; Theresa M. McBride, 'The Long Road Home: Women's Work and Industrialization', in ibid., pp. 282–4; Louise A. Tilly and Joan Scott, *Women, Work, and Family* (New York: Holt, Rinehart and Winston, 1978), pp. 127–9.

97. Pinchbeck, ch. 12; Snell, pp. 272–83, 294–304.

98. Thompson, *Making*, pp. 202–3.

99. Harold Perkin, *The Origins of Modern English Society 1780–1880* (Toronto: University of Toronto Press, 1969), p. 89.

100. I have discussed this issue with respect to Locke and the first Whigs in 'Locke, Levellers, and Liberty: Property and Democracy in the Thought of the First Whigs', *History of Political Thought* 10 (1989), pp. 17–40.

101. John Rule, *The Experience of Labour in Eighteenth Century Industry* (London: Croom Helm, 1981), pp. 124–33; Peter Linebaugh, 'Labour History without the Labour Process: a Note on John Gast and His Times', *Social History* 7 (1982), pp. 319–27;

C.R. Dobson, *Masters and Journeymen: A Prehistory of Industrial Relations 1717–1800* (London: Croom Helm, 1980), pp. 27–9.

102. Michael Ignatieff, *A Just Measure of Pain: The Penitentiary in the Industrial Revolution 1750–1850* (Harmondsworth: Penguin, 1987), pp. 27, 108; Rule, p. 131.

103. Linebaugh, p. 321.

104. See Rule, ch. 4; Snell, pp. 256–7; Iorwerth Prothero, *Artisans and Politics in Early Nineteenth-Century London* (Folkestone, Kent: Dawson, 1979), pp. 31–4.

105. Snell, pp. 236, 253, 259–62.

106. On the decline in artisan wages, see Rule, p. 68; and Snell, p. 245. On the apprenticeship campaign waged by artisans, see Prothero, ch. 3; Rule, pp. 111, 117; and T.K. Derry, 'The Repeal of the Apprenticeship Clauses of the Statute of Apprentices', *Economic History Review* 3 (1931), pp. 67–87.

107. As cited by Derry, p. 75.

108. J. Chitty, *A Practical Treatise on the Law Relative to Apprentices and Journeymen, and to Exercising Trades* (1812), as cited by Prothero, p. 58.

109. Derry, pp. 73, 58.

110. As cited by ibid., p. 78, my emphasis.

111. Rule, p. 95.

112. See Paul Richards, 'The State and Early Industrial Capital: The Case of the Handloom Weavers', *Past and Present* 83 (1979), pp. 91–115; and Thompson, *Making*, pp. 300–301.

113. Chapman, *Early Factory Masters*, pp. 167–70. On the penal origins of factory design, see Ignatieff, p. 32.

114. Wadsworth and Mann, p. 391; Neil McKendrick, 'Josiah Wedgwood and Factory Discipline', *Historical Journal* 4 (1961), p. 51.

115. In addition to McKendrick, see E.P. Thompson, 'Time, Work-Discipline and Industrial Capitalism', in *Essays in Social History*, eds M.W. Flinn and T.C. Smout (Oxford: Oxford University Press, 1974); and Sidney Pollard, 'Factory Discipline in the Industrial Revolution', *Economic History Review*, 2nd series, 16 (1963–4); Douglas A. Reid, 'The Decline of Saint Monday 1766–1876', *Past and Present* 71 (1976), pp. 76–101.

116. As cited by McKendrick, pp. 35–6, emphasis in original.

117. Sidney Pollard, *The Genesis of Modern Management: A Study of the Industrial Revolution in Great Britain* (London: Edward Arnold, 1965), pp. 207–8.

118. Ibid., p. 189.

119. Pollard, p. 263; McKendrick, pp. 40–46, 52; Parliamentary committee, as cited by Pollard, p. 258.

120. See E.P. Thompson, *Whigs and Hunters: The Origin of the Black Act* (New York: Pantheon, 1975); and Douglas Hay et al., *Albion's Fatal Tree: Crime and Punishment in Eighteenth-Century England* (New York: Pantheon, 1975).

121. As cited by Ignatieff, pp. 25, 26.

122. Ibid., pp. 84, 87, 154, 179.

123. All three of these representative statements are cited in ibid., pp. 46, 72, 74. The eighteenth-century 'technologies' of punishment are the focus of Michel Foucault's insightful but frustratingly idealist *Discipline and Punish: The Birth of the Prison*, trans. Alan Sheridan (New York: Vintage, 1979).

124. Jeremy Bentham, 'Letter to Lord Pelham' (London, 1806), p. 6.

125. Ignatieff, pp. 168, 175–7, 184–5.

126. Karl Polanyi, *The Great Transformation* (Boston: Beacon Press, 1957), p. 141.

2. Justice and Markets: Adam Smith

1. As cited by J.L. Hammond and Barbara Hammond, *The Skilled Labourer 1760–1832*, 2nd edn (London: Longmans, Green, 1920), p. 123.

2. For a discussion of the term 'Smithian socialists', see Noel Thompson, *The People's Science: the popular political economy of exploitation and crisis 1816–1834* (Cambridge: Cambridge University Press, 1984), ch. 4.

3. F.A. Hayek, *The Political Order of a Free People*, 2nd edn (Chicago: University of Chicago Press, 1981), p. 158.

4. F.A. Hayek, *Knowledge, Evolution and Society* (London: Adam Smith Institute, 1983), pp. 32, 39; *Social Justice, Socialism and Democracy* (Turramurra: Centre for Independent Studies, 1979), p. 21; *Law, Legislation and Liberty*, vol. 2 (London: Routledge and Kegan Paul, 1976), pp. 142–7.

5. F.A. Hayek, *New Studies in Philosophy, Politics, Economics and the History of Ideas* (Chicago: University of Chicago Press, 1978), pp. 268, 269; idem, *Knowledge*, p. 19.

6. This is the expression used by George Davie in a discussion of 'Berkeley, Hume, and the Central Problem of Scottish Philosophy', in *McGill Hume Studies*, eds David Fate Norton, Nicholas Capaldi and Wade L. Robinson (San Diego: Austin Hill Press, 1976), p. 44. It is a central argument of my *Political Essay and the Rise of Capitalism: A Reinterpretation* (Berkeley: University of California Press, 1988), ch. 4, that Smith produced the most sophisticated, although ultimately flawed, attempt at such a reconciliation. For one of the best treatments of this problem see J. Ralph Lindgren, *The Social Philosophy of Adam Smith* (The Hague: Martinus Nijhoff, 1973).

7. Ludwig von Mises, *Theory and History* (New Haven: Yale University Press, 1957), p. 168.

8. Max Lerner, Introduction to Adam Smith, *The Wealth of Nations*, ed. Edwin Cannan (New York: Modern Library, 1937), p. ix; Joseph Cropsey, 'Adam Smith and Political Philosophy', in *Essays on Adam Smith*, eds Andrew Skinner and Thomas Wilson (Oxford: Oxford University Press, 1975), p. 132.

9. Istvan Hont and Michael Ignatieff, 'Needs and Justice in the *Wealth of Nations*', in *Wealth and Virtue: The Shaping of Political Economy in the Scottish Enlightenment*, eds Istvan Hont and Michael Ignatieff (Cambridge: Cambridge University Press, 1983), p. 2; Michael Ignatieff, 'Smith, Rousseau and the Republic of Needs', in *Scotland and Europe, 1200–1850*, ed. T.C. Smouth (Edinburgh: John Donald, 1986), p. 193.

10. Among the most important examples of this interpretation, see Quentin Skinner, *The Foundation of Modern Political Thought*, 2 vols (Cambridge: Cambridge University Press, 1978); Duncan Forbes, *Hume's Philosophical Politics* (Cambridge: Cambridge University Press, 1975); James Tully, *A Discourse of Property: John Locke and his Adversaries* (Cambridge: Cambridge University Press, 1980); Knud Haakonssen, *The Science of a Legislator: The Natural Jurisprudence of David Hume and Adam Smith* (Cambridge: Cambridge University Press, 1981); and Richard Teichgraber, III, *'Free Trade' and Moral Philosophy: Rethinking the Sources of Adam Smith's 'Wealth of Nations'* (Durham: Duke University Press, 1986). For a critique of the conclusions arrived at in this approach with respect to Locke, see David McNally, 'Locke, Levellers and Liberty: Property and Democracy in the Thought of the First Whigs', *History of Political Thought* 10 (1989), pp. 17–40.

11. This is the view especially of Samuel Hollander, *The Economics of David Ricardo* (Toronto: University of Toronto Press, 1979), pp. 652–60, a position which is repeated, not surprisingly, by another subscriber to the 'jurisprudential' approach, Biancamaria Fontana, *Rethinking the Politics of Commercial Society: the 'Edinburgh Review' 1803–1832* (Cambridge: Cambridge University Press, 1985), p. 80. For my critique

of Hollander's interpretation of Smith, see McNally, *Political Economy*, pp. 242–8.

12. Donald Winch, 'Adam Smith's "Enduring Particular Result": a Political and Cosmopolitan Perspective', in Hont and Ignatieff, p. 268.

13. Hayek, *New Studies*, p. 252.

14. Gladys Bryson, *Man and Society: The Scottish Enquiry of the Eighteenth Century* (Princeton: Princeton University Press, 1945), p. 8.

15. Bernard Mandeville, *The Fable of the Bees*, 2 vols, ed. F.B. Kaye (Oxford: Oxford University Press, 1924).

16. Ibid., p. 369.

17. See the discussion in McNally, *Political Economy*, pp. 164–7.

18. Adam Smith, 'Letter to the *Edinburgh Review*', in his *Essays on Philosophical Subjects* (London: Oxford University Press, 1980), pp. 250, 251.

19. Adam Smith, *The Theory of the Moral Sentiments* (Indianapolis: Liberty Classics, 1969), pp. 47, 487, 493. This work is hereafter cited as *TMS*.

20. Adam Smith, *Lectures on Jurisprudence*, ed. R.L. Meek, D.D. Raphael and P.G. Stein (Oxford: Oxford University Press, 1978), p. 352 (hereafter cited as *LJ*); Smith, *TMS*, p. 54. The human need for communication and conversation is a much neglected aspect of Smith's thought. For more on this point, see McNally, *Political Economy*, pp. 178–81.

21. Adam Smith, *Lectures on Rhetoric and Belles Lettres*, ed. John M. Lothian (Carbondale: Southern Illinois University Press, 1971), p. 51.

22. Smith, *TMS*, p. 501.

23. Ibid., p. 531.

24. It is worth noting that such a position represents a unique synthesis of Hutcheson's largely naturalistic and Hume's essentially rationalistic explanations of moral behaviour, one which Smith thinks overcomes the weakness in the positions of his predecessors.

25. Smith, *TMS*, p. 67.

26. Ibid., p. 162.

27. Adam Smith, *The Wealth of Nations*, 2 vols, eds R.H. Campbell and A.S. Skinner (Oxford: Oxford University Press, 1976), pp. 25–6. This work is hereafter cited as *WN*. On the origins of the propensity to exchange in our inclination to persuade, see Adam Smith, *LJ*, p. 352.

28. See McNally, *Political Economy*, pp. 210–11.

29. Smith, *TMS*, p. 162.

30. McNally, *Political Economy*, pp. 225–7. On Smith's growing pessimism as reflected in the 1790 edition of the *Moral Sentiments*, see John Dwyer, *Virtuous Discourse: Sensibility and Community in Late Eighteenth-Century Scotland* (Edinburgh: John Donald, 1987), ch. 7; and Ralph Anspach, 'The Implications of the *Theory of the Moral Sentiments* for Adam Smith's Economic Thought', *History of Political Economy* 4 (1972), pp. 176–206.

31. Smith, *WN*, 1, pp. 22, 29, 30.

32. Ibid., 1, pp. 22, 24.

33. Ibid., 1, p. 99, 2, p. 660, 1, p. 283. See also Samuel Hollander, *The Economics of Adam Smith* (Toronto: University of Toronto Press, 1973), p. 146.

34. Smith, *WN*, p. 96.

35. Smith, *LJ*, p. 333. On this point, despite some theoretical shortcomings, see Thomas J. Lewis, 'Adam Smith: The Labor Market as the Basis of Natural Right', *Journal of Economic Issues* 11 (1977).

36. Smith, *WN*, 1, p. 101.

37. See ibid., p. 18.

38. It is true, of course, that Smith does use examples of nail-making and pin-

making manufacture, but these are mere illustrations of his argument for the productivity generated by division of labour; they do not affect the core model he employs in these early chapters (which indicates his tendency to conflate the division of labour in industry with social division of labour in general). On Smith's neglect of fixed capital, see McNally, *Political Economy*, pp. 240–43.

39. This shift in model is crucial to Smith's description of an 'adding up' theory of value based on the respective contributions of land, labour and capital in place of a simple labour theory of value. I have argued elsewhere that Smith acquired the triadic model from the physiocrats. See McNally, *Political Economy*, pp. 234–50.

40. Smith, *WN*, 1, p. 83.

41. Ibid., pp. 84–5, 157–8, 114–15.

42. Smith, *LJ*, p. 497.

43. Adam Smith to Andreas Holt, October 1780 in *The Corespondence of Adam Smith*, eds Ernest Campbell Mossner and Ian Simpson Ross (Oxford: Clarendon Press, 1977), p. 251.

44. Smith, *WN*, 1, p. 267.

45. Ibid., 1, pp. 144, 267, 2, pp. 471, 493, 2, p. 613.

46. See McNally, *Political Economy*, pp. 223, 231–2.

47. Smith, *WN*, 2, p. 654. Smith's reference to 'the rich and the powerful' can be found in ibid., p. 644.

48. Marian Bowley, *Studies in the History of Economic Theory Before 1870* (London: Macmillan, 1973), pp. 127–8.

49. E.P. Thompson, 'The Moral Economy of the English Crowd in the Eighteenth Century', *Past and Present* 50 (1971), pp. 89–91; Hont and Ignatieff, pp. 18–21.

50. Smith, *WN*, 1, p. 534.

51. Ibid., pp. 526–39.

52. Ibid., pp. 154, 156, 157.

53. Ibid., p. 157. Gertrude Himmelfarb, *The Idea of Poverty: England in the Early Industrial Age*, (New York: Vintage, 1985), p. 111.

54. Smith, *WN*, 2, p. 644.

55. Ibid., 1, p. 493.

56. Ibid., pp. 461–2, 265.

57. Smith's discussion this group can be found in *TMS*, p. 127. For a fuller discussion of Smith's profound worries in this respect, see J. Ralph Lindgren, *The Social Philosophy of Adam Smith* (The Hague: Martinus Nijhoff, 1973), chs 4–6; and McNally, *Political Economy*, pp. 180–208.

58. Nicholas Philipson, 'Adam Smith as Civic Moralist', in *Wealth and Virtue: The Shaping of Political Economy in the Scottish Enlightenment*, eds Istvan Hont and Michael Ignatieff, p. 197.

59. E.P. Thompson, 'The Moral Economy Reviewed', in *Customs in Common: Studies in Traditional Popular Culture*, New York: The New Press, 1991), p. 269. While Thompson is not always fully attentive to the strains and ambiguities in Smith's work, his insistence on the social context of political economy is a refreshing corrective to the propensity of Hont and Ignatieff in particular to reconstruct Smith in the context of a disembodied, desocialized, academicized realm of ideas. See Thompson's telling remarks to this effect, ibid., p. 275.

3. The Malthusian Moment

1. Henry Cockburn, *Memorials of His Time* (Edinburgh, 1856), p. 80.

2. *Sir James Mackintosh* by his own son, 2nd edn, 2 vols (London, 1836), 1, p. 87.

3. E.P. Thompson, *The Making of the English Working Class* (New York: Vintage, 1963), p. 90.

4. Thomas Paine, 'The Rights of Man', in *The Thomas Paine Reader*, eds Michael Foot and Isaac Kramnick (Harmondsworth: Penguin, 1987), p. 269.

5. Gwyn A. Williams, *Artisans and Sans-Culottes: Popular Movements in France and Britain during the French Revolution* (London: Edward Arnold, 1968), p. 17.

6. Paine, 'Rights of Man', pp. 349, 356.

7. Ibid., pp. 336, 337. See also Paine, 'Agrarian Justice', in *The Thomas Paine Reader*, p. 477.

8. Thompson, pp. 107–8; Edward Royle and James Walvin, *English Radicals and Reformers 1760–1848* (Sussex: Harvester, 1982), p. 54; Williams, p. 67.

9. Williams, pp. 58–61, 66–70; Royle and Walvin, pp. 50–51.

10. As cited by Royle and Walvin, p. 54.

11. Williams, p. 70. On France's second revolution, see Georges Lefebvre, *The French Revolution. Volume 1: From its Origins to 1793*, trans. Elizabeth Moss Evanson (New York: Columbia University Press, 1962), pp. 227–47; and Albert Soboul, *The French Revolution 1781–1799. Volume 1: From the Storming of the Bastille to the Fall of the Girondins*, trans. Alan Forrest (London: New Left Books, 1974), pp. 241–51.

12. Royle and Walvin, p. 62.

13. Walter M. Stern, 'The Bread Crisis in Britain, 1795–96', *Economica*, new series, 31 (1964), pp. 168–9; Roger Wells, 'The Development of the English Rural Proletariat and Social Protest, 1700–1850', *Journal of Peasant Studies* 6 (1979), p. 121.

14. Royle and Walvin, pp. 74–5; Thompson, pp. 142–3, 132–7.

15. Thompson, p. 160. Thelwall is in fact one of the great representatives during this period of a radical plebeian perspective based on the assumption of common interests of wage-labourers, independent artisans and small capitalist employers – a sort of rugged petty bourgeois socialism. For an interesting treatment of Thelwall in terms of his theory of natural rights, see Iain Hampsher-Monk, 'John Thelwall and the Eighteenth-Century Radical Response to Political Economy', *Historical Journal* 43 (1991), pp. 1–20.

16. As cited in Thompson, p. 159. As Hampsher-Monk points out (pp. 14–16), the key move in Thelwall's position is his treatment of property in one's labour as the foundational right to which all other property rights are subordinate.

17. [Arthur Young], *A Plain and Earnest Address to Britons* (Ipswich, 1792), as cited by Gregory Claeys, 'The French Revolution Debate and British Political Thought', *History of Political Thought* II (1990), p. 73.

18. This point is well brought out by Claeys, ibid., who fails, however, to connect the attribution to Paine of 'levelling' tendencies to the deepening plebeian radicalism of the mid 1790s.

19. Thomas Spence, 'The Real Rights of Man', in *The Political Works of Thomas Spence*, ed. H.T. Dickinson (Newcastle upon Tyne: Avero Publications, 1982), p. 2.

20. Spence to Charles Hall, 28 June 1807, as cited by G.I. Gallop, 'Introductory Essay: Thomas Spence and the Real Rights of Man', in *Pig's Meat: Selected Writings of Thomas Spence* (Nottingham: Spokesman, 1982), p. 23.

21. Thomas Spence, 'The Restorer of Society to its Natural State', in *Pig's Meat*, pp. 157, 163.

22. See Roger Wells, *Insurrection: The British Experience 1795–1803* (Gloucester: Alan Sutton, 1986), pp. 23, 44–5, 55–6, 130–33. The most accurate biographical information on Spence, including the dating of his arrival in London, is provided by Malcolm Chase, *'The People's Farm': English Radical Agrarianism 1775–1840* (Oxford: Clarendon, 1988), chs 2–3. P.M. Ashraf, *The Life and Times of Thomas Spence* (Newcastle upon Tyne: Frank Graham, 1983) is also useful.

23. Thomas Spence, 'The End of Oppression', in *Political Works of Thomas Spence*, p. 36; and Spence, 'Restorer', p. 141. On the naval mutinies of 1797, see Wells, *Insurection*, ch. 5.

24. Spence, 'Restorer', p. 154; Watson, as cited by Chase, p. 86.

25. Thompson, p. 181.

26. Iain McCalman, *Radical Underworld: Prophets, Revolutionaries and Pornographers in London, 1795–1840* (Cambridge: Cambridge University Press, 1988), pp. 1–2.

27. See Spence, 'The Rights of Infants', in *Political Works of Thomas Spence*, pp. 46–53. On the Spenceans and women's rights, see Thompson, pp. 162–3; Chase, pp. 57–8; and Barbara Taylor, *Eve and the New Jerusalem: Socialism and Feminism in the Nineteenth Century* (London: Virago, 1984), pp. 7–8. On the important involvement of Janet Evans, whose husband Thomas was Spence's most important follower in the radical movement of the time, see McCalman, pp. 32–3, 125.

28. See especially McCalman; and Chase.

29. The view I am attacking here is that of Gareth Stedman Jones, 'Rethinking Chartism', in his *Languages of Class: Studies in English working class history 1832–1982* (Cambridge: Cambridge University Press), pp. 90–178.

30. Thomas Evans, *Christian Policy, the Salvation of the Empire* (1816), as cited by McCalman, p. 108.

31. Chase, p. 67. On the plebeian base of the Spencean movement, and its predisposition towards revolutionary politics, see ibid., pp. 78, 88, 93–120.

32. Eric Hobsbawm and George Rudé, *Captain Swing: A social history of the great English agricultural uprising of 1830* (New York: W.W. Norton, 1975), p. 47.

33. Karl Marx, 'A Review of Guizot's Book, *Why Has the English Revolution Been Successful?*', in Karl Marx and Frederick Engels, *Articles on Britain* (Moscow: Progress, 1971), p. 93.

34. On the crisis of 1800, see Wells, *Insurrection*, ch. 9.

35. On the Speenhamland system, see Hobsbawm and Rudé, pp. 47–51; and J.L. Hammond and Barbara Hammond, *The Village Labourer*, (London: Longman, 1978), pp. 107–11. The argument that the system was not widespread is ably put by J.R. Poynter, *Society and Pauperism: English Ideas on Poor Relief, 1795–1834*, (London: Routledge and Kegan Paul, 1969), pp. 77–84.

36. On Whitbread's scheme see Hammond and Hammond, pp. 91–4; and Raymond Cowherd, *Political Economists and the English Poor Laws* (Athens: Ohio University Press, 1977), pp. 12, 17–18.

37. As cited by Cowherd, p. 18.

38. A point made by Gertrude Himmelfarb, *The Idea of Poverty: England in the Early Industrial Age* (New York: Vintage, 1985), pp. 70–71.

39. Edmund Burke, 'Thoughts and Details on Scarcity', in *The Works of Edmund Burke*, 4th edn, vol. 5 (Boston: Little, Brown, 1871), pp. 133, 136.

40. Ibid., pp. 140, 141, 142, 147, 152.

41. Ibid., pp. 167–8, 156–7.

42. Cited by Wells, *Insurrection*, p. 254.

43. On Pitt's plan, see Hammond and Hammond, pp. 98–102; and Poynter, pp. 62–76. For Malthus's *Investigations* and his *Letter to Samuel Whitbread*, see *The Pamphlets of Thomas Robret Malthus* (New York: Augustus M. Kelley, 1970).

44. Poynter, p. xv. Perhaps one of the more interesting conversions to 'humanitarianism', during the period of the French Revolution was that of the famous advocate of enclosure and large farms, Arthur Young, who in 1800 began a campaign for land allotments to all those who lost land or access to commons as a result of enclosure. But Young's position too was an isolated one, and was attacked by Malthus in his *Essay on the Principle of Population*. On Young's plan, see Poynter, pp. 100–103.

45. Thomas Robert Malthus, *An Essay on the Principle of Population*, ed. Anthony Flew (Harmondsworth: Penguin, 1970), p. 121. See also pp. 67, 171. Henceforth this work will be cited as *FE* for *First Essay*.

46. Donald Winch, *Malthus* (Oxford: Oxford University Press, 1967), p. 17.

47. Malthus, *FE*, p. 172.

48. Ibid., pp. 77, 79.

49. Ibid., p. 133.

50. An important exception is Himmelfarb, ch. 4.

51. Malthus, *FE*, 184–5.

52. Ibid., pp. 97, 948.

53. [Robert Southey], *Analytical Review*, vol. 2, pp. 298–9.

54. A point that is made by Thomas Sowell, 'Malthus and the Utilitarians', *Canadian Journal of Economics and Political Science*, 28 (1962), pp. 268–74.

55. See 'An Essay on the Principle of Population', in *The Works of Thomas Robert Malthus*, eds E.A. Wrigley and David Souden (London: William Pickering, 1986), vol. 3, pp. 340–6, 548–51. This edition follows the sixth edition of 1826 while providing alternative passages from the second to fifth editions.

56. Ibid., 3, pp. 501, 502, 503.

57. Ibid., p. 505. On the attribution of such a position to Paine, see Claeys, pp. 60–61, 73–8.

58. Robert M. Young, 'Malthus and the Evolutionists: The Common Context of Biological and Social Theory', *Past and Present*, 43 (1969), p. 119.

59. The chronology of subsequent editions of the *Essay* is 1803 (second), 1806 (third), 1807 (fourth), 1817 (fifth), 1826 (sixth, posthumous). The most substantial changes were introduced in 1803.

60. Malthus, *FE*, pp. 202, 205, 210.

61. As cited by J.M. Pullen, 'Malthus' Theological Ideas and Their Influence on His Principle of Population', in *Thomas Robert Malthus: Critical Assessments*, 4 vols, ed. John Cunningham Wood (London: Croom Helm, 1986), 2, p. 210. See also E.N. Santurri, 'Theodicy and Social Policy in Malthus' Thought', ibid., 2, pp. 402–17.

62. Malthus, 'Essays', *Works*, 3, pp. 342, 465, 471.

63. Ibid., pp. 516–17.

64. Ibid., pp. 480.

65. Ibid., 2, pp. iii, 16.

66. Ibid., 3, pp. 484, 500.

67. Ibid., pp. 488–9.

68. Sowell, p. 271.

69. Malthus, 'The Amendment of the Poor Laws', in *The Works of Thomas Robert Malthus*, 4, p. 10.

70. Sowell, p. 273.

71. A good treatment of these shifts in economic analysis across the editions of the *Essay* is provided by G. Gilbert, 'Economic Growth and the Poor in Malthus' *Essay on Population*' in *Thomas Robert Malthus: Critical Assessments* vol. 2, pp. 402–18. It is worth noting that Malthus's shift away from anti-industrialism became more pronounced over time.

72. Malthus, 'Essay on the Principle of Population', 3, pp. 392, 401.

73. Ibid., p. 442.

74. Ibid., p. 447.

75. Malthus, *Principles of Political Economy*, in *The Works of Thomas Robert Malthus*, 6, pp. 288, 290; on the notion of 'proportions', see ibid., p. 300.

76. Ibid., 6, pp. 317–19.

77. Ibid., p. 342.

78. James, p. 303.

79. Morton Paglin, *Malthus and Lauderdale: The Anti-Ricardian Tradition* (New York: Augustus M. Kelley, 1961), pp. 134–5.

80. Robert Torrens, *Essay on the External Corn Trade* (London, 1815), pp. xi–xii.

81. B. Semmel, 'Malthus: "Physiocracy" and the Commercial System' in *Thomas Robert Malthus: Critical Assessments*, vol. 4, p. 116; Poynter, p. 237; James, pp. 168, 346; Young, p. 114.

82. Nassau Senior, *Two Lectures on Population*, as cited by James, p. 438.

83. On the reception of Malthus in the journals of the time, see Kenneth Smith, *The Malthusian Controversy* (London: Routledge and Kegan Paul, 1951), p. 49; and James, pp. 65, 110. Brougham's comment is cited by Peter Dunkley, *The Crisis of the Old Poor Law in England 1795–1834 – An Interpretive Essay* (New York: Garland, 1982), p. 121.

84. Paglin, p. 141.

85. Malthus, 'Essay', in *Works*, 3, pp. 697–8. See also ibid., pp. 556–7, 584, 589.

86. Ibid., 3, pp. 516, 517, 515.

87. Ibid., p. 373.

88. Ibid., pp. 385, 528.

89. Malthus, 'Essay', in *Works*, 3, p. 342.

90. Ibid., p. 468.

91. Malthus, 'A Summary view of the Principles of Population', in *First Essay*, pp. 245, 268–9.

92. Malthus, 'Essay', in *Works*, 3. pp. 575–6.

93. R.A. Soloway, *Prelates and People: Ecclesiastical Social Thought in England 1783–1852* (London: Routledge and Kegan Paul, 1969), p. 33.

94. As cited in ibid., p. 63, n5; for a discussion of the clerical desire to destroy Paineite thought, see also ibid., p. 129.

95. Both cited in ibid., pp. 74, 66.

96. As cited in ibid., p. 131.

97. As cited by Poynter, p. 229; cited by Soloway, p. 133; see also ibid., pp. 95–101, 107–8.

98. As cited in ibid., pp. 138, 140.

99. Thomas Chalmers, *Problems of Poverty: Selections from the Economic and Social Writings of Thomas Chalmers* (London: Thomas Nelson and Sons, 1912).

100. Frank W. Fetter, 'The Rise and Decline of Ricardian Economics', *History of Political Economy*, 1 (1969), p. 70.

101. David Ricardo, *On the Principles of Political Economy and Taxation*, in *The Works and Correspondence of David Ricardo*, eds Piero Sraffa and M.H. Dobb, vol. 1 (Cambridge: Cambridge University Press, 1951), p. 106.

102. David Ricardo, speeches to the House of Commons of 25 March 1819 and 17 May 1819, in *The Works and Correspondence of David Ricardo. Volume V: Speeches and Evidence* (Cambridge: Cambridge University Press, 1962), pp. 1, 7.

103. Ricardo, speech of 29 June 1820, in ibid., 6, pp. 68–9. On Maxwell's campaign, see Barry Gordon, *Political Economy in Parliament 1819–1823* (New York: Barnes and Noble, 1977), pp. 88–9; and Paul Richards, 'The State and Early Industrial Capitalism: The Case of the Handloom Weavers, *Past and Present* 83 (1979), pp. 91–115.

104. Gordon, p. 170.

105. Ricardo, speeches of 9 May 1823 and 21 May 1823, in *Works*, 6, pp. 292, 296.

106. Ricardo, speech of 9 June 1823, in ibid., 6, p. 307.

107. Ricardo to Place, 9 September 1821, *Works*, 9, p. 52; speech of 8 May 1821, *Works*, 5, p. 114.

108. Cited by James, p. 374.

109. John Clive, *Scotch Reviewers: The Edinburgh Review, 1802-1815* (London: Faber and Faber, 1957), p. 131.

110. S. Smith, 'Nares' *Sermon*', *Edinburgh Review* 1 (October 1802), pp. 83-90.

111. As cited by Biancamaria Fontana, *Rethinking the Politics of Commercial Society: the Edinburgh Review 1802-1832* (Cambridge: Cambridge University Press, 1985), p. 55; as cited by Dunkley, pp. 120-21.

112. Horner to Thomas Thomson, 15 August 1803, in *Memoirs and Correspondence of Francis Horner, M.P.*, ed. Leonard Horner (London, 1843), vol. 1, p. 229.

113. Cowherd, p. 150; Fontana, pp. 74, 78.

114. Marian Bowley, *Nassau Senior and Classical Economics* (New York: Octagon, 1967), pp. 277-81; Richards, pp. 111-14.

115. Nassau Senior, *Three Lectures on the Rate of Wages*, 2nd edn (New York: Augustus M. Kelley, 1959), pp. xiv-xv.

116. Dunkley, pp. 1, 46-7.

117. Hobsbawm and Rudé, p. 51; see also Poynter, p. 281.

118. Andrew Charlesworth, *An Atlas of Rural Protest in Britain 1548-1900* (Philadelphia: University of Pennsylvania Press, 1983), pp. 139-45.

119. Ibid., pp. 146-51. See also A.J. Peacock, 'Village Radicalism in East Anglia 1800-50', in *Rural Discontent in Nineteenth-Century Britain*, ed. J.P.D. Dunbabin (London: Faber and Faber, 1974).

120. Hobsbawm and Rudé, pp. 77-81.

121. The best study remains Hobsbawm and Rudé.

122. As cited by ibid., pp. 100-101.

123. S.G. Checkland and E.O.A. Checkland, eds, *The Poor Law Report of 1834* (Harmondsworth: Penguin, 1974), p. 410. This document will hereafter be cited as *PLR*.

124. As cited by Anthony Brundage, *The Making of the New Poor Law* (London: Hutchinson, 1978), p. 55.

125. See Dunkley, pp. 15, 40, 89, 167; Brundage, pp. 15, 183; Poynter, p. 296.

126. As cited by K.D.M. Snell, *Annals of the Labouring Poor: Social Change and Agrarian England* (Cambridge: Cambridge University Press, 1985), p. 121. For an insightful discussion of the landed gentry's acceptance of the basic principles of the Poor Law Report well in advance of 1834, see Peter Mandler, 'The Making of the New Poor Law Redivivus', *Past and Present* 117 (1987), pp. 131-57.

127. Cowherd, p. 215.

128. Poynter, p. 318.

129. *PLR*, p. 82.

130. John Knott, *Popular Opposition to the 1834 Poor Law* (London: Croom Helm, 1986), p. 26.

131. *PLR*, pp. 325, 335, 372-8.

132. But not entirely; see ibid., p. 167.

133. Ibid., pp. 146, 167, 353, 329.

134. Ibid., p. 325.

135. Ibid., p. 219.

136. Ibid., pp. 123, 408.

137. Ibid., pp. 135, 156.

138. Brundage, pp. 33-4, 41, 52, 159, 163, 170-2, 178-9; as cited in ibid., p. 52. On gentry concerns about centralization, and their weakening after 1817, see Mandler, pp. 143-56.

139. Anne Digby, 'Malthus and Reform of the English Poor Law', in *Malthus and His Time*, ed. Michael Turner (London: Macmillan, 1986), p. 167.

140. As cited by James, p. 451.

141. Knott, p. 116.

4. Exploitation, Inequality and the Market

1. For Cobbett's 'Letter to Parson Malthus', see *The Opinions of William Cobbett*, eds G.D.H. Cole and Margaret Cole (London, 1944), pp. 187–95. A useful overview of Cobbett's views on Malthus can be found in Herman Ausubel, 'William Cobbett and Malthusianism', *Journal of the History of Ideas* 13 (1952), pp. 250–6. For introductions to Cobbett's politics, see Gertrude Himmelfarb, *The Idea of Poverty: England in the Early Industrial Age*, (New York: Vintage, 1985), ch. 9; and Raymond Williams, *Cobbett* (Oxford: Oxford University Press, 1983).

2. Malcom Chase, *'The People's Farm': English Radical Agrarianism 1775–1840* (Oxford: Clarendon, 1988), p. 132; Iorwerth Prothero, *Artisans and Politics in Early Nineteenth-Century London: John Gast and His Times* (Folkestone, Kent: Dawson and Son, 1979), p. 207.

3. On the *Trades' Newspaper*, see Prothero, pp. 183, 206–9, 216–31. I shall discuss *The Poor Man's Guardian* at more length below; the best introduction is Patricia Hollis, *The Pauper Press: A Study in Working Class Radicalism of the 1830s* (Oxford: Oxford University Press, 1970), especially ch. 7.

4. Biancamaria Fontana, *Rethinking the Politics of Commercial Society: the 'Edinburgh Review' 1802–1832* (Cambridge: Cambridge University Press, 1985), pp. 2, 4, 8. See also John Clive, *The Scotch Reviewers: The 'Edinburgh Review' 1802–1815* (London: Faber and Faber, 1957).

5. Henry Brougham, *Practical Observations on the Education of the People, addressed to the Working Classes and their Employers* (London, 1825), Preface; Thomas Chalmers, 'On Mechanics' Schools and on Political Economy as a Branch of Popular Education', *Glasgow Mechanics' Magazine* 5 (3 June 1826), p. 221; Nassau Senior, 'Political Economy', *Westminster Review*, 8 (July 1827), p. 183; as cited by Noel Thompson, *The People's Science: The popular political economy of exploitation and crisis 1816–1834* (Cambridge: Cambridge University Press, 1984), pp. 59, 59, n85.

6. Harold Perkin, *The Origins of Modern English Society 1780–1880* (Toronto: University of Toronto Press, 1969), p. 305. See also Prothero, pp. 191–203; and Elie Halévy, *Thomas Hodgskin*, ed. and trans. A.J. Taylor (London: Ernest Benn, 1956), pp. 86–91.

7. Francis Place, *Illustrations and Proofs of the Principle of Population* (London, 1822), p. 279. On Owen's confrontation with political economy, see Gregory Claeys, *Machinery, Money and the Millenium: From Moral Economy to Socialism, 1815–1860* (Princeton: Princeton University Press, 1987), pp. 48–50.

8. E.P. Thompson, *The Making of the English Working Class* (New York: Vintage, 1963), p. 727.

9. The classic statement is, of course, E.P. Thompson, 'The Moral Economy of the English Crowd in the Eighteenth Century', *Past and Present* 50 (1971), pp. 76–136. A useful supplement is Noel Thompson, *The Market and its Critics: Socialist Political Economy in Nineteenth Century Britain* (London and New York: Routledge, 1988), ch. 2.

10. *Trades Newspaper*, 13 November 1825, and 12 February 1826, as cited by Prothero, p. 229; and *Trades Newspaper*, 13 November, 1824, as reprinted in *Class and Conflict in Nineteenth-Century England, 1815–1850*, ed. Patricia Hollis (London: Routledge and Kegan Paul, 1973), p. 46.

11. See Cobbett's 'Address', in *The Opinions of William Cobbett*, pp. 201–17; and his

Tour of Scotland (1833), cited by Thompson, *Making*, p. 761.

12. Williams, *Cobbett*, p. 34; Thompson, *Making*, p. 757.

13. Thomas Evans, *Christian Policy, the Salvation of the Empire* (London, 1816), p. 14.

14. Thomas Spence to Charles Hall, 28 June 1807, in Gregory Claeys, 'Four Letters Between Thomas Spence and Charles Hall', *Notes and Queries* 226 (August 1981), p. 320; Iain McCalman, *Radical Underworld: Prophets, Revolutionaries and Pornographers in London, 1795–1840* (Cambridge: Cambridge University Press, 1988), p. 102.

15. See 'Four Letters Between Thomas Spence and Charles Hall', p. 320; and G.I. Gallop, 'Introductory Essay: Thomas Spence and the Real Rights of Man', in *Pig's Meat: The Selected Writings of Thomas Spence, Radical and Pioneer Land Reformer*, ed. G.I. Gallop (Nottingham: Spokesman, 1982), pp. 23–5. On this point I dissent from the view of Ian Hampsher-Monk, 'John Thelwall and the Eighteenth-Century Radical Response to Political Economy', *Historical Journal* 34 (1991), p. 14, who sees Spence as a nostalgic agrarian radical opposed to modernization.

16. On political anatomy and political arithmetic, see my *Political Economy and the Rise of Capitalism* (Berkeley: University of California Press, 1988), pp. 43–8.

17. As quoted by William Stafford, *Socialism, Radicalism, and Nostalgia: Social Criticism in Britain, 1775–1830* (Cambridge: Cambridge University Press, 1987), p. 109.

18. William Godwin, *Enquiry Concerning Political Justice*, ed. Isaac Kramnick (Harmondsworth: Penguin, 1985), pp. 793, 622. The notion of the capitalist as a middleman within the sphere of exchange, not as an employer of labour-power, is characteristic of the period.

19. As we have noted, he corresponded with Thomas Spence; see note 15 above.

20. Charles Hall, *The Effects of Civilization on the People in European States* (London, 1805), pp. 70, 103, 111.

21. Ibid., pp. 73, 70.

22. Stafford, pp. 158–9, emphasis in original.

23. See Thomas Paine, 'Dissertations on Government, the Affairs of the Bank, and Paper Money', in *The Thomas Paine Reader*, eds Michael Foot and Isaac Kramnick (Harmondsworth: Penguin, 1987), pp. 167–200. On Cobbett's alleged debt to Paine in this respect, see Himmelfarb, p. 209. On his views on money, see also Noel Thompson, *The Market*, pp. 41–4.

24. Cobbett, 'The Monied Interest', in *The Opinions' of William Cobbett*, pp. 69–70.

25. Cobbett, 'Paper-Money', in ibid., p. 282, emphasis in original.

26. Thompson, *Making*, p. 806.

27. James H. Treble, 'The Social and Economic Thought of Robert Owen', in *Robert Owen: Aspects of his Life and Work*, ed. John Butt (New York: Humanities Press, 1971), p. 42; Gregory Claeys, 'Paternalism and Democracy in the Politics of Robert Owen', *International Review of Social History*, 27 (1982), pp. 185–90; Robert Owen, 'A New View of Society', in his *A New View of Society and Report to the County of Lanark*, ed. V.A.C. Gatrell (Harmondsworth: Penguin, 1969), pp. 95, 99, 102; Owen, 'On The Employment of Children in Manufactories', in his *A New View of Society and Other Writings*, ed. G.D.H. Cole (London: J.M. Dent and Sons, 1927), pp. 133–4; W. Hamish Fraser, 'Robert Owen and the Workers', in *Robert Owen: Aspects of his life and work*, pp. 79–82; Chushichi Tsuzuki, 'Robert Owen and Revolutionary Politics', in *Robert Owen: Prophet of the Poor*, eds Sidney Pollard and John Salt (Lewisburg: Buckness University Press, 1971), p. 29; Ralph Miliband, 'The Politics of Robert Owen', *Journal of the History of Ideas* 15 (1954), p. 237.

28. Karl Marx and Frederick Engels, 'Manifesto of the Communist Party', in Karl

Marx, *The Revolutions of 1848*, ed. David Fernbach (Harmondsworth: Penguin, 1973), pp. 94–6.

29. John F.C. Harrison, *Quest for the New Moral World: Robert Owen and the Owenites in Britain and America* (New York: Charles Scribner's Sons, 1969), p. 196; Prothero, p. 239.

30. Harrison, p. 214. On the rise and fall of the GNCTU, see ibid., pp. 207–13.

31. Eileen Yeo, 'Robert Owen and Radical Culture', in *Robert Owen: Prophet of the Poor*, pp. 89–91.

32. Thompson, *Making*, p. 789. It is also worth noting, as Prothero, p. 255, does, that much of Owen's economic critique had been anticipated by artisan radicals.

33. Carpenter's *Letter to Wilmot Horton*, probably published in December 1830, as cited by Patricia Hollis, *The Pauper Press: A Study in Working-Class Radicalism of the 1830s* (Oxford: Oxford University Press, 1970), p. 217.

34. Owen, 'Report to the County of Lanark', in *A New View of Society and Report to the County of Lanark*, pp. 204, 207, 225–6.

35. Ibid., pp. 231–3, 251–2.

36. Ibid., pp. 205–10.

37. Ibid., pp. 221–3. On determining the average value input of labour, see also p. 207.

38. On Owen's acceptance of profit on capital, see Noel Thompson, *People's Science*, pp. 78, 78, n44, 79, n47; Hollis, p. 217; Treble, p. 41.

39. Owen, *Report*, pp. 207, 222–3.

40. I have chosen to refer to these as works of 'popular political economy'. Like Noel Thompson in *People's Science*, I reject the term 'Ricardian socialists', since all of these writers considered themselves to be anti-Ricardian. Thompson's term of choice, 'Smithian socialism', has much more to commend it since the theoretical approach of these writers owed much to Smith. Yet it cetainly does not fit Thomas Hodgskin, who was an individualist and anti-socialist. All of these writers, however, considered that they were writing on the side of the productive sections of society, and against the political economy of the idle and exploiting classes. In this sense, they considered their political economy to be 'popular', and following the lead of Hodgskin's *Popular Political Economy*, I have selected this term as that which most accurately describes their orientation.

41. I am largely in agreement with Noel Thompson (*People's Science*, p. 83) on this point, although I would qualify his position on a few counts as should become clear below.

42. Prothero, p. 208; Place, in Noel Thompson, *People's Science*, p. 20; James Mill to Henry Brougham, 3 September 1832, in Alexander Bain, *James Mill a Biography* (London: Longmans, Green, 1882), pp. 364–5. Mill's mis-spelling of Hodgskin's name was not idiosyncratic; it was a commonplace of the time.

43. See Elie Halévy, *Thomas Hodgskin*, ed. A.J. Taylor (London: Ernest Benn, 1956), pp. 31–9, 52–4, 113, 118, 125, 130, 133, 145, 148–9, 165; and C.H. Driver, 'Thomas Hodgskin and the Individualists', in *The Social and Political Ideas of Some Representative Thinkers of the Age of Reaction and Reconstruction*, ed. F.J.C. Hearnshaw (New York: Barnes and Noble, 1967), pp. 191–220.

44. Max Beer, *A History of British Socialism*, 2 vols (London: G. Bell and Sons, 1929), 1, p. 266.

45. Thomas Hodgskin, *Labour Defended Against the Claims of Capital* (1825; rpt London: Labour, 1922), pp. 60, 71–3, 91, 66. Two modern writers have treated Hodgskin's theory of capital as the theoretical predecessor of that of Marx, and of the latter's notion of fetishism. In so doing they commit an error which I shall examine below in discussing Marx's critique of petty bourgeois socialism. See E.K. Hunt,

'Value Theory in the Writings of the Classical Economists, Thomas Hodgskin, and Karl Marx', *History of Political Economy* 9 (1977), p. 341; and J.E. King, 'Utopian or Scientific? A Reconsideration of the Ricardian Socialists', *History of Political Economy* 15 (1983), p. 355.

46. On the political foundation of capitalist profit, see ibid., pp. 80, 86.

47. Hodgskin to Place, 28 May 1820, as reproduced by Halévy, pp. 72–5.

48. Hodgskin, *Labour Defended*, p. 91.

49. See Halévy, pp. 149, 145, and Hodgskin's 'A Lecture on Free Trade', reprinted as an appendix to his *Popular Political Economy* (1827); rpt New York: Sentry Press, 1966).

50. In addition to Hodgskin's letter to Place of 28 May 1820, evidence for his abiding debt to Smith can be found in *Popular Political Economy*, pp. x, xxii, 6, 19, 40, 100–101, 107, 178, 196, 220.

51. Driver, p. 219.

52. Richard K.P. Pankhurst, *William Thompson: Britain's Pioneer Socialist, Feminist, and Co-operator* (London: Watts, 1954), p. 23. On his importance in the co-operative movement, see Prothero, pp. 239–40, and on his support for the emancipation of women, see his *Appeal of One Half the Human Race* (1825; rpt New York: Burt Franklin, 1970), which staked out a much more radical position than that of Mary Wollstonecraft. See also Pankhurst, pp. 63, 70–79, 95; and Barbara Taylor, *Eve and the New Jerusalem* (London: Virago, 1983), pp. 17, 23–9, 50, 54.

53. Pankhurst, pp. 32, 207. The question as to how Thompson's views were taken up by others is a point to which we shall return.

54. William Thompson, *An Inquiry into the Principles of the Distribution of Wealth* (London, 1824), pp. 95, 4. On his Benthamite point of departure, see ibid., pp. v, 3, 4–6.

55. Ibid., pp. 45, 48–51, 56n–57n.

56. Ibid., pp. 165–7, 180, 244, 254, 424, 252. As with Hodgskin, Thompson does not clarify the actual mechanisms of labour exploitation.

57. As Marx pointed out, Owen actually transcends commodity production and exchange by presupposing 'directly socialized labour'. See Karl Marx, *Capital*, vol. 1, trans. Ben Fowkes (Harmondsworth: Penguin, 1976), p. 188, n1.

58. Ibid., pp. 368, 369.

59. Ibid., pp. 404, 399. It must have been with these arguments in mind that Marx described Thompson's *Inquiry* as a work which transcended the horizons of petty bourgeois socialism. See Karl Marx, *A Contribution to the Critique of Political Economy*, trans. S.W. Ryazanskaya (Moscow: Progress, 1970), p. 86.

60. William Thompson, *Labor Rewarded* (1827; rpt New York: Augustus M. Kelley, 199), pp. 4, 97.

61. Ibid., pp. 33–6, 12, 16, 13.

62. Ibid., p. 33.

63. Ibid., p. 109. Thompson's co-operative design was set forth in his *Practical Directions for the Speedy and Economical establishment of Communities, on the Principles of Mutual Cooperation, United Possessions and Equality of Exertions and of the Means of Enjoyment* (Cork, 1830), which is discussed by Pankhurst, ch. 15. As Pankhurst shows (e.g. p. 171), Thompson advocated a much more democratic approach to building co-operative communities than did Owen. In chapter 6 I shall discuss the radical difference beween commodity exchange and exchange of the products of socialized labour.

64. Ibid., pp. 73, 87, 12, 110, 92–3.

65. Claeys, *Machinery*, p. 110. For Thompson's defence of Gray, see Pankhurst, p. 171.

66. John Gray, *A Lecture on Human Happiness* (London: Sherwood, Jones, 1825),

pp. 5–6, 34, emphasis in original (I have omitted emphasis in the original from the first part of this citation).

67. Ibid., pp. 15–30.

68. Ibid., pp. 68, 70. Note that the last part of this citation does contain a vague notion of labour exploitation, but again it is one that is market-based.

69. Ibid., pp. 26–7; see also ibid., p. 43.

70. Ibid., pp. 57, 39.

71. Ibid., p. 60.

72. See Janet Kimball, *The Economic Doctrine of John Gray – 1799–1883* (Washington: Catholic University of America Press, 1948), pp. 6–7; David E. Martin, 'Gray, John (1799–1883), Early English Socialist and Currency Reformer', in *Dictionary of Labour Biography*, eds John Saville and J. Bellamy, vol. 6, p. 122; Claeys, *Machinery*, p. 118.

73 John Gray, *The Social System: A Treatise on the Principle of Exchange* (1831; rpt Clifton: Augustus M. Kelley, 1973), 1973), p. 19, emphasis omitted, pp. 25, 57, 90 emphasis in original.

74. Ibid., pp. 371, 58, 95, 127 emphasis in original.

75. Ibid., pp. 60, 195, 273, 274 emphasis in original, pp. 33, 16.

76. Ibid., pp. 31–7.

77. This point seems to me to have been largely missed by Noel Thompson, *The Market*, p. 109, who treats Gray as an advocate of a form of state socialism. It is not clear, however, in what sense Gray's position remained socialist by this time. In later works, as we shall see, he explicitly rejected socialism; moreover, even at this point, state regulation did not involve public ownership of the means of production. Private ownership was to remain the basis of economic life, and competition its motive force, in Gray's social system.

78. Ibid., pp. 99, 100 emphasis in original, pp. 103, 104.

79. Noel Thompson, *People's Science*, p. 180.

80. John Gray, *An Efficient Remedy for the Distress of Nations* (Edinburgh: Adam and Charles Black, 1842), pp. x, 2–5, 103, 5, 8–11, 16–25. See also Kimball, pp. 84–91.

81. John Gray, *Lectures on the Nature and Use of Money* (Edinburgh: Adam and Charles Black, 1848), pp. 282–3. On his embrace on Smith, see ibid., pp. 52–3; see also *Social System*, p. 340.

82. Martin, p. 123.

83. Beer, 1, p. 236.

84. John Francis Bray, *Labour's Wrongs and Labour's Remedies* (Leeds: David Green, 1839), pp. 17, 170. See Karl Marx, *The Poverty of Philosophy* (New York: International, 1963), p. 69, where he refers to Bray as 'an English *Communist*', and his book as 'his remarkable work'. Marx described Bray as a 'Communist' in contradistinction to the English 'Socialists' because of his support for communal property arrangements.

85. On Bray's life, see H.J. Carr, 'John Francis Bray', *Economica* 7 (1940), pp. 397–415, who shows that into his eighties Bray continued to participate in the American socialist and working-class movements.

86. Bray, *Labour's Wrongs*, pp. iv, 214 emphasis in original, pp. 8, 28, 30, 33.

87. Ibid., pp. 49, 50, 59, 61, 69, 80, 84.

88. James P. Henderson, '"An English Communist", Mr. Bray [and] his remarkable work', *History of Political Economy* 17 (1985), pp. 73–95, an interesting article which, however, thoroughly misconstrues central Marxian concepts like capital, relative surplus value and money.

89. Bray, *Labour's Wrongs*, pp. 78, 146, 88, 172.

90. Ibid., pp. 117, 124, 133, 134, 136, 128, 163, 168, 203, 193–4.

91. Ibid., pp. 193–4, 194–208.

92. See Gareth Stedman Jones, 'Rethinking Chartism' in his *Languages of Class: Studies in English working class history 1832–1982* (Cambridge: Cambridge University Press, 1983), pp. 90–178. I have put forward a critique of this piece in my 'Popular Political Economy and English Radicalism: The Case of Bronterre O'Brien', forthcoming.

93. As cited by Alfred Plummer, *Bronterre: A Political Biography of Bronterre O'Brien 1804–1864* (Toronto: University of Toronto Press, 1971), pp. 38–9. On O'Brien, see also Eva H. Haraszti, *Chartism* (Budapest: Akadamiai Kiado, 1978), pp. 68–77.

94. O'Brien, *Poor Man's Guardian*, 5 July 1834, hereafter cited as *PMG*.

95. Charles Gide and Charles Rist, *A History of Economic Doctrines*, 2nd edn, trans. R. Richards (London: George G. Harrap, 1948), p. 251. On the upsurge of co-operative experiments during this period, see Harrison, pp. 195–232, and G.D.H. Cole, *Century*, ch. 2.

96. See *PMG*, 7 January 1832, 18 February 1832.

97. W. King, *The Working of Capital, at present represented by money* (London, 1831), as cited by Noel Thompson, *People's Science*, p. 176.

98. *PMG*, 21 July 1832.

99. W.H. Oliver, 'The Labour Exchange Phase of the Cooperative Movement', *Oxford Economic Papers*, n.s., 10 (1958), pp. 357–8).

100. Davenport, as cited by E.P. Thompson, *Making*, p. 798; for O'Brien's initial scepticism and subsequent enthusiasm, see *PMG*, 22 September 1832, 2 November 1833.

101. Harrison, p. 205. For the participation of artisans see Oliver, pp. 358–62; E.P. Thompson, *Making*, p. 791.

102. *PMG*, 29 September 1832.

103. Oliver, p. 362; E.P. Thompson, *Making*, p. 792.

104. Benjamin Warden, 'Rewards of Industry', in *Owenism and the Working Class: Six Pamphlets and Four Broadsides 1821–1834* (New York: Arno Press, 1972), n.p.

105. Cole, *Century*, p. 31. See also Harrison, p. 206; Oliver, pp. 366–7; Gide and Rist, p. 252, n.1.

106. Oliver, pp. 362–3, 366.

107. Cited by Noel Thompson, *Market*, p. 99, n30.

5. Proudhon did Enormous Mischief

1. Maximilien Rubel, 'A History of Marx's "Economics"', in *Rubel on Karl Marx: Five Essays*, eds Joseph O'Malley and Keith Algozin (Cambridge: Cambridge University Press, 1981), p. 119.

2. Karl Marx, 'Letter to J.B. Schweitzer, 24 January 1865', in Karl Marx, *The Poverty of Philosophy* (New York: International, 1963), pp. 194–6.

3. P.J. Proudhon, *What is Property*, trans. Benjamin R. Tucker (New York: Dover, 1970), pp. 70–71, 82, 109, 112.

4. Ibid., pp. 133, 167, 121–4.

5. Ibid., pp. 239, 285, 286. See also the Introduction to this work by George Woodcock, p. xiv.

6. P.J. Proudhon, *System of Economical Contradictions or, The Philosophy of Misery* (New York: Arno Press, 1972), p. 282. See also ibid., p. 97, and idem, *General Idea of the Revolution in the Nineteenth Century*, trans. John Beverley Robinson (New York: Haskel House, 1969), p. 227.

7. As cited by Robert L. Hoffman, *Revolutionary Justice: The Social and Political Theory of P.J. Proudhon* (Urbana: University of Illinois Press, 1972), p. 283.

8. Proudhon, *General Idea*, p. 268; Edward Hyams, *Pierre-Joseph Proudhon* (London: John Murray, 1979), p. 219.

9. Proudhon, *System*, pp. 127, 303.

10. Proudhon, *General Idea*, p. 228.

11. Proudhon, 'The Solution of the Social Problem', pp. 45–8, and 'System', pp. 49–51, in *Proudhon's Solution of the Social Problem*, ed. Henry Cohen (New York: Vanguard Press, 1927).

12. See Hyams, p. 280.

13. Proudhon, *General Idea*, pp. 273, 242–4; and *System*, pp. 225–7, 229, 240–41; Hyams, pp. 142, 192; and Proudhon, *System*, pp. 259–61, 270–71.

14. Proudhon, *System*, pp. 396, 398, 149. See also Hyams, p. 107; and Henry Collins and Chimen Abramsky, *Karl Marx and the British Labour Movement: Years of the First International* (London: Macmillan, 1965), p. 117, n1. On Proudhon's 1865 work, see Karl Marx, 'Political Indifferentism', in Karl Marx, *The First International and After*, ed. David Fernbach (Harmondsworth: Penguin, 1974), pp. 330–31.

15. As cited by J. Hampden Jackson, *Marx, Proudhon and European Socialism* (London: The English Universities Press, 1957), p. 84.

16. As cited by Hyams, pp. 102, 125.

17. Cited by Hyams, p. 166; Jackson, p. 131.

18. Hyams, pp. 147, 150, 204. For Marx's comments on Proudhon's analysis of Louis Bonaparte's coup, see 'The Eighteenth Brumaire of Louis Bonaparte', in Karl Marx, *Surveys from Exile*, ed. David Fernbach (Harmondsworth: Penguin, 1973), pp. 143–4. The most systematic critique of Proudhon from a Marxist perspective has been developed by Hal Draper, *Karl Marx's Theory of Revolution. Volume IV: Critique of Other Socialisms* (New York: Monthly Review Press, 1990), ch. 5.

19. Hyams, pp. 272–4, 63; Collins and Abramsky, p. 119.

20. Marx to Kugelmann, 9 October 1866, in *Selected Correspondence of Marx and Engels*, 2nd edn (Moscow: Progress, 1965), pp. 183–4.

21. Collins and Abramsky, p. 85.

22. *Mémoire des délégués français au Congrès de Génève*, as quoted in ibid., p. 117, n1; ibid., p. 118.

23. Ibid., p. 128. At Brussels the following year, Marx's ideas were sufficiently influential to block mutualist resolutions.

24. Ibid., pp. 151, 171, 252–3.

25. Marx to F. Bolte, 23 November 1871, as cited in ibid., p. 249.

26. Karl Marx, 'Communism and the Augsburg *Allgemeine Zeitung*', in *Collected Works of Marx and Engels* (hereafter cited as *CW*), 1, p. 220. The 'non-committal' character of Marx's discussion at this point is noted by W. Pickles, 'Marx and Proudhon', *Politica* 3 (1938), pp. 242–3.

27. Frederick Engels, 'Progress of Social Reform on the Continent', in *CW*, 3, p. 399. For an interesting discussion of Proudhon's influence on Engel's *Outlines*, see Gregory Claeys, 'Engels's *Outlines of a Critique of Political Economy* (1843) and the Origins of the Marxist Critique of Capitalism', *History of Political Economy* 16 (1984), pp. 207–32. The influence of this work on Marx is discussed, in occasionally exaggerated terms, by Terrell Carver, *Marx and Engels: The Intellectual Relationship* (Bloomington: Indiana University Press, 1983), ch. 2

28. Karl Marx, 'Economic and Philosophic Manuscripts', in *CW*, 3, pp. 241, 280.

29. Ibid., pp. 316, 317.

30. Marx and Engels, *The Holy Family*, in *CW*, 4, pp. 32, 34, 35.

31. Ibid., pp. 31, 42–3.

32. Oscar J. Hammen, *The Red '48ers: Karl Marx and Friedrich Engels* (New York: Charles Scribner's Sons, 1969), pp. 142–3; David McLellan, *Karl Marx: His Life and Thought* (New York: Harper and Row, 1973), pp. 159–60.

33. Marx to Schweitzer, in Marx, *Poverty*, p. 202.

34. Marx, *Poverty*, p. 55, and generally pp. 45–69. At this point Marx considered exchange-value to be determined by the minimum labour-time necessary to the production of a commodity, as opposed to the socially necessary labour-time (which approximates the social average). He also had not yet fully theorized the relationship between the measure and the substance of value.

35. Ibid., pp. 64–5, 68.

36. Ibid., pp. 77, 78.

37. Ibid., pp. 79, 81. Marx directly discusses the issue of labour exchanges in 79n.

38. Ibid., p. 114.

39. Ibid., pp. 115, 122, 125–6; Karl Marx and Friedrich Engels, *Manifesto of the Communist Party* in Karl Marx, *The Revolutions of 1848*, ed. David Fernbach (Harmondsworth: Penguin, 1973), p. 80.

40. Marx, *Poverty*, pp. 172–4. On the principle of working-class self-emancipation in Marx's theory, see Hal Draper, *Karl Marx's Theory of Revolution. Volume One: State and Bureaucracy* (New York: Monthly Review Press, 1977), ch. 10. For a discussion of Marx's 'optimistic fatalism' with respect to the development of working-class consciousness, see John Molyneux, *Marxism and the Party* (London: Pluto, 1978), ch. 1.

41. Marx to Engels, 14 August 1851 and 13 October 1851, in Karl Marx and Friedrich Engels, *Letters on 'Capital'* (London: New Park, 1983), pp. 28–30, 31; Marx to Engels, 24 November 1851 and Marx to Wedermeyer, 13 December 1851, as cited by Rubels, p. 139.

42. Marx to Engels, 10 January 1857, in *Letters on 'Capital'*, p. 41.

43. Karl Marx, *Grundrisse*, trans. Martin Nicolaus (Harmondsworth: Penguin, 1973), pp. 115–238.

44. Ibid., pp. 115, 122–3, 127.

45. Ibid., pp. 136–40.

46. Ibid., pp. 141, 145, 157, 145.

47. Ibid., p. 151. What Marx has in mind here is that his *Grundrisse* discussion treats the many concrete determinations which make up capitalism as emanating from the nature of money and its apparently innate drive to self-expansion. *Capital*, however, begins with a much more concrete and determinate point of departure – the commodity, the immediate form of appearance of capital. On this point see John Mepham, 'From the *Grundrisse* to *Capital*: The Making of Marx's Method', in *Issues in Marxist Philosophy. Volume One: Dialectics and Method*, eds John Mepham and D.H. Ruben (Atlantic Highlands, N.J.: Humanities Press, 1979), pp. 145–73.

48. Ibid., pp. 153–6, 171.

49. Ibid., p. 172.

50. Marx to Engels, 2 April 1858; Marx to Wedermeyer, 1 February 1859; Marx to Engels, 22 July 1859, in *Letters on 'Capital'*, pp. 59, 61, 66, 65, 68.

51. Karl Marx, *A Contribution to the Critique of Political Economy* (Moscow: Progress, 1970), pp. 84–5.

52. Ibid., p. 86.

53. Marx to Lassalle, 28 March 1859, in *Letters on 'Capital'*, p. 68.

54. Karl Marx, *Capital*, vol. 1, trans. Ben Fowkes (Harmondsworth: Penguin, 1976), pp. 150, 153. The previous three paragraphs draw upon the whole discussion on pp. 125–50.

55. Ibid., p. 166.

56. Marx, *Grundrisse*, pp. 159, 160.

57. Marx, *Capital*, 1, p. 161, n26. See also ibid., p. 181, n4.

58. Ibid., p. 196. Marx does not deal at this point with the added complication of divergences of prices from immanent value brought about by equalization of the rate of profit in the context of variations in the organic composition of capital (the value relation of means of production to living labour); he takes these points up only in the third volume of *Capital*.

59. Ibid., p. 199.

60. Ibid., p. 236.

61. This confusion received sustenance from Engels's 'Supplement and Addendum to volume 3 of *Capital*', which applies Marx's law of value to all acts of exchange irrespective of mode of production. See Karl Marx, *Capital*, vol. 3, trans. David Fernbach (Harmondsworth: Penguin, 1981), pp. 1027–47. An excellent critique of Engels's position is set forth by John Weeks, *Capital and Exploitation* (Princeton: Princeton University Press, 1981), pp. 50–62.

62. Marx, *Capital*, 1, pp. 729–30.

63. Ibid., p. 731.

64. Ibid., p. 733. See also Marx, *Capital*, vol. 2, trans. David Fernbach (Harmondsworth: Penguin, 1978), p. 196.

65. Ibid., p. 734, n10.

66. Frederick Engels, *Anti-Dühring* (Moscow: Progress, 1969), p. 368. Engels notes the similarity between Dühring and Proudhon, ibid., p. 370.

6. Beyond the Market

1. Karl Marx, *Grundrisse*, trans. Martin Nicolaus (Harmondsworth: Penguin, 1973), pp. 158–9.

2. Both terms quoted come from Alec Nove, *The Economics of Feasible Socialism* (London: George Allen and Unwin, 1983), pp. 203, 42. Nove's book is littered with this sort of denunciation and dismissal – a poor substitute for rigorous confrontation with key Marxian concepts (which are continually misunderstood throughout his text). *The Economics of Feasible Socialism* must stand as a prime example of what Geras describes as 'that volume of caricature, ill-informed oversimplification and generally facile disputation in the treatment of Marxian thought', which characterizes so much discussion on the Left at the moment. See Norman Geras, 'Seven Types of Obloquy: Travesties of Marxism', *Socialist Register 1990: The Retreat of the Intellectuals*, eds Ralph Miliband and Leo Panitch (London: Merlin, 1990), p. 6.

3. It is not only Nove who talks of commodities, prices, money and profit under socialism. So, albeit with some qualifications to be discussed below, do Wlodimierz Brus, *The Market in a Socialist Economy* (London: Routledge and Kegan Paul, 1972); and Diane Elson, 'Market Socialism or Socialization of the Market?', *New Left Review* 172 (1988). Brus's earlier caution in this area has largely disappeared in his latest effort, with Kazimierz Laski, *From Marx to the Market: Socialism in Search of an Economic System* (Oxford: Oxford University Press, 1989).

4. Nove, p. 211; Alan Carling, 'Rational Choice Marxism', in *Approaches to Marx*, eds Mark Cowling, Lawrence Wilde and Milton Keynes (Philadelphia: Open University Press, 1989), p. 194; Robin Blackburn, 'Fin de Siècle: Socialism After the Crash', *New Left Review* 185 (1991), pp. 15, 41, and 31–63 generally. It is instructive that the theory of value Nove employs here is derived from neo-classical bourgeois economics. Carling's approach at least has the merit of consistency – it consistently subscribes to

the tenets of liberal individualism. For critical assessments of Carling and 'rational choice Marxism', see Ellen Meiksins Wood, 'Rational Choice Marxism: Is the Game Worth the Candle?', *New Left Review* 177 (1989); and Michael Lebowitz, 'Is "Analytical Marxism" Marxism?', *Science and Society* 52 (1988).

5. Nove, pp. 210–15.

6. Ludwig von Mises, 'Economic Calculation in the Socialist Commonwealth', in *Collectivist Economic Planning*, ed. Friedrich A. von Hayek (London: Routledge and Sons, 1935), pp. 105, 111, 112.

7. Brus and Laski, p. 151, Preface, n.p., pp. 105–17, 151.

8. Frederic Jameson, 'Postmodernism and the Market', *Socialist Register 1990*, p. 98.

9. Ludwig von Mises, *Human Action* (New Haven: Yale University Press, 1949), pp. 590, 591.

10. Karl Marx, *Capital*, vol. 1, trans. Ben Fowkes (Harmondsworth: Penguin, 1976), p. 733.

11. Karl Marx, *Theories of Surplus Value*, Part 3, trans. Jack Cohen and S.W. Ryazanskaya (Moscow: Progress, 1971), p. 74. It should be remembered that independent commodity producers (including peasants) whose reproduction is market-dependent – i.e. they have market-determined money rents, must buy both producer and consumer goods on the market, and are thus compelled to raise cash through commodity production – are also governed by the market.

12. Marx, *Grundrisse*, pp. 421n, 424.

13. Marx, *Capital*, 1, pp. 436–7.

14. Ibid., p. 742.

15. Karl Marx, 'Immediate Results of the Process of Production', in *Capital*, 1, p. 989; *Grundrisse*, p. 513. Of course, all of this entails *some* form of private ownership and/or control of the means of production; but this need not mean that certain individuals have a legal claim over the means of production, only that the latter are not owned *and controlled* by society. Alienated labour and the commodity form do entail asocial (and hence private, particularistic) forms of ownership and control – but these forms are multifaceted, a point to which I return.

16. Karl Marx, *Capital*, vol. 3, trans. David Fernbach (Harmondsworth: Penguin, 1981), p. 571.

17. Marx, *Grundrisse*, p. 512. It is on this basis that Marx and Engels could talk of the state playing the role of capitalist. See Karl Marx, 'Marginal Notes on Wagner', in *Value: Studies by Marx*, trans. Albert Dragstedt (London: New Park, 1976), p. 216; and Friedrich Engels, *Anti-Dühring* (Moscow: Progress, 1947), pp. 329–31.

18. For good empirical evidence, see Andrew Zimblast and Howard J. Sherman, *Comparing Economic Systems* (Orlando: Academic Press, 1984), pp. 428–34; Laura D'Andrea Tyson and Egon Neuberger, 'The Impact of External Economic Disturbances on Yugoslavia: Theoretical and Empirical Explorations', *Journal of Comparative Economics*, 3 91979), pp. 346–74; and Diane Flaherty, 'Economic Reform and Foreign Trade in Yugoslavia', *Cambridge Journal of Economics* 6 (1982), pp. 105–43. For a first-rate account of the evolution of Yugoslavia from market Stalinism to disintegration, see Duncan Blackie, 'The Road to Hell', *International Socialism* 53, n.s. (1991), pp. 29–56.

19. Diane Flaherty, 'Self-Management and Socialism: Lessons from Yugoslavia', *Science and Society* 56:1 (1992), pp. 92–108.

20. Arthur Diquattro, 'Alienation and Justice in the Market', in *Marxism and the Good Society*, eds John P. Burke, Lawrence Crocker and Lyman H. Legters (Cambridge: Cambridge University Press, 1981), p. 134.

21. On this point, see Hal Draper, *Karl Marx's Theory of Revolution. Volume One: State*

and Bureaucracy (New York: Monthly Review Press, 1977), chs 9 and 10.

22. Karl Marx, 'Inaugural Address of the International Workingmen's Association', in Karl Marx, *The First International and After: Political Writings, Volume Three* (Harmondsworth: Penguin, 1974), p. 79.

23. Marx, *Theories of Surplus Value*, 3, pp. 255, 257.

24. Marx, *Grundrisse*, p. 706.

25. Marx, 'Inaugural Address', p. 79; *Capital*, 3, p. 571.

26. Karl Marx, 'Instructions for the Delegates of the Provisional General Council. The Different Questions', in *Minutes of the General Council of the First International, 1864–66* (Moscow: Foreign Languages, n.d.), p. 346, as cited by Michael Lebowitz, *Beyond Capital: Marx's Political Economy of the Working Class* (New York: St. Martin's Press, 1992), p. 72. The whole of chapter 4 of Lebowitz's important study is directly relevant to these issues.

27. Marx, 'Inaugural Address', pp. 79, 80. I emphasize here that I am discussing *tendencies*. Capitalism also breeds that fetishism which takes the capital/wage-labour relation as natural, and this is a central part of the tendency towards reformism in the working-class movement.

28. One can see here the consistency of Nove, who argues (p. 42) against any alternative to the market and the state and thus accepts the necessity of both.

29. Marx, *Capital*, 3, p. 370; and *Capital*, 1, p. 172.

30. Marx, *Grundrisse*, p. 172; and Karl Marx, *Critique of the Gotha Programme* (New York: International, 1966), p. 8.

31. I will leave a further objection – the capacity of socialism to provide a means of rational economic calculation – to the next subsection of this chapter. I am not addressing in this study the most frequent objection: the view that the experience of the 'command economies' of eastern Europe has proved the disastrous consequences of any commitment to economic planning. As indicated at the outset of this work, I subscribe to the powerful case that has been made to the effect that these regimes can best be characterized as 'state capitalist' in nature. And it should be said that this case involves not mere sloganeering, but an impressive body of theoretical and empirical analysis. The outstanding work of Chris Harman over the past twenty years or so should serve as ample illustration. See especially 'The Eastern Bloc', in *World Crisis: Essays in Revolutionary Socialism*, eds Nigel Harris and John Palmer (London: Hutchinson, 1971); *Bureacracy and Revolution in Eastern Europe* (London: Pluto, 1974), updated as *Class Struggles in Eastern Europe* (London; Bookmarks, 1985); 'Poland: the Crisis of State Capitalism', Parts I and II, *International Socialism* 93 and 94, November–December 1976, January 1977; with Andy Zebrowski, 'Glasnost Before the Storm', *International Socialism* 39, n.s., Summer 1988; 'The Storm Breaks', *International Socialism* 46, n.s., Spring 1990.

32. Jean Cohen, *Class and Civil Society: The Limits of Marxian Critical Theory* (Amherst: University of Massachusetts Press, 1982), p. 184.

33. Marx, *Grundrisse*, p. 197, my emphasis, and p. 706; *Capital*, 3, p. 1016; *Wages, Price and Profit* (Moscow: Progress, 1947), p. 47. These examples are so numerous that a full-length study could be devoted to their enumeration and clarification. For a work that recognizes the centrality of 'free individuality' to Marx's position, see Carol Gould, *Marx's Social Ontology: Individuality and Community in Marx's Theory of Social Reality* (Cambridge, Mass.: MIT Press, 1978).

34. Marx, *Grundrisse*, p. 158. See also *Capital*, 3, pp. 1015–16.

35. Kate Soper, *On Human Need: Open and Closed Theories in a Marxist Perspective* (Sussex: Harvester, 1981), pp. 134, 91–2, 99, 108, 194.

36. G.W.F. Hegel, *Philosophy of Right*, trans. T.M. Knox (London: Oxford University Press, 19520, p. 11. For one of the very few studies which understands the

centrality to Marx's thought of the notion of immanent critique, see Patrick Murray, *Marx's Theory of Scientific Knowledge* (New Jersey: Humanities Press, 1988).

37. For an excellent discussion of this, see Lebowitz, pp. 23–7.

38. Karl Marx and Frederick Engels, 'Manifesto of the Communist Party', in Karl Marx, *Political Writings. Volume One: The Revolutions of 1848* (Harmondsworth: Penguin, 1973), p. 87. On Marx's schematization of stages of economic history *from the standpoint of free individuality*, see Gould, pp. 3–30; and Tony Smith, *The Logic of Marx's 'Capital': Replies to Hegelian Criticisms* (Albany: State University of New York Press, 1990), pp. 62–70. It must be emphasized that this categorization has a particular problematic: the development of the free social individual. It is entirely distinct from an historical delineation of modes of production.

39. Marx, *Grundrisse*, pp. 158, 159.

40. Nove, pp. 15–16.

41. Marx, *Capital*, 3, p. 958–9; *Capital*, 1, p. 667.

42. Marx, *Capital*, 3, pp. 958–9. As well as prioritizing the reduction of social labour, Marx is equally concerned that the process of social production itself be disalienated to the greatest extent possible – a point to which I return below.

43. Marx, *Grundrisse*, p. 172. This point seems to me essential to rounding out the insightful discussion of the issue of abundance in Norman Geras, 'The Controversy About Marx and Justice', in his *Literature of Revolution: Essays on Marxism* (London: Verso, 1986), pp. 51–4.

44. Marx, *Capital*, 2, p. 544; *Capital*, 2, pp. 544–5. See Nove, Part 1; and Blackburn, pp. 46–8.

45. Nove, pp. 19, 215, 229, 233, 225.

46. On Marx's anti-elitist aversion to blueprints, see Draper, ch. 10.

47. On this important point, see Alex Callinicos, *The Revenge of History: Marxism and the East European Revolutions* (Oxford: Polity, 1991), pp. 118–20.

48. Marx, *Grundrisse*, p. 171.

49. Marx, *Capital*, 1, p. 188, n1. See also *Capital*, 2, p. 434.

50. Blackburn, pp. 31–55.

51. Israel M. Kirzner, *The Meaning of Market Process: Essays in the Development of Austrian Economics* (London: Routledge, 1992), p. 201. The quote from Joseph Schumpeter can be found in his *History of Economic Analysis* (New York: Oxford University Press, 1954), pp. 986–7.

52. Israel M. Kirzner, *Prime Mover of Progress* (London: Institute of Economic Affairs, 1980), p. 146; Kirzner, *Meaning*, ch. 13.

53. Perhaps nowhere is this clearer than in the so-called 'philosophical' works of the later Hayek. See chapter 2 above, notes 3–5.

54. E.K. Hunt, 'A Radical Critique of Welfare Economics', in *Growth, Profits, and Property*, ed. E. Nell (Cambridge: Cambridge University Press, 1980), p. 244. For an excellent treatment of 'Crusoe economics', see Stephen Hymer, 'Robinson Crusoe and the Secret of Primitive Accumulation', ibid., ch. 2.

55. Robin Hahnel and Michael Albert, *Quiet Revolution in Welfare Economics* (Princeton: Princeton University Press, 1990), p. 218.

56. Harvey Leibenstein, *General X-Efficiency Theory and Economic Development* (New York: Oxford University Press, 1978); and *Inside the Firm: The Inefficiencies of Hierarchy* (Cambridge, Mass.: Harvard University Press, 1987).

57. See Mark Blaug, *Economic Theory in Retrospect*, 3rd edn (Cambridge: Cambridge University Press, 1978), ch. 12.

58. William J. Baumol, *Welfare Economics and the State* (London: London School of Economics and Political Science, 1965), pp. 131–2.

59. J. De V. Graaff, *Theoretical Welfare Economics* (Cambridge: Cambridge University Press, 1963), p. 105.

60. On the neo-Austrian rejection of general equilibrium theory, see Kirzner, *Meaning*, ch. 2; and Alexander H. Shand, *The Capitalist Alternative: An Introduction to Neo-Austrian Economics* (Brighton: Wheatsheaf, 1984), pp. 37–41. Robin Blackburn seems entirely to have missed the fact that the neo-Austrian theory of calculation of which he is enamoured entails a theory of economic instability and disequilibrium.

61. Graaff, p. 99.

62. Thomas R. De Gregori, 'Power and Illusion in the Marketplace: Institutions and Technology', in *The Economy as a System of Power*, 2nd edn, eds Marc R. Tool and Warren J. Samuels (New Brunswick, N.J.: Transaction, 1989), p. 39.

63. Ibid., p. 40.

64. Amartya Sen, *Poverty and Famines* (Oxford: Oxford University Press, 1981), pp. 161–2.

65. Ernest Mandel, 'In Defence of Socialist Planning', *New Left Review* 159 (1986), pp. 10, 11. Mandel's useful article suffers from one huge deficiency: failure to discuss the labour market and the commodification of labour-power as the crucial feature of a market-regulated economy. His critique of market socialism is thus severely weakened.

66. Pat Devine, *Democracy and Economic Planning* (Cambridge: Polity, 1988), p. 242.

67. This point is hinted at by Pat Devine, who correctly insists on distinguishing between market exchange (which socialism can accept within limits) and market forces (which are antithetical to socialism however much they might have to be tolerated and hemmed in for a period of time). Unfortunately, Devine undermines much of his own case by accepting the need for a labour market (and hence the commodification of labour-power) and by giving market prices an exaggerated role in the allocative process. See ibid., pp. 22–3, 197, 238–41.

68. Wlodzimierz Brus, *The Economics and Politics of Socialism* (London: Routledge and Kegan Paul, 1973), p. 55. This is far and away Brus's best book on the economics of socialism. In fact, this book – especially chapter 4, 'Commodity Fetishism and Socialism' – is much superior to his best-known work, *The Market in a Socialist Economy*, trans. Angus Walker (London: Routledge and Kegan Paul, 1972). While the latter has some interesting things to say about 'regulated prices', it betrays a thorough misunderstanding of the applicability of the law of value to socialism, a defect which plays havoc with the whole discussion. Brus's latest writings move dramatically in the direction of Alec Nove's position. See, for example, 'Socialism – Feasible and Viable', *New Left Review* 153 (1985), pp. 43–62.

69. Marx, *Grundrisse*, p. 706; *Capital*, 3, p. 959.

70. Marx, *Theories of Surplus Value*, 3, p. 255.

71. Quality control inspectors would have to be accountable to public agencies. Poor quality products which were rejected by these inspectors would thus involve increased hours on the part of workers who failed to meet established standards.

72. Marx, *Grundrisse*, p. 409.

73. Ibid. See also Lebowitz, pp. 17–26; and Istvan Meszaros, 'Marx "Philosopher"' in *The History of Marxism. Volume One: Marxism in Marx's Day*, ed. Eric J. Hobsbawm (Bloomington: Indiana University Press, 1982).

74. Marx, *Capital*, 3, p. 959. It should be remembered that Marx rejected the notion of a fixed human nature. The human nature at issue here is socially and historically formed.

75. Marx, 'Economic and Philosophical Manuscripts', in *Collected Works of Marx and Engels*, vol. 3, pp. 276, 275, 277.

76. Frederick Engels, *Dialectics of Nature*, 2nd edn (Moscow: Progress, 1954), pp. 183, 180; Marx, *Capital*, 1, p. 638.

77. Oskar Lange, 'On the Economic Theory of Socialism', in Oskar Lange and Fred M. Taylor, *On the Economic Theory of Socialism* (New York: McGraw Hill, 1964), p. 61.

78. Joseph Schumpeter, *Capitalism, Socialism and Democracy*, 3rd edn (New York: Harper and Row, 1975), pp. 172, 196. This is not to embrace Schumpeter's hypothetical socialist model. Like Lange, Taylor and Dobb, Schumpeter is too ready to accept the terms of debate thrown up by Mises and Hayek. On this point, however, he is clearly correct.

79. See Mandel, pp. 10–18.

80. Oskar Lange, 'The Computer and the Market', in *Socialism, Capitalism and Economic Growth: Essays presented to Maurice Dobb* (Cambridge: Cambridge University Press, 1967), p. 161. While differing with Lange's model of socialist planning, I see no flaw in his argument on this point.

81. Maurice Dobb, *Welfare Economics and the Economics of Socialism* (Cambridge: Cambridge University Press, 1969), p. 165. On the use of labour inputs generally as a means of calculation, see ibid., chs 8–9.

82. Diane Elson, 'Market Socialism or Socialization of the Market?', *New Left Review* 172 (1988), p. 28.

83. Ibid., pp. 27, 12, 11, 27.

84. Marx, *Grundrisse*, p. 160.

85. Elson's confusion in this area is not new. In an often insightful essay on Marx's theory of value from the late 1970s, she consistently confused matters by suggesting that abstract labour is a transhistorical concept, one applicable to any and all forms of economy. In so doing, she failed to grasp Marx's insistence that abstract labour refers to the purely formal and alienated universality of human labour under capitalism. Unlike social labour, which is a concept applicable to all forms of economy, the notion of abstract labour is specific to the reified forms of capitalist economy. See Elson, 'The Value Theory of Labour', in *Value: The Representation of Labour in Capitalism*, ed. Diane Elson (London: CSE, 1978), pp. 149–50.

86. Elson, pp. 43–4. This is not to disparage Elson's many valid insights. She is right to point out, for instance, that Mandel fails to incorporate the household and the labour performed therein into his model. Her own approach to this issue, however, is too uncritical. She fails to discuss the prospect of socializing large amounts of this kind of necessary social labour through the development of communal kitchens, dining facilities, laundries and childcare centres.

87. Depiction of socialism as spruced-up liberalism is the basic thrust of both 'rational choice Marxism' and the trendy 'post-Marxism' of Laclau and Mouffe. For critiques of the former, see Ellen Meiksins Wood, 'Rational Choice Marxism'; and Michael Lebowitz, 'Is "Analytical Marxism" Marxism?' The classic of 'post-Marxism' is Ernesto Laclau and Chantal Mouffe, *Hegemony and Socialist Strategy* (London: Verso, 1985). For important rejoinders, see Ellen Meiksins Wood, *The Retreat From Class* (London: Verso, 1986); and Norman Geras, *Discourses of Extremity* (London: Verso, 1990), chs 3 and 4. The most significant attempt to assess Marxism in the aftermath of the events in Eastern Europe is Callinicos, *Revenge of History*.

88. Pat Devine, 'Self-Governing Socialism', in *The Future of Socialism: Perspectives from the Left*, ed. William K. Tabb (New York: Monthly Review Press, 1990), pp. 201–202.

Conclusion

1. Edmund Burke, 'Thoughts and Details on Scarcity', in *The Works of Edmund Burke*, 4th edn, vol. 5 (Boston: Little, Brown, 1871), p. 142; Thomas Robert Malthus,

'Essay on Population', 2nd edn, in *Works of Thomas Robert Malthus*, eds E.A. Wrigley and David Souden (London: William Pickering, 1986), 3, p. 516.

2. As cited by K.D.M. Snell, *Annals of the Labouring Poor: Social Change and Agrarian England 1660–1900* (Cambridge: Cambridge University Press, 1985), p. 171. The equation here of wage-labour with labour in general is a symptom of the reification of capitalist social relations.

3. Karl Polanyi, *The Great Transformation* (Boston: Beacon Press, 1957), p. 83. See also ibid., p. 82.

4. Karl Marx, *Theories of Surplus Value*, Part One, trans. Emile Burns (Moscow: Progress, 1963), p. 43.

5. Malthus, 'Essay', in *Works*, 3, pp. 575–6.

6. Karl Marx, *Capital*, vol. 1, trans. Ben Fowkes (Harmondsworth: Penguin, 1976), p. 874. Let me again emphasize that the separation of labour and capital can exist even in the context of workers' co-operatives producing according to the imperatives of a market system – labour in such a context remains subordinated to (thus separated from) the accumulative imperatives imposed by the market.

7. Karl Marx, *The Poverty of Philosophy* (New York: International, 1963). Of course, extra-economic force only 'pulls back' from centre-stage. It is always in the wings waiting to be used when economic compulsion alone does not suffice to maintain the stability of capital accumulation.

8. Karl Marx, *A Contribution to the Critique of Political Economy*, trans. S.W. Ryazanskaya (Moscow: Progress, 1970), p. 85. Marx is here referring specifically to John Gray.

9. G.W.F. Hegel, *Realphilosophie*, vol. 1, pp. 239ff., as cited by Georg Lukacs, *The Young Hegel*, trans. Rodney Livingstone (London: Merlin, 1975), p. 333. I prefer this translation of Hegel's passage to that provided in G.W.F. Hegel, *System of Ethical Life and First Philosophy of Spirit*, eds and trans. H.S. Harris and T.M. Knox (Albany: State University of New York Press, 1979), p. 249.

10. Hegel, *System*, p. 248.

11. For a clear discussion of the undialectical nature of Hegel's 'resolution' of bourgeois antagonisms, see Herbert Marcuse, 'The Concept of Negation in the Dialectic', *Telos* 8 (1971), pp. 30–2.

12. For an exceptionally clear explanation of the links between market reform, economic collapse and political crisis in Yugoslavia, see Duncan Blackie, 'The Road to Hell', *International Socialism* 53 (1991). My argument here should not be taken in any way to imply the superiority of the older state-capitalist arrangements in the Stalinist bloc. The very crisis that the market is exacerbating grew out of precisely those arrangements. My point is simply that the market is the key instrument of capitalist restructuring, be it in North America, Africa or Eastern Europe. Data on Africa come from John Stackhouse, 'African Economy in Peril, UN Says', *Globe and Mail* (Toronto), 29 December 1991.

13. I refer here not only to the destruction of the natural environment, but also to the capitalist drive to war. It is worth recalling Bukharin's statement that 'war in capitalist society is only one of the methods of capitalist competition', a view which formed a core element of Lenin's theory of imperialism. See Nikolai Bukharin, *Imperialism and World Economy* (New York: Monthly Review Press, 1973), p. 54. No one has developed this insight more powerfully than Chris Harman, who writes that 'total war is the ultimate horrific expression of the world of alienated labour, in which human beings become dominated by the products of their own past activity'. See his *Explaining the Crisis: A Marxist Reappraisal* (London: Bookmark, 1984), p. 72.

14. Rosa Luxemburg, 'Social Reform or Revolution', in *Selected Political Writings of Rosa Luxemburg*, ed. Dick Howard (New York: Monthly Review Press, 1971), p. 116, emphasis in original.

Index

able-bodied poor 100–102
abstract labour 160–61, 177–8
abundance 190-92
accumulation
    Malthus and Smith 77
    wage labour and market
        regulation 175–84
    see also capitalism
Act of Settlement (1662) 23
Africa 222–3
agriculture
    development of capitalism 7–24
    Malthus 77, 83–4
    with rural industry 24–5
    Swing riots 97–9, 102
Ainsworth, T. 43
Albert, M. 199
Alcock, T. 24
Anglican social thought 80, 91–3
apprenticeship debate 35–7
Association for the Preservation of
        Liberty and Property against
        Republicans and Levellers
        65–6
Attwood, T. 138

banking 142
Beer, M. 118
Bentham, J. 41, 74, 103, 122
Black Act (1723) 39
Blackburn, R. 1–2, 171, 173, 192,
    197
Blackstone, Sir W. 40
Blomfield, C.J. 100
Bonaparte, Louis 144

Bowley, M. 57
Bray, J.F. 117, 131–3, 151–2, 170
Brougham, H. 87, 95, 105
Brus, W. 2, 173–4, 205–6
bureaucracy 193–4
Burke, E. 24, 67, 218
    French Revolution 62
    and poverty 73–4, 75
    and radicalism 67, 74, 75

calculation 118, 197–213
    see also planning
Calder Valley 28
capitalism
    fetishism 220–21
    Hodgskin 118–19
    Marx 7, 159–69, 174–84, 190,
        221
    origins of 5–42
        agriculture 7–24
        battle for discipline 34–42
        manufacturing 24–34
    Smith and agrarian 60
Carling, A. 170–71
Cavaignac, General 144
Chadwick, E. 100
Chalmers, T. 92, 105
Chambers, J.D. 21
children 79, 81, 88, 93, 95
Chitty, J. 36
Clapham, J.H. 12, 15
class, social
    differentiation among petty
        producers 29–30
    Smith and 59–61

see also working class
class struggle 70, 143, 153–4
   see also working-class movement
Cobbett, W. 104, 107–8, 111–12
Colquhoun, P. 126
combinations 55
   see also trade unions
commodities, Marx and 160–61
commodity fetishism 5, 162, 214,
   220–21
commodity/money relation 156–9,
   161–5
commons, access to 18–19
   see also enclosure
communication 49, 50–53
competition 6, 142, 179, 214
   popular political economy
      123–4, 124, 128, 133
   proletarianization and 30–34
compulsion 218–20
computers 210
concrete labour 160–61, 177–8
Condorcet, M. 76
consumption
   Smith and wealth 52, 55–6
   social 194–7, 201
co-operative movement
   Marx and factories 184, 185–6
   Owen 113–14, 135
   popular political economy
      117–33
Copleston, E. 92
correction, penal 41
corruption 47
cotton industry 27–8, 29, 43, 94
Coulson, W. 100
Cowherd, R. 100
crime 39–42
crises *see* economic crisis; subsistence
   crises
Crouzet, F. 30
currency reform 130–31, 132, 138,
   155

Dariman, A. 155
Davenport, A. 136
Day, W. 99
demand
   food supply and 85–6

   planning 202–5
demarketization of subsistence
   202–3
democracy 191, 193, 202, 209
dependence 53–5
development
   economic 77
      individual 185, 189–90, 191–2,
         206–7
Devine, P. 204
dialectics 152–3
Diquattro, A. 183
discipline, labour 34, 37–9
distribution 194–7
Dobb, M. 211
Driver, C.H. 121

Eastern Europe 216, 223, 252
   economic crisis
      global 222–3
      Gray 127–8, 129
      Marx 164–5
economic regulation 129–30
Edinburgh Review 95–6, 105
efficiency *see* productivity
Elson, D. 213–16, 255–6
embezzlement 35, 39
employers, Smith and 55–6, 59–60,
   60–61
employment, rising 43
   see also labour market
enclosure 12–15, 19–21, 34, 219
Engels, F. 147, 148, 148–9, 208
environment 207–8
equality, voluntary 124
equity 55–7
Evans, T. 70–71, 108
evil, moral 47, 80–81
exchange 115, 117–33
   Bray and unequal 131–2, 151–2
   Gray 128–9
   market regulation 175–8
   Marx 150–52, 166–7
   Proudhon 140, 141, 151
   sympathy, communication
      and 50–53
exchange-value 160–61, 175, 178
exploitation 109–10, 183
   competition and proletarianiz-
      ation 31–4

Hall 110–11
Marx 165–6, 179–81
Owen 116
popular political economy 119–20, 125, 126–7
Proudhon 141–2
self- 181
Smith 55–7
externalities 199

factory system 6
competition and proletarianization 31–4
labour discipline 37–9
famine 80, 96, 202–3
farmer-craftsmen 25–6
fatalism 80
Ferguson, A. 53
fetishism, commodity 5, 162, 214, 220–21
feudalism 7–24, 53
Fielden's Bill 37
First International 144–6
First Western Co-operative Union 135
food supply 76, 85–6
French Revolution 62, 65, 75, 76
French workers' movement 143–6

General Motors 222
German communism 148–9
global economic crisis 222–3
Godwin, W. 76, 106, 109–10
Goodchild, J. 28
Gough, J.W. 26
grain 58, 61, 66
Grand National Consolidated Trade Union (GNCTU) 114
Gray, J. 117, 126–31, 138, 159, 170, 145–6
Grun, K. 149

Hahnel, R. 199
Halifax, 28
Hall, C. 110–11
Hallas, B. 28
Hardy, T. 65, 66
Hayek, F. von 1–2, 44, 46–7, 171, 197

Heaton, H. 26
Hegel, G.W.F. 150, 221
Himmelfarb, G. 59
Hobsbawm, E. 72
Hodgskin, T. 106, 117–21, 170 243–4
Hodgson, G. 2
Hone, G. 92
Horner, F. 96
Horner, J. 95
Horsley, S. 91
Hoskins, W.G. 17
Howard, J. 40
Huddersfield 26, 27, 28, 28–9
humanitarianism 71–5
Hume, D. 46, 53
hunger 80, 96, 202–3
Hunt, E.K. 199
Hutcheson, F. 46, 47, 48, 53

IBM 222
immanent critique 189
improvement, social 76–7, 79, 82, 84
individualism 188–90, 199
Malthus and individual agency 80–81
personal development 185, 189–90, 191-2, 206–7
Industrial Revolution 24–34
working class and 34–42
inequality
Malthus and social 89–90, 91
Spenceanism and economic 71
information, access to 213, 214, 216
International Monetary Fund 222–3
International Workingmen's Association 144–6
inventory control systems 204, 212
investment, planning 199–201

Jacobinism, British 63–71
James, P. 86–7
Jameson, F. 174
joint stock companies 133
Jones, G.S. 133–4

Kames, Lord 53
King, G. 15, 16

labour
    commodification of 5, 31,
        107–8, 174, 218–22
    commodity/money relation
        157–8, 159
    concrete and abstract 160–61,
        177–8
    exploitation *see* exploitation
    Hodgskin 119
    Marx 147–8, 150–52, 156,
        157–8, 160–61
    planning and 187, 211
    popular political economy
        117–33
    productive and unproductive
        126–7
    productivity 179–81, 191, 206–8
    Proudhon 140
    value and 115–17, 137–8,
        150–51
    see also labour market
labour banks 135, 146
labour certificates 184–6
labour exchange experiment 133–8
labour market 218–20
    accumulation and market
        regulation 175–84
    creating 4, 5–42
        agriculture 7–24
        battle for discipline 34–42
        manufacturing 24–34
    Malthus 90–91, 220
    Marx 165–9
    Mises 5, 6, 174
    moral economy 58–9
    Smith 53–5, 219
labour notes 135, 137
Lachmann, R. 9,16
Lancashire 26, 29
land
    farm size and enclosure 14–15
    ownership 9–11
        Spenceanism 108–9
    right to 68–9
    see also enclosure; subsistence
landed class 60, 61, 72
Lange, O. 209, 210
Laski, K. 2, 173–4
Leeds 28

living standards 68, 84, 94
Locke, J. 120
London 94, 135
London Corresponding Society
    (LCS) 65, 66, 66–7
London United Trades Associa-
    tion 136
Lovett, W. 121
Luxemburg, R. 223–4

Mackintosh, J. 62
Malthus, T.R. 3, 4, 24, 74–103,
    218, 220
    Chair in Political Economy 105
    essays on population 75–91
    hostility to 104
    legacies 91–103
    Smithian economics 6, 44, 61,
        76–7, 84
Mandel, E. 204
Mandeville, B. 45, 47, 48
Mann, J. de L. 29–30
manufacturers 27, 56, 59–60, 60–61
manufacturing 24–34
Marcet, J. 106
market interference 59, 63–4
market reformism 216–17
market regulation 202
    socialism and 172–4
    socialization and 215
    wage-labour, accumulation
        and 175–84
market socialism 4, 170–74
    and labour market 168–9, 222
    and state socialism 2–3
markets, nature of 198–200
Martineau, H. 106
Marx, K. 3, 4, 61, 170, 217, 221
    agricultural proletariat 18
    capital relation 7, 180–81
    commodification of labour-
        power 5, 31, 174, 221–2
    commodity fetishism 162, 214,
        221
    enclosure 13
    exchange-value 160–61, 248
    market regulation 202
    political economy of working
        class 184–8

productivity and the environment 207–8
and Proudhon *see* Proudhon
socialism *see* socialism
state 186–7, 221–2
on Steuart 219
wealth as disposable time 206
Maxwell, J. 94
McCulloch, J.R. 96, 105
Mechanics' Institutes 106
mechanization 31–2, 39
mercantilism 56–7
merchants
    development from petty production 27–30
    Smith and 54–5, 56, 59–60, 60–61
metalworking industry 26, 27
Midlands, industrial 26–7, 27, 29
Mill, J. 87, 105, 118
Mill, J.S. 46, 87
Millar, J. 53
Mingay, G.E. 14, 21
Mises, L. von 45, 171
    labour market 5, 6, 174
    planning 1–2, 173, 197
monetary reform 130–31, 132, 138, 155
money 117–33, 178, 213–14
    Bray 132
    Cobbett 111–12
    Gray 128–9
    Marx 152, 155–6
        commodity/money relation 156–9, 161–5
    Owen 115–16, 117
    Proudhon 142, 152
monoopolistic practices 56–7
monopoly, political 63–4
moral economy 58–9
moral evil 80–81
moral restraint 81–2, 83
mutualism 142

National Chamber of Commerce 129
National Equitable Labour Exchange Association of the Industrious Classes 136

National Reform League 146
needs 188–90, 202–3
New Poor Law 102–3, 219
Norwich Patriotic Society 67
Nove, A. 2, 170, 171, 190, 192, 193–4

O'Brien, J.B. 121, 134–5, 136, 138, 146
Ogilvie, W. 109
Operative Builders' Union 138
overproduction 192–3
Otter, Bishop 103
outdoor relief 100–102
Owen, R. 94, 106, 112–17, 121
    currency reform 138
    and Gray 126
    labour exchange experiment 135–6
    Malthus and 76, 78

Paglin, M. 86
Paine, T. 62, 91–2, 111
    Malthus and 78, 87
    popular radicalism 63–6
    and right to subsistence 67, 68
Paley, W. 81
Pare, W. 130–31
participation 191, 193, 202, 209
payments in kind 22
peasant-workers 25–6
peasantry, transformation of 8–10
penitentiaries 40–41
pensions 64
People's Bank 142, 155
Perkin, H. 34
perquisites 35
petty bourgeois socialism 123, 139
    Marx's 150–54, 158–9, 160, 168–9
        commodity/money relation 163, 164, 165
    see also Proudhon
petty producers 69, 123, 139, 140
    development of labour market 24–34, 168
    Smith 53–5
    Spenceanism 108–9
Philipson, N. 60

Pig's Meat 69
Pinchbeck, I. 32–3
Pitt, W. 73, 74
Place, F. 67, 103, 105, 106, 110, 118
planning, economic 1–2, 252
    calculation 197–213
    Marx 187–8, 192-3
    Nove 193–4
    objectives guiding 208–9
    Thompson 124–5
'planning prices' 209–11, 212
Polanyi, K. 42
political economy 104–6
    Malthus's legacy and classical 93–7, 103
    Owenism and 112–17
    popular *see* popular political economy
    respectability 104–5
        of the working class 184–8
Political Economy Club 100
political monopoly 63–4
Pollard, S. 38–9
Poor Law Commission 93, 99–100
    Report (1834) 19, 20, 92, 96–7, 100–103
poor laws 22–4, 95
    Burke 73, 74–5
    debate 97–103, 219–20
    Malthus 77–91
    New Poor Law 102–3, 219
    Ricardo 93, 95
    Senior 96
poor relief 21, 22–4, 92
    costs 23, 97
    see also poor laws; poverty
popular political economy
    forerunners 106–12
    labour exchange experiment 133–8
    labour, exchange, money and co-operation 117–33
popular radicalism 62–3, 104
    Burke and 67, 74, 75
    Malthus and 75, 76, 78–9, 90
    and poverty debate 63–71
population, Malthus's essays 75–91
Porteus, B. 91

possession, property and 140
poverty
    Africa 222–3
    debate
        Anglican social thought 92–3
        humanitarianism 71–5
        Malthus 75–91, 220
        popular radicalism 63–71
    enclosure and 14, 19, 21
    Smith 59, 60–61
    see also poor laws; poor relief
Poynter, J.R. 75, 86, 100
Pretyman, Bishop 92
prices 172, 213–14
    commodification of labour 177-9
    grain 58, 66
    Hodgskin 119–20
    market socialism 172–3
    planning and 197
        'planning prices' 209–11, 212
        regulation by public policy 205
    Proudhon and just 141
    Smith and 55–7, 58
    value and 156, 163–4
prisons 40–41
productivity 179–81, 191, 206–8
profit 55–6, 119–20, 132
proletarianization 948, 168
    agriculture 12–18, 20–21
    competition and 30–34
property
    crime, punishment and 39–42
    labour market and 34–42, 218–19
    Malthus 89–90
    popular political economy 120–21, 126, 131-2, 133
    popular radicalism 67–8, 69, 71, 108
    Proudhon 139–46
    Marx's critique 147–8, 166–8
    see also enclosure; land
Proudhon, P.J. 170, 171
    Marx and 139–69
        Capital 159–69
        development of critical views 146–9
        Economy 154–9

Poverty of Philosophy 150–54
property and political
   economy 139–46
public works programmes 85–6
punishment 40–41
putting-out system 28–30

radical societies 65–71
   see also popular radicalism
rationality, economic 1, 6, 21, 171,
   173, 200–201
   see also calculation; planning
Reeves, J. 66
reform, by prisons 41
regulation
   economic 129–30
   market *see* market regulation
revolution *see* class struggle
Ricardo, D. 46, 87, 93–5, 119, 150
Robertson, J.C. 106
Roebuck, J. 27
Romilly, S. 74
Rousseau, J.J. 48
Rubel, M. 139
Rudé, G. 72
rural industries 24–6
   see also petty producers

Saville, J. 16
Say's Law 84
Schumpeter, J. 1948, 210
Select Committee on Enclosures
   19–20
self-control 50
self-development 185, 189–90,
   191–2, 206–7
self-exploitation 181
selfish passions 47–8
self-management 181–2, 183–4
Semmel, B. 86
Sen, A. 203
Senior, N. 87, 96, 100, 105
service in husbandry 21–2
settlement laws 23, 58–9
Sheffield 26, 27, 67
Sheffield Constitutional Society 65
silk industry 94
Single, T. 107
Slaney, R.A. 99

Smith, A. 3, 4, 43–61, 63, 119, 219
   Act of Settlement 23
   dependence and wage-labour
      53–5
   Edinburgh Review 95–6
   exploitation and equity 55–7
   Malthus and 6, 44, 61, 76–7, 84
   moral economy 58–9
   social classes 59–61
   sympathy, communication and
      exchange 50–53
   virtue and commerce 46–50
Smith, S. 95
Snell, K. 23
social consumption 194–7, 201
social contract 141
social foresight 186, 187
   see also planning
social production 185–7
social reform 112–13
social services 64
socialism 4
   defect of 1
   market *see* market socialism
   Marxian 169; objections
      to 188–97
   Owenite 113, 114
   Spencean 109
   transition to 2, 194–7
   'true' 148–9
socialization of decision-making 202
socialized markets 213–17
socialized sector 204–5, 212
Soper, K. 188–9
Southey, R. 78, 82
Sowell, T. 83
specialization 52, 98
Speenhamland system 73
Spence, T. 68–70, 108, 109
Spenceanism 68–71, 76, 78, 108
Spitalfields silk industry 94
starvation 80, 96, 202–3
state 39
   Marx 186–7, 221–2
   Smith 59–60
Statute of Artificers and Apprentices
   (1563) 35–6, 37
Steuart, Sir J. 219
strikes 143, 145

Sturges-Bourne, W. 93, 100
subsistence
    demarketization of 202–3
    right to 23–4, 107
        Burke 74
        Malthus 75–8, 79, 87–9
        poor law debate 97, 98–9,
            101
        popular radicalism 66, 67–8,
            71
subsistence crises 67, 72, 77
Sumner, J.B. 81, 92, 99
surplus-value 165–8, 180
Swing riots 97–9, 99, 102
sympathy 48–50, 50–53

Ten Hours Bill 184, 185
textile industries 26, 27–8, 28–9
Thelwall, J. 66, 67–8, 236
Thirsk, J. 17
Thompson, E.P. 33–4, 61, 63, 67,
        108, 114
Thompson, W. 117, 121–6
time
    labour discipline 38
    productivity and self-
        development 119–2, 206–7
Tolain, H.L. 145
Torrans, R. 86, 87, 105
Townsend, J. 24
trade unionism 114, 143, 145, 154
'true socialism' 148–9

universal suffrage 134
use-value 160–61, 178
utilitarianism 122

Vagrancy Act (1744) 39–40
value 170
    capitalism and 175
    exchange-value and use-
        value 160–61, 178
    Hodgskin 119–20
    labour and 115–17, 137–8,
        150–51
    market regulation 178–9
    Marx and 155–7, 168–9
    Owen 115–17

and price 156, 163–4
'value problem' 192
vices 47
virtue 45–6, 46–50

Wadsworth, A.P. 29–30
wage-labour see labour market
wages
    Gray 129–30
    Malthus 89
    market regulation 182–3
    minimum 73
    Ricardo 94
    right to work at a living wage
        107–8
    Smith 43
Watson, Dr 70
wealth, consumption and 52, 55–6
Wedgwood, J. 38, 4-41
West Bromwich 27
Whitaker, T. 92
Whitbread, S. 73, 74–5
Williams, G.A. 65
Williams, R. 108
Winch, D. 75
women 32–3, 144
woollen industry 26, 27, 28, 28–9
Wordie, J.R. 15
workhouses 101, 102, 103
working class
    and Industrial Revolution 33–4
    battle for discipline 34–42
    political economy of 184–8
working-class movement 217
    control of production 181–2,
        183–4
    French 143–6
    Marx 153–4
    Owen 113–15
    see also class struggle

yeomen-clothiers 26
yeomen farmers 9–10
Yorkshire 26, 28
Young, A. 18–19, 24, 68, 237
Young, R. 87
Yugoslavia 182, 223